12/25
STRAND PRICE
$5.00

Unleashing Social Justice through EU Public Procurement

The dramatic results of the 2014 European Parliament elections have highlighted the European Union's urgent need for a review of the scope and purpose of its social objectives and for a reordering of European priorities.

This book advocates a radical and original alternative to the current philosophy that determines the set of rules for the awarding of EU public procurement contracts. It calls for a reordering of the EU's economic and social priorities. In doing so, it advocates for a social dimension to be placed at the core of public procurement, which could elicit a social model of integration in the EU in which the European citizen is the key actor. This is achieved through an analytical approach as well as concise and contextualised explanations relating to free trade theories, poverty and public interest theories.

This book will be of key interest to students and scholars of the European Union, political theory and EU law.

Antoinette Calleja is Director, International Affairs and Policy Development with the Ministry for Health, Malta.

Critical European Studies
Edited by Hartmut Behr
University of Newcastle, UK
and Yannis A. Stivachtis
Virginia Tech, USA

1   **Mapping European Empire**
    Tabulae Imperii Europaei
    Russell Foster

2   **Revisiting the European Union as an Empire**
    Edited by Hartmut Behr and Yannis A. Stivachtis

3   **Unleashing Social Justice through EU Public Procurement**
    Antoinette Calleja

Unleashing Social Justice through EU Public Procurement

Antoinette Calleja

LONDON AND NEW YORK

First published 2016
by Routledge
2 Park Square, Milton Park, Abingdon, Oxon OX14 4RN

and by Routledge
711 Third Avenue, New York, NY 10017

Routledge is an imprint of the Taylor & Francis Group, an informa business

© 2016 Antoinette Calleja

The right of Antoinette Calleja to be identified as author of this work has been asserted by her in accordance with sections 77 and 78 of the Copyright, Designs and Patents Act 1988.

All rights reserved. No part of this book may be reprinted or reproduced or utilised in any form or by any electronic, mechanical, or other means, now known or hereafter invented, including photocopying and recording, or in any information storage or retrieval system, without permission in writing from the publishers.

Trademark notice: Product or corporate names may be trademarks or registered trademarks, and are used only for identification and explanation without intent to infringe.

British Library Cataloguing in Publication Data
A catalogue record for this book is available from the British Library

Library of Congress Cataloging in Publication Data
Calleja, Antoinette.
Unleashing social justice through EU public procurement / Antoinette Calleja.
  pages cm. – (Critical European studies ; 3)
  1. Government purchasing–European Union countries. 2. Public contracts–European Union countries. 3. Social justice–European Union countries. 4. Public-private sector cooperation–European Union countries. 5. European Union countries–Social policy. I. Title. II. Title: Unleashing social justice through European Union public procurement.
  JN30.C347 2015
  352.5'32114–dc23   2015014738

ISBN: 978-1-138-93089-6 (hbk)
ISBN: 978-1-315-68009-5 (ebk)

Typeset in Times New Roman
by Wearset Ltd, Boldon, Tyne and Wear

Contents

List of illustrations viii
Preface ix
Acknowledgements xiii
List of abbreviations xiv

PART I
The status quo 1

1 **Introduction** 3
 1.1 Background 3
 1.2 Theoretical perspectives on social formation – a general idea 11
 1.3 On theories of social justice 14
 1.4 On Europe's social model 21
 1.5 Social Europe on the move 23
 1.6 On the power of social protection expenditure 25
 1.7 The case for a reordered public procurement regime 28
 1.8 Concluding remarks 30

2 **European integration and the interplay with public procurement** 41
 2.1 Introduction 41
 2.2 The relationship between the EU's social and economic dimensions 43
 2.3 The beginnings of the development of EU public procurement regulation and its role in European integration – an overview 50
 2.4 Advancing a socially just model of European integration through public procurement 54
 2.5 Concluding remarks 56

3 The effectiveness of EU public procurement — 64
3.1 Introduction 64
3.2 EU public procurement and its impact on transparency 66
3.3 EU public procurement and its impact on cross border procurement 72
3.4 EU public procurement and its impact on small- and medium-sized enterprises 75
3.5 EU public procurement and its impact on the international public procurement market 76
3.6 Concluding remarks 77

4 Free trade: what about it – myths or realities? — 82
4.1 Introduction 82
4.2 On framing economic theories 85
4.3 The theory of comparative advantage – a general idea 86
4.4 Moving beyond theory – free trade and the Europe 2020 strategy 91
4.5 The liberalisation of the network industries as an illustration of the EU's overriding and unconditional attitude towards the Single Market project 93
4.6 Concluding remarks 98

5 Poverty and natural law theory in context — 105
5.1 Introduction 105
5.2 Poverty across the EU – a snapshot 106
5.3 The nature of poverty – definitions abound 111
5.4 Freedom for human flourishing as conceived through natural law theory 115
5.5 Respect for human dignity – a legally enforceable fundamental right 120
5.6 The quest for poverty reduction – putting EU public procurement into perspective 121
5.7 Concluding remarks 124

PART II
Closing the gap — 133

6 The mission of serving the public: services of general interest and community law — 135
6.1 Introduction 135
6.2 The European Commission and its plethora of soft law 136

6.3 *Services of general economic interest – forging a bond between European economic efficiency and social cohesion? 137*
6.4 *Services of general interest – an endeavour in untangling chaos in the free-thinking zone 142*
6.5 *Concluding remarks 158*

7 Public procurement as the EU's safety valve 171
7.1 *Introduction 171*
7.2 *The EU as a decentred State 172*
7.3 *Marchés publiques as sui generis markets 176*
7.4 *To what extent is the EU public procurement regime serving the public interest? 178*
7.5 *Concluding remarks 184*

PART III
The solution 191

8 On public-private partnerships: a European theory of a socially just alternative 193
8.1 *Introduction 193*
8.2 *On public-private partnerships 194*
8.3 *UK, London: Thameslink rolling stock procurement programme – the case in a nutshell 195*
8.4 *Arguing for a European theory of social justice 203*
8.5 *Concluding remarks 210*

9 Conclusions 215
9.1 *The validity of our actions needs to be limited by time and concrete results 216*
9.2 *On a plane of practical reasonableness 218*

Index 228

Illustrations

Figure

7.1	Conceptual forces underpinning the EU legal order: a binary distinction on the conduct of the State	174

Tables

1.1	Youth unemployment rate – annual average percentage	26
2.1	A general concept of social integration	58
5.1	At risk of poverty or social exclusion, 2012	108
5.2	Relative median at-risk-of-poverty gap, evolution in percentage points, 2012–13 and 2008–13	110
5.3	Summary description of the basic requirements of practical reasonableness, as postulated by Finnis	118
5.4	Summary description of the seven basic goods, as postulated by Finnis	120

Preface

Unleashing Social Justice through EU Public Procurement responds to the European Union's urgent need for a review of the scope and purpose of its social objectives. It seeks to foster novel and critical thinking that challenges the current predominant mindset linked to the EU public procurement regime, and provokes for the very first time a shift in its paradigm. It advocates a radical and original alternative to the current EU philosophy that drives the rule set concerning the awarding of public procurement contracts that fall within its legal jurisdiction. This alternative is for the EU public procurement regime to have a social dimension standing at its core, one that extends into a social model of European integration in which the European citizen becomes the key actor in the integration process. It is argued that the intertwined social threads constitute the very fabric of Europe's economic dimension, and that Europe's building capacity is located within this space – potentially weaving the way towards European integration.

Public procurement expenditure across the EU is estimated at 19 per cent of EU GDP. Its regulation plays a vital role in the integration programme of the single European market. Preferential public procurement is considered as State aid and this is generally prohibited by the Treaty unless it can be justified for reasons of general economic development. In essence, governments are not allowed to support individual companies gain competitive advantages since this would distort trade between Member States. Such market intervention and institutionalised controls are commensurate with neoliberal principles which do not reflect upon the distributive objectives of societal welfare.

However, this book presents a fundamental departure from such logic for it argues on the basis of a socially just alternative that takes into account the distributive objectives of societal welfare – albeit in a limited manner as far as public procurement contracts are concerned. Through a journey of *'verstehen'*[1] this book culminates by advancing a European theory of social justice. Such a theory finds philosophical underpinnings that are grounded on natural law theory, and is institutionalised through the public-private partnership regime by putting into operation principles derived from John Rawls' in *Justice as Fairness*. This social model is in alignment with the European Union's founding values, and it operates on the basis of principles and conditions that enable the flourishing of its citizens through the incorporation of key values that themselves are tightly enmeshed and that cannot be disentangled. Such values are mutually reinforcing, and include the respect for human dignity, equality and the freedom of participatory action. These key values correspond to the fight against poverty. In essence, this socially just model calls for a reordering of the European Union's economic and social policy dimensions, as far as the EU public procurement regime is involved. Such reordering primarily calls for a change in attitude – one that moves away from the overriding and unconditional approach that embraces a European economic efficiency logic in which the individual is used as a means to an end. Instead, a socially just alternative is called for – an alternative in which the individual is seen as an end in itself. There remains a significant amount of unexploited potential within EU public procurement to utilise strategic investment in both an economic *and* a social policy dimension. Optimising the benefits of this approach can be achieved through the institutionalisation of a reordered public procurement regime that extends into a socially just model of European integration – one in which the European citizen becomes the key actor in the integration process.

EU public procurement is the product of various exogenous forces and therefore one cannot rely solely on its own terms but needs to incorporate the substance provided by other disciplines in order to better grasp understandings – or in other words '*verstehen*'. In order to capture a broad and explanatory map, this book incorporates the substance provided by other disciplines – drawing on understandings from, historical, legal, social, marketing, management, economics and philosophical perspectives. On a plane of practical reasonableness the analysis and synthesis of source materials attempt to present fair and holistic understandings. This novel critical approach cuts through various disciplines while simultaneously maintaining linkages with the EU public procurement regime – and in so doing, validates the legitimacy of this book and stamps out its very distinctive mark.

This book is organised into three main themes:

Part I: 'The Status Quo' revisits the premises that provide the current justifications for the regulation of EU public procurement. The case for a reordered public procurement regime which extends to a socially just model of integration is presented. As the tensions between the EU's social and economic dimensions – and the challenges involved – are put into perspective, a socially just model of European integration through public procurement is advanced. The general concept of what is meant by social integration, and how a socially just model of integration emerges within the pan European social space, is discussed. EU public procurement plays a vital role in the EU plan to integrate Member States through the single market imperative. The move towards the single market is based on neoliberal economics, at the heart of which rests the theory of comparative advantage. When one delves into this theory and the way it evolved over the years – starting from the very early logic postulated by Adam Smith during the mid-eighteenth century, to the Ricardian model of the early nineteenth century, and other modifications that were incorporated during the twentieth and twenty-first centuries – one finds that the concept, even today, remains under scrutiny. The author questions the rationale and justifications of the European Union in devoting so much attention, energy and resources to policies which directly promote a concept that, despite its power, is put in check by economists. Such overriding and unconditional attitudes come at the expense of promulgating social policies that tap at the very heart of the EU's social dimension. The question of poverty is also put into context. Poverty across Europe is a real problem and a major obstacle to social cohesion, harmonious development, the attainment of acceptable standards of living and, last but not least, EU integration objectives. Poverty is fundamentally linked with the question of how society distributes and redistributes its resources and opportunities, and it therefore exposes the inadequacy of our current systems. Indeed, poverty exposes the depth of the gap that has emerged in pursuit of European integration objectives. The themes under discussion are tackled in Chapters 1 to 5.

Part II: 'Closing the Gap' sets out to closely examine the attempts of the European Union to close the integration gap in its drive towards the attainment of European integration. It does so by examining the provision of public services and how these have become captured at the European level by way of services of general economic interest. The ever-increasing commercialisation of the EU citizen's everyday life, which serves to subordinate public policies to market forces, is seen by the author as a major obstacle when it comes to attaining European integration aims. The author reveals how concepts that embrace utilitarianism are incompatible with claims maintaining that at the heart of Community policies lies the interest of its citizens. For utilitarianism is concerned with the achievement of aggregate utility. Individual freedom, autonomy, rights and quality of life are only valuable insofar as they increase aggregate utility. Hence, it is argued that a European social model can only emerge if we distance ourselves from utility-based concepts. These themes are taken up in Chapters 6 and 7.

Part III: 'The Solution' presents the author's vision for a socially just European model that bridges the gap between economic liberal theories and poverty. It identifies with a reordered EU public procurement regime as the most likely bridge for preserving the ideal market economy – identified by the author as 'one that exploits the potential and provides the greatest opportunities for all those wanting to engage in it in a sustained manner'. Public procurement's ability to bridge this gap manifests itself through its flexibility as an instrument of public policy, serving both domestic and EU-wide public interest needs. The formulation of an umbrella concept that captures key fundamental values, and which embraces the fight against poverty, social exclusion and enabling the participatory engagement of citizens, underpins the author's vision for a European theory of a socially just alternative. The respect for human dignity, equality and freedom of participatory action emerge as the key fundamental values that are captured within this umbrella concept, explicating Europe's social model. These three values are tightly enmeshed and cannot be disentangled. Any attempt to treat them separately deprives the very essence of their integrity. A European social model that incorporates sizeable enhancements of these values will create a telling case, and one that pronounces even more strongly the value of respect for human dignity. These themes are discussed in Chapters 8 and 9.

Note

1 That is, rational comprehension of the motivations that underlie behaviour.

Acknowledgements

I owe gratitude to all those who, in various ways, have supported and encouraged me over the years – especially, mum, Paul, Joseph and Mark.

I also wish to express my deep gratitude to Professor Christopher Bovis. Special thanks go to Marica Shepherd and Dr Joseph Calleja.

I also wish to express my thanks to the Malta Government Scholarship Scheme Grant for having part-funded my research studies.

Abbreviations

BRIC	Brazil, Russia, India and China
CAN	Contract Award Notice
CN	Contract Notice
DG	Director General
EC	European Community
ECJ	European Court of Justice
ECSC	European Coal and Steel Community
ECU	European Currency Unit
EDC	European Defence Community
EEC	European Economic Community
EPC	European Political Cooperation
EU	European Union
EURATOM	European Atomic Energy Community
GATT	General Agreement on Tariff and Trade Rules
GDP	Gross Domestic Product
GPA	Government Procurement Agreement
NAFTA	North American Free Trade Agreement
OECD	Organisation for Economic Cooperation and Development
OEEC	Organisation for European Economic Cooperation
OMC	Open Method of Coordination
PIN	Prior Information Notice
PPP	Power Purchasing Parity
PPPs	Public-Private Partnerships
PSO	Public Service Obligation
SEM	Single European Market
SGEI	Services of General Economic Interest
SGI	Services of General Interest
SMEs	Small- and Medium-Sized Enterprises
SSGI	Social Services of General Interest
TED	Tenders Electronic Daily
TEU	Treaty of the European Union
TFEU	Treaty on the Functioning of the European Union
US	United States
USO	Universal Service Obligation
VFM	Value For Money

Part I
The status quo

1 Introduction

1.1 Background

This book attempts to prove how the development of European integration could be further advanced through a socially just model of integration in the European Union, achieved through a reordered public procurement regime in which the European citizen is the key actor in the integration process.

The motive behind public procurement regulation in the European Union goes beyond the eradication of discriminatory practices and protectionist behaviour. Rather, it forms part and parcel of Europe's drive to create an integrated political and economic union (Cox 1993: 9). In this respect, history enlightens us further. The Treaty of Rome which led to the creation of the European Economic Community (EEC) signed on 25 March 1957, although politically motivated, has primarily an economic focus with anticipated spillover effects. Its rationale draws from neofunctionalist theory which sees initial cooperation on non-controversial technical sectors as bringing about a gradual spillover effect to other sectors. This in due course is expected to lead towards greater political cooperation that calls for a gradual reduction in the power of national governments while concurrently increasing centralisation of powers for dealing with sensitive and politically charged issues (Craig and De Búrca 2011).[1] Neofunctionalist arguments were eventually challenged – most prominently by liberal intergovernmental theory. This theory held that States rather than supranational institutions were the key actors in the integration process (Craig and De Búrca 2011). Such a rationale guided the actions that were taken in reinforcing the Single European Market, and which led to the signing of the Single European Act (SEA) in 1986 and which came into force in 1987 (Craig and De Búrca 2011). The Single European Act (SEA), which embodied the White Paper, represented Member States' willingness to accept Treaty reform and the political commitment to removing (before the 1992 deadline) the long list of identified barriers to the Single European Market. The adoption of the SEA also reflected a shift in intellectual, political and economic thinking in favour of neoliberalism (Cox 1993).

At the time, the liberalisation of public procurement was said to play a key role in European integration via the single market initiative, even though it comprised only one of the 282 legislative proposals for reform. According to the European Commission the 'continued partitioning of individual national markets is one of the most evident barriers to the achievement of a real internal market' (COM 85 (310) 1985: 23) It was argued that as long as Member States maintained preferential national public procurement patterns to protect their own domestic industries from competition there would always be vested interests that would act to resist an integrated political and economic union – thereby eradicating any hope that Europe could ever become properly integrated, either politically or economically (Cox 1993: 11). In addition, in view of the fragmented European market, it was argued that European firms were operating in relatively small domestic markets that lacked the necessary economies of scale, and that this situation prevented them from competing successfully in world markets (Cox 1993).

The legislative reforms proposed by the 1985 White Paper presented the European Commission with the long awaited opportunity to conduct studies that would give further impetus in sharpening their resolve for liberalising public procurement, thus enabling the proper functioning of the European Single Market (Cox 1993: 58). In effect, the Atkins Report on *The Costs of Non-Europe in Public Sector Procurement* (Atkins 1988) and the Cecchini Report on *The European Challenge, 1992* (Cecchini 1988) provided much of the rationale for the public procurement recommendations found in the Single Market Initiative (Cox 1993: 13). The reform extended the scope of the public procurement rules to previously excluded areas, to henceforth include public services procurement and public utilities procurement (the utilities sector included entities operating in the water, energy, transport and telecommunication sectors).[2] While building on the framework of the previous Directives,[3] the new Directives were aimed at coordinating the effective establishment of a competitive public procurement regime. Additional safeguards designed to introduce transparency and to monitor compliance were introduced. Worth noting here is that the first Community Directives that were enacted in 1971 and in 1977 – which essentially sought to institutionalise the liberalisation of public procurement practices – failed in their scope. According to the Atkins Report (Atkins 1988) only 2–5 per cent of public purchasing could be attributed to cross border trade. Member States did not comply with the public procurement rules, and the lack of an effective enforcement and remedy regime did not prove to be helpful either (COM 85 (310) 1985; Van Hamme 1990; Cox 1993).

Key arguments emerging from both the Atkins Report and the Cecchini Report were that significant economic gains could be achieved if more aggressive liberalisation policies were to be instituted by the Community (Cox 1993: 13). According to the Atkins Report failures on the demand side created suboptimal supply side outcomes, thereby reducing intra Community trade integration (Cox 1993: 17). The Cecchini Report, described as 'a solid body of scientifically-assembled evidence' (Cecchini 1988: xvii) projected efficiency gains amounting to 0.5 per cent of 1986 Community GDP ($c.$17.5 billion ECUs, or 21.5 billion ECUs if defence procurement was included) (Cecchini 1988: 17).

Other projections emanating as a result of the removal of all formal and informal barriers to intra European Union (EU) trade included major reductions in chronic European unemployment, opportunities for growth, stable prices and greater consumer choice. In his opening statement to the Cecchini Report Lord Cockfield, then Vice President of the European Commission, stated that the completion of the Internal Market 'will give a permanent boost to the prosperity of the people of Europe and indeed of the world as a whole' (Cecchini 1988: p. xiii).

In line with the main objectives for the creation of an integral public market, the integration dynamics of the European Union have maintained recourse to neoliberal economic theories wherein the creation of the Single European Market has served as a major focus – with the ultimate aim that this would eventually lead to an integrated European economic and political union. In this respect EU Directives 2004/18/EC and 2004/17/EC, and the respective implementing national public procurement regulations currently in force,[4] need to be examined in the light of the rules and principles resulting from the European Treaties – particularly as regards the freedom of establishment and freedom to provide services (Article 49 TFEU and Article 56 TFEU respectively), which encompass, in particular, the principles of transparency, equality of treatment, proportionality and mutual recognition. In essence, the regulation of public procurement exposes an economic and a legal approach to the integration of public markets in the EU with the aim of enhancing competition and unobstructed market access. In its proposal for a Directive to the European Parliament and the Council on public procurement, the European Commission claimed that public authorities in Europe spend *c.*18 per cent of GDP on supplies, works and services (COM (2011) 896 final). In 2004, public procurement spending was estimated at 16 per cent of the EU's GDP (European Commission 2004).

It could be argued that public procurement, as a vital public policy tool that operates within *sui generis* markets, is concerned with the delivery of public services. Ultimately, the goal is to award government contracts in a way that 'adds value', and therefore results in better outcomes for the communities that governments serve. The provision of public services is a crucial societal role, and one that cannot be left solely to the whims of market forces. One cannot ignore the fact that European jurisprudence has recognised this point. Hence, in the Corbeau judgement of 1993 (Case C-320/91) it was acknowledged that the granting of special or exclusive rights to public undertakings might hinder the competition rules of the treaty. However, the Court also acknowledged that Article 106 (2) TFEU allowed Member States to grant such rights in order to ensure that the necessary services of general economic interest were provided, even if this meant that such rights were to restrict or even exclude all competition (Case C-320/91: para. 14). In the BFI case (1998) the Court held that bodies that are governed by public law, and established for the specific purpose of meeting public interest needs, 'may choose to be guided by other than economic considerations' (Case C-360/96: para. 43). In these instances, 'such a body might consider it appropriate to incur financial losses' (Case C-360/96). 'The fact that there is competition is not sufficient to exclude the possibility that a body financed or controlled by the State, territorial authorities or other bodies governed by public law may choose to be guided by other than economic considerations' (Case C-360/96). For 'the needs in question are ones which, for reasons associated with the general interest, the State itself chooses to provide or over which it wishes to retain a decisive influence' (Case C-360/96: para. 51).

Public purchasing is inextricably linked with national policies, and in particular social policy (Bovis 2006). It has proven to be a dedicated follower of political fashion. Historically, there have been consistent links between public procurement and the government policy of the day – EU public procurement did not always have economic and open market access objectives. In 1989 the European Commission published a communication on the regional and social aspects of public procurement (COM (1989) 400 final). It claimed that opportunities deriving from the liberalisation of public procurement could not be realised as long as Member States maintained protectionist behaviour and refrained from adopting appropriate restructuring measures. For instance, in the case of the UK and Germany, the Commission held as follows:

> In neither the British nor the German case is there reliable evidence of the preference schemes having made a significant contribution to the development of the regions concerned. At the same time, there is no evidence either of them giving rise to significant distortions to trade whether within those countries or between them and other Member States.
> (COM (1989) 400 final: para. 35: 9)

Although preference schemes may have contributed 'to a more balanced functioning of the economy, by helping to limit the widening of regional disparities through guaranteeing certain markets' (COM (1989) 400 final: para. 40: 10), and despite the 'absence of evidence, one way or the other, concerning the effect of these schemes' (COM (1989) 400 final), it was concluded that regional preference schemes were problematic because they privileged certain enterprises at the expense of others. This was perceived as impinging upon fundamental Community procurement policy, and upon the Treaty itself, because such schemes 'do not operate in a way which ensures that similarly situated enterprises are treated equally' (COM (1989) 400 final: para. 41, p. 10). Such protectionist behaviour was considered to threaten the transparency and fairness of public procurement procedures, thereby delaying the achievement of the Single European Market. Indeed neoliberalism has had a profound impact upon the development and interpretation of EU public procurement: 'the Commission's actions were, from the latter part of the 1980s and during much of the 1990s, hostile to the incorporation of social aspects into procurement. The demise of the social use of procurement was widely predicted.' (McCrudden 2007: 361). According to the European Commission, 'It is implicit in the programme for the establishment of the single market in public procurement that removal of internal barriers will give rise to changes in the distribution of contracts and therefore to more efficient procurement' (COM (1989) 400 final: para. 16, p. 5).

At the time, in 1989, the Commission also asserted that 'while the overall consequences for economic demand and employment will be positive, the distribution of the pain and gain between firms, groups and regions will only become apparent with time' (COM (1989) 400 final: para. 17, p. 6). Twenty years after the anniversary of the Single Market, the distribution of this 'pain' and 'gain' across the EU in the public procurement market has become very apparent. The following are among the salient issues that are worth highlighting:

1 When it comes to the participation of small- and medium-sized enterprises (SMEs) in public procurement, they have remained consistently underrepresented. In the period 2006–08 (PwC *et al.* 2014) an estimated 60 per cent of above-EU threshold contracts were awarded to SMEs. This accounted for 34 per cent of the market share in terms of value (GHK 2010).[5] For the period 2008–11, SMEs accounted for 29 per cent of market share in terms of value (PwC *et al.* 2014). When SMEs' participation was considered through other award routes – as in joint bid arrangements, or as subcontractors – the aggregate public procurement value for the above-EU threshold procurement awards was estimated at 46 per cent of market share.

2 Over the past 20 years, cross border public procurement has remained relatively low – over 98 per cent of contracts awarded according to EU rules have been won by national bidders (SEC (2011) 1586 final).[6]

3 When it comes to the international scenario, EU suppliers in the utilities public procurement market are facing discriminatory practices that in effect close off their export opportunities (COM (2009) 592). The economic crisis has served to increase such practices (COM (2009) 592 final: 18).[7]

4 The Court of Auditors of the European Union, in their audits concerning projects co-financed by Regional Development Funds and Cohesion Funds, has on various occasions identified irregularities relating to public procurement contracts. For instance, for the years 2006–09, such irregularities have accounted for 41 per cent of the cumulative quantifiable errors (SEC (2011) 1179 final).[8] In its declaration of assurance by Director General (DG) Regional Policy concerning the regularity and legality of the applicable EU budget in 2011, DG Regional Policy noted various reservations – one of which was in respect of 'serious deficiencies in the management and control systems with regard to the compliance of the operations with the public procurement rules' (European Commission 2012).[9]

5 Member States are obliged to forward to the Commission yearly statistical reports of the preceding year by end of 31 October, in order to facilitate an assessment of the results of applying the EU Directives to public procurement. However, the European Commission has consistently presented *estimates* in lieu of actual data reports, in view of the fact that a large proportion of public procurement[10] data is unavailable (European Commission 2010: 3).

6 Transparency has been regarded as a mandatory element for the elimination of preferential and discriminatory purchasing behaviour. Points 2, 4 and 5

8 *The status quo*

(above) can be viewed as important considerations that shed light upon the extent of transparency – or lack of it when it comes to the implementation of EU public procurement policy.

7 In 2011 the Commission claimed that the EU public procurement Directives had helped generate savings and improvements in the quality of procurement outcomes. Open and competitive public procurement has driven down costs by around 4%, generating savings of approximately €20 billion. This far exceeds the costs generated by the regulatory framework, which are estimated to be €5 billion.

(IP/11/785 2011)

It is argued that such claimed savings are highly unreliable estimates because they rely on data that captures nothing more than the award price as published in the Contract Award Notices in the *Official Journal of the European Union* through the Tenders Electronic Daily database (TED). To rely on this method can be highly misleading. What counts is the *actual* final price that the public purchaser pays by the end of the contractual period. This is highly relevant, especially for works and service contracts where cost overruns can emerge during the contractual period. In the case of large construction projects cost overruns are a common feature due to various unforeseens such as inflation (wages and materials) and the need for additional works. As the Commission notes, '[T]he ultimate test of the effectiveness of public procurement legislation is the impact on prices actually paid for goods and services by public procurement authorities' (European Commission 2004: 14). However, measuring actual prices that incorporate the variations that arise during the contractual period would appear to be a mammoth task.

The above points are some of the salient issues that reflect upon the ineffectiveness of the public procurement regulations, and their consequent failure to create an integrated and efficient EU public procurement market. Notwithstanding such, in this journey of *verstehen* the matter is taken a few steps further as it endeavours to capture a more integrated and explanatory map. In this respect, and in order to understand better the discourses surrounding EU public procurement, one cannot rely solely on its own terms because public procurement is the product of various exogenous forces. It is therefore important that insights from other sources are drawn upon. Monodisciplinary perspectives frame too narrow a social inquiry and leave too much that is of significance out of the picture (Peterson 1998).[11] Authoritative claims that influence policy-making bear an impact on society at large (Giddens 1976). This in turn leads us to enquire whether or not communities are becoming any better off from a general viewpoint.

According to the poverty data nearly one in seven people in the EU are at risk of poverty, i.e. below the poverty threshold (Antuofermo and Di Meglio 2012; Frazer 2009: 7).[12] In the years 2012, 2011, 2010 and 2009 the percentage of people at risk of poverty (17 per cent; 17 per cent; 16 per cent; 16 per cent, respectively) was not so different from the former Member States in the previous decade (17 per cent in 1995; 16 per cent in 1997; 15 per cent in 2001), or for the EU as a whole (15 per cent in 2002) (Antuofermo and Di Meglio 2012; Frazer 2009). The concept of poverty raises important political questions because it is fundamentally linked with how society distributes and redistributes its resources and opportunities. It reflects upon the extent of the failure of the State in relation to its system of welfare.

Poverty exposes the depth of the gap that limits European integration aims. The persistent levels of poverty across the EU, as well as current social injustices, are indicative of the systematic failure of market regulation – which is too heavily based on neoliberal economics. European economic efficiency logic has its limits. The Single Market route is not the only one that is capable of leading Europe towards full integration; that is, political and economic integration. The *European citizen* is the fulcrum that stands at the heart of reaching European integration aims and paves the way to various potential market routes – all of which are available, and all of which are there for the taking. Such routes need not necessarily be bound by those economic liberal theories that essentially underpin the Single Market dogma, for what in effect is economic integration about? According to Myrdal, economic integration refers to economic life within the existing Nation States (Myrdal 1956). This is not to be interpreted as a call for nationalism, but rather a recognition that European citizens are the expression of how life is actually lived. Therefore the social dimension cannot be neglected. Enabling European citizens to attain for themselves reasonable objectives constitutes the common good (Finnis 2011).[13] And the conditions that need to be obtained if each citizen is to attain her or his objectives, relate to the common good of the political community (Finnis 2011) – a matter that needs to be addressed by both the EU and its Member States.

It is within this context that the argument for a reordered EU public procurement regime is presented. Such reordering entails an EU public procurement regime that ropes in a clear public interest function – a public interest function that capitalises on Member States' diversity whilst also operating on the basis of principles and conditions that enable its citizens to flourish. This is made possible by incorporating a key umbrella concept that embraces three core values; namely, the respect for human dignity, equality and freedom of participatory action. Simply put, the public interest function that operates in a reordered public procurement regime treats the individual as an end in itself. This is in contrast to the system that is presently in place. As the analysis in this book shows, as far as public procurement is concerned, when it comes to promulgating the EU's internal market the individual is used as the means towards this end.

Indeed, preferential procurement – alongside state aid – reflects the sort of market intervention on the part of the public sector that is commensurate with neoliberal principles, and less on the distributive objectives of societal welfare. This book, however, presents a fundamental departure from such logic by demonstrating how public procurement through a reordered regime can also operate as the means by which, *ex ante*, welfare distribution might be attained. This has been made possible by advancing a European theory of a socially just alternative that draws heavily from Rawls in a property-owning democracy. According to Rawls a property-owning democracy is necessary in order to realise the principles of justice as fairness. This he distinguishes from welfare state capitalism. It is argued that while welfare state capitalism secures a social baseline through *ex post* redistributive taxation, a property-owning democracy sets limits to the accumulation of wealth across a concentrated and narrow band of citizens. It achieves this by dispersing capital holdings across the population, therefore making use of *ex ante* redistribution of capital.

> The intent is not simply to assist those who lose out through accident or misfortune (although that must be done), but rather to put all citizens in a position to manage their own affairs *on a footing of a suitable degree of social and economic equality*.
>
> (Rawls 2001: 138)

But while Rawls grounds his arguments in favour of a property-owning democracy, there have been others who believe that both welfare state capitalism and property-owning democratic regimes can complement each other; and that a property-owning democracy can be regarded as 'useful extensions of, rather than replacements for, the welfare state' (O'Neill 2009: 390).[14] This view is congruent with that of the author, who also attempts to demonstrate how Rawls' principles of justice as fairness – through the regime of a property-owning democracy – could be realistically institutionalised via public procurement. Hence, the intellectual rationale underpinning the logic of a public procurement contract takes into consideration the distributive objectives of societal welfare – albeit in a limited manner as far public procurement is concerned. This is made possible by way of:

- broadening the concept of 'equality' so that it is not confined solely to ensuring *equal access to opportunities* as interpreted by the European Commission; but rather adopts a more encompassing interpretation, one that recognises the individual in its totality – the individual as a physical and social being at whose core lies human dignity. It recognises the human being as an end in itself and not as a means to an end;[15]
- broadening the concept of the *value-for-money* principle by incorporating objectives that go beyond the whole-of-life costs and the quality of the good or service being purchased; instead seeking the most efficient *mix* of costs that can lead to cost savings while at the same time increasing social welfare gains;[16]
- instituting systems that safeguard against conflicts of interest, favouritism and corruption in public procurement.[17]

Such logic engages in a social justice model that seeks to define and meet the ends of its citizens and capitalise on Member States' diversity. It operates on the basis of principles and conditions that enable the flourishing of its citizens by incorporating three key values: the respect for human dignity,[18] equality[19] and freedom of participatory action.[20] These key values – which combine to form a key umbrella concept – add content to the notion of the *public interest*, and correspond to embracing the fight against poverty and social exclusion, while also enabling the participatory engagement of citizens.

Very often, claims on behalf of the public interest form the basis for justifying actions or decisions at various levels of government policy. Although this term is very well used the notion of the public interest remains vague – well used, but abused. It is thus imperative that we are clear from the outset on how we configure this term in order to instil within it content that is capable of leading to workable meanings. When it comes to the EU public procurement regime it is apparant that the public interest function draws largely from the sort of neoliberalism that takes into consideration aggregative conceptions of the *common good*. However, what is presented here marks a fundamental departure from such a conception, since it endorses and sets forth a public interest function that seeks to achieve a common good in which the interdependent and harmonious flourishing or fulfilment of each individual in the community can only be made possible through cooperation and coordination within and between communities. It calls for the incorporation of the key umbrella concept, as mentioned above, and as elaborated further on in this book, to underpin and thus guide such public interest functions.

Both the EU and its Member States can make optimum use of public procurement when this is allowed to operate in the reordered format elaborated in this book. The scope for strategic investments at EU and Member State level can be guided by both social and economic reasons. In this reordered format it is possible to operate a public procurement regime which, on the one hand, seeks open market access opportunities by reinforcing transparency, objectivity and non-discrimination between those taking part in competitive tenders at EU-wide level; while on the other hand it seeks to take into account the domestic distributive objectives of societal welfare – albeit in a limited manner as far as public procurement contracts are concerned. It is argued here that during this process, and when seeking to derive optimum benefit through the use of a reordered public procurement regime, a socially just model of European integration emerges as a by-product.

1.2 Theoretical perspectives on social formation – a general idea

With a view to derive a better understanding of the diverse standpoints underpinning social formation within a political community,[21] this section presents a very brief overview of some of the theoretical viewpoints. We start with *individualistic* conceptions of society. The interaction between the individual and society, and where the balance between the individual and the community is located, have been the subject of major ideological controversies. *Individualtistic conceptions* of society are based on the belief that individuals have an inalienable right to pursue their own interests in their own way. The individual is seen to stand at the heart of any political theory or social explanation. Although individuals pursue their interests through collective entities such as businesses and trade unions, the drive to pursue self-interest is considered to be the cementing factor that leads to a natural balance among competing individuals and groups in society (Heywood 2004: 15–50). This theory is best reflected in classical liberalism as it seeks to obtain the greatest possible individual freedom (Heywood 2004).

Collectivism, on the other hand, ascribes primacy to collective action. It recognises the individual as a social animal and hence its capacity for collective action that is cemented through collective identity. This viewpoint adopts a holistic approach to society, one that is made up of complex networks of relationships (Heywood 2004). The state acts as the central agent controlling collective action in the interest of society (Heywood 2004). There have been varying interpretations concerning the role of the state from the standpoint of collectivism. On the one hand it is regarded as representing orthodox states in which the State exerts coercive authority – thus restricting individual liberty. This conception therefore stands in stark contrast to individualism. On the other hand, rather than adopting a coercive role, the State is seen as advancing the cause of individual self-development – as is the case when it provides education. From this viewpoint collectivism is conceived as compatible with the concept of indiviualism (Heywood 2004).

While the above theories assume an underlying social consensus, other theories add the notion of conflict (Heywood 2004). One such influential theory is *Marxism*. Marxism focuses on class relations and social conflicts. It holds that private property is the fundamental cause of social conflict, which in turn leads to irreconcilable class conflict (Heywood 2004). In Marx's view, classes are major political actors that are destined to overcome capitalism once a certain level of class consciousness is achieved (Heywood 2004). Classical Marxian thought makes use of three intellectual tools:

1 historical materialism – a methodological approach for understanding social change through economic development and class struggle;
2 dialectic materialism – a method for understanding social transformation that combines dialectics with philosophical materialism;
3 Marxian economics – a school of economic thought as the basis for understanding the exploitation of class and class struggle within capitalism.

According to the classical Marxian viewpoint, social change is based upon a contradiction between the means of production and those who own and control such means. Althusser rejected such a viewpoint, and instead presented a more complex view of society based on his concept of *overdetermination*. The concept of overdetermination refers to

> the effects of the contradictions in each practice constituting the social formation on the social formation as a whole, and hence back on each practice

and each contradiction, defining the pattern of dominance and subordination, antagonism and non-antagonism of the contradictions in the structure in dominance at the given moment.

(Althusser 1977: 253)

Thus, for Althusser, society is made up of multiple contradictions and non-contradictions. Change is brought about through uneven development, since ruptures in the social structure occur when contradictory aspects overcome non-contradictory ones. Although various elements exert an influence in the course of such development, the economic structure of society is believed to maintain a dominant causative relation with all other aspects of society. Nonetheless, 'the economic dialectic is never active in the pure state' (Althusser 1977: 113).

The concept of overdetermination was reformulated by Resnick and Wolff, who dismissed the causative dominance of economic life and philosophical materialism. Accordingly, '[T]he world is not to be comprehended as a complex of ready-made things, but as a complex of processes' (Resnick and Wolff 1987: 56). Each social process is itself determined either in contradiction or in support of other social processes. Nonetheless, such social processes cannot be described as one superseding another, or one being more fundamental than another, when determining a given social outcome. Resnick and Wolff's theory has been simply described as 'everything determines everything', and that 'nothing is privileged over anything else in causal hierarchy; thus, everything is equal' (Hyun Woong Park 2013: 326).

From this fleeting glimpse of theoretical understandings about social formation, and given the multitude of competing theoretical perspectives, it could be argued that it would be incorrect to reduce social formation to any single form of determinism. According to Unger, in his theory of *false necessity*, the social world represents an artifact of human endeavours (Unger 2004). For Unger there is no pre-set institutional arrangement that societies must abide by. On the contrary, there are an infinite number of ways of resisting social and institutional constraints, which can in turn lead to an infinite number of outcomes. Unger develops a progressive alternative to neoliberalism and social democracy – one in which institutional innovation plays a crucial role.

Various theories attempt to explain the process of social formations within the EU. Major contributions have come from within the political science subfield of international relations. Political integration, defined as the 'process by which nation-states selectively pool their sovereignty and set up institutions of supranational governance' (Peterson 2001), has also led to the creation of a common European *social space* (Bach 2000). This space exists in parallel to national societies (Bach 2000).

> At the same time, citizens are part of at least two social spaces, their national society and the European social space. How intense the interactions within these two social spaces are is an empirical questions [sic]. Presumably, the

European social space is still quite 'empty', compared to the national ones – but it may turn out that it is far away from being a vacuum, thanks to business contacts, holiday travel, student exchange, song contests and sporting events.

(Delhey 2004: 7)

In 2012 the European social space comprised 504 million inhabitants spread across the EU28 (Eurostat 2014b). By 2020 the total number of inhabitants across the EU28 is projected to stand at 512 million (Eurostat 2014b). But even as the EU increases competencies that were once the preserve of its constituent Nation States, still the EU remains far from being a fully fledged Nation State. Any attempts to harmonise a 'European' welfare state would require major and fundamental structural and institutional changes that would undoubtedly be met with fierce opposition (Scharpf 1997). That said, the EU has its own very distinctive mark which sets it apart from other international organisations. One major contributing factor is that the EU citizen is capable of enforcing common EU legislation through the doctrines of *direct effect* and *supremacy*. These were developed by the European Court of Justice and ensure that EU law takes precedence over domestic law. This fact distinguishes the EU from other international organisations. While other international organisations give due recognition to states over individuals, the EU recognises its citizens (Delhey 2004). Therefore, within this common EU social space, the European citizen plays a crucial role. And it is within this pan European social space that a socially just model of European integration has the potential to be realised – one in which the European citizen maintains the key actor role. The sections and chapters that follow will further endeavour to explain how a socially just model of European integration can be brought about in real terms.

1.3 On theories of social justice

Our concern here is with justice and its social application. It is not concerned with the actions of individuals, but 'as a predicate of societies – particularly of such societies called nations – and of their acts and institutions' (Frankena 2003: 63). Social justice came to stand out as a distinctive concept in the early nineteenth century. Being more concerned with who should get what in terms of the moral distribution of societal benefits or rewards, it represents a shift from the more classical ideal of justice in which the main concern is with legal penalties and punishment (Heywood 2004). Social justice is thus more concerned with social well-being.

Justice is said to constitute one of the four 'cardinal virtues' of classical moral philosophy, together with courage, temperance (self-control) and prudence (efficiency). All these virtues are concerned with elevating the dignity and sovereignty of the human person (Centre for Economic and Social Justice 2010). It has been argued that in order for a society to be fully just, social justice needs to be considered both from its formal aspect – that is, the legal aspect – and its informal aspect including cultural institutions, conventions, moral rules and moral sanctions (Frankena 2003).

A review of the theories of social justice reveals that there are a range of disagreements within political philosophy. There are various competing conceptions of what, exactly, constitutes justice. These include libertarian, utilitarian, egalitarian, contractarian and various other conceptions. This is definitely a stumbling block, particularly when it comes to examining and generating public policy. The following discussion will provide an outline of two influential theories of social justice, focusing on principles of distributive justice that entail the distribution of benefits and burdens of economic activity across society. An attempt to understand how these theories translate into real-life policy issues will also be undertaken.

It appears that there never has been, and never will be, a society whose distribution could be said to be in conformity with one of the proposed theories (Lamont and Favor 2007). Indeed, we lack a single determinate concept of justice and instead are confronted with fundamentally different ones. The theories vary, but attempt to provide us with an explanation of various fundamental issues. For instance, when it comes to distribution, what should be considered as the subject for distribution? Should it be income, jobs, opportunities or welfare? The theories also attempt to explain the basis upon which the distribution should be made. There are theories that argue for maximisation of utility, while others argue in favour of equality. But what do we mean by 'equality'? Equality of what? How can one go about specifying what constitutes a minimum standard of living? In the midst of such theoretical confusion, Hayek argues that social justice is a 'weasel word' used to evade or mislead, an excuse for increasing state control and government interference (Heywood 2004).[22] Because social justice also represents a political ideal; and pivotal to the political debate comes the role of the State (Lister 2007).

1.3.1 Utilitarianism

In classical utilitarianism, in order to obtain the social good, social institutions are to be arranged so as to maximise the *greatest happiness* – this being the sum total of individual 'utilities'. The principle of *utility*, as developed in particular by Jeremy Bentham, is understood as pleasure, happiness, or preference-satisfaction (Bentham 1907), and is inspired by the slogan 'the greatest happiness of the greatest number' (Mill 1962). Bentham sometimes used this slogan to describe the principle of utility. However, utilitarianism is solely concerned with those actions that yield the greatest aggregation of utility among all citizens irrespective of its distribution, i.e. ignoring distributional inequalities.[23] According to the utilitarian viewpoint social *injustice* results in the aggregate loss of utility which could have been achieved. Indeed, utilitarians insist on the principle of equality. That is to say, when it comes to calculating the *greatest utility* each person's utility counts equally with that of each and every other person (Mill 1962: 251–321). Everyone counts as one. The notion of the equality of people in utilitarianism serves as a means in the methodology when calculating the aggregate sum. Thus, for instance, individual freedom, autonomy, rights and quality of life are only valuable insofar as they increase aggregate utility. In other words, such values acquire a subordinate status in relation to the maximisation of aggregate utility, notwithstanding the fact that in the calculation of the aggregate utility all desires are encapsulated – including 'selfish' and 'external' preferences (Dworkin 1977: 234). Intrusion on the individual's autonomy and rights, according to utilitarians, is justified when one considers that the total benefits will be outweighed by such intrusions (Wright 2000).

It has been claimed that utilitarian logic is mirrored in the golden rule of Jesus of Nazareth. Mill affirms, 'In the golden rule of Jesus of Nazareth, we read the complete spirit of the ethics of utility. "To do as you would be done by," and "to love your neighbor as yourself," constitute the ideal perfection of utilitarian morality' (Mill 1963). Accordingly, utilitarians hold self-interests equally with those of others, be it family, friends or groups. However, this interpretation of the golden rule has been criticised and considered implausible (Wright 2000: 1869).[24] For, it is argued, to maintain a complete impartiality of interest goes against the thoughts and actions of rational individuals since it ultimately leads to self-abnegation and destruction. Indeed, one cannot expect people to sustain their desires at the expense of others (Kymlicka 1990). Utilitarianism, therefore, fails to provide a proper interpretation of the equal respect for each individual (Rawls 1971).

According to classic utilitarianism, the success or otherwise of States and their policies in generating *total happiness* needs to be determined according to three distinct informational components (Sen 1999). First of all, actions, rules, institutions and so on are to be judged by their results. This first component is referred to as 'consequentialism'. However, it appears that the main bone of contention here is what to include in the list of so-called consequences; and how can one determine whether such consequences are attributable to certain decisions. Second, judgements are to be restricted to the utilities generated in their respective States. This second component is referred to as 'welfarism'. The third component, referred to as 'sum-ranking', simply requires the summation of the utilities of different people so as to reach an aggregate utility of the entire citizenry.

But the subject of interpersonal comparisons of happiness received major criticism because it was argued that happiness as experienced by one person could not be compared with that of another because 'no common denominator of feeling was possible' (Robbins 1938). Consequently, such criticisms gave way to what has become known as 'the new welfare economics', often referred to as '*welfarism*' (Sen 2009: 278). Although the notion of pleasure/happiness remains the driving force behind the theory, it concurrently dispenses of the interpersonal comparisons of utilities.

Modern forms of utilitarianism appear to have shifted their focus towards desire fulfilment instead of happiness generation. What becomes relevant is the strength of the desire that is being fulfilled. Nevertheless, because of the difficulties encountered in measuring happiness and desire, according to modern economic analysis the measurement of utility is represented by a person's observable choices.[25] The methodology does not make use of interpersonal comparisons, and, as such, cannot accommodate the *sum-ranking* approach other than ones that invoke *welfarism* and *consequentialism*. It is for this reason that the method has been regarded as deficient and as a consequence a major demerit in the utilitarian calculus (Sen 1999).

Despite the debate on the various demerits of utilitarianism, Sen draws out two particular insightful points that are worth noting. Utilitarianism necessitates that in judging social arrangements one needs to take into consideration *results* and the *well-being* of people (despite the disagreements on the 'utility-centred mental-metric') (Sen 1999: 60). This, he argues, is highly relevant, especially when most institutions are advocated on the basis of their constitutive features without taking into consideration their consequential outcomes.

Drawing on utilitarian theories economic liberal arguments support the idea that the distribution of social resources produced by market exchanges is innately fair and just – as long as those market exchanges are unfettered. Standing at the heart of the theory is the assumption that all human decision-making is driven in pursuit of individual pleasure/happiness (utility) and its maximisation. Therefore, it is argued that as long as individual decision-making is allowed to occur without government interference there will be a just and fair distribution of social resources. The theory thus advocates a minimal role in the economy for the government. At the macroeconomic level, government policy is necessary to regulate fiscal and monetary policy; while at the microeconomic level there are those who argue in favour of a laissez-faire attitude by government; while yet others advocate regulation in order to remove market distortions. Consequently, when a state of perfect competitive market equilibrium is reached this is said to be Pareto efficient. However, this should not be taken to mean that the efficient distribution of resources has been allocated in a socially desirable manner (Sen 1993; Barr 2004). Indeed, as discussed above, utilitarian concern is with the maximum distribution of wealth rather than how such distribution affects the individual.

Economic liberal arguments hold that wealth is the result of hard work and thrift, while those who become poor do so because of their recklessness and laziness. It is argued that the provision of a social minimum policy regime reduces incentives to work or to save, and dampens entrepreneurship (White 2010). On the one hand, it is alleged that the rich would want to work less because otherwise they will have to pay more tax to support the social minimum policy regime. On the other hand, the poor need not work hard and can afford to save less because they know that ultimately they can fall back on a welfare-based safety net. This is, broadly speaking, the utilitarian argument against the enactment of a social minimum policy regime. Such were the arguments underlying the principles of the UK's 1834 New Poor Law, and they explain why nineteenth century utilitarian reformers such as Edwin Chadwick had serious reservations about enacting a social minimum. Accordingly, while conceding that there was a need for some kind of safety net for the very poor, state assistance was set at a very low level and on deliberately punitive terms (Roberts 1960).

1.3.2 Egalitarian liberal perspectives

Within contemporary political philosophy, John Rawls' *A Theory of Justice* (1971) has had profound impact in shaping modern liberal and social democratic concepts of social justice.[26] Rawls' theory of justice as fairness is considered as the most influential theory of justice in modern moral philosophy (Sen 200: 5). According to Rawls, justice is founded on the demands of fairness. Justice as fairness constitutes Rawls' basic idea for justice in a liberal society – a society in which citizens are free, hold equal basic rights, and cooperate within an egalitarian economic system. Justice as fairness aims to describe the just arrangements of major social institutions (political constitution, legal system, the economy, the family and so on) in a liberal society. For Rawls the arrangement of these institutions forms the basic structure of society, and it is within this basic structure that justice is located. Accordingly, justice is about 'the way in which the major social institutions distribute fundamental rights and duties and determine the division of advantages from social co-operation' (Rawls 1971: 6). Given that such institutions have a major impact on the lives of people, their justification becomes imperative. In a well-ordered society vested interests are put aside.

In order to derive principles of justice that are based on the notion of fairness, Rawls employs the device of the social contract[27] and sets off from an ideal world by making use of ideal theory. Ideal theory assumes that people are willing to comply with whatever principles of justice are chosen. It also assumes reasonably favourable social conditions, free from historical, cultural and empirical barriers – thus making it possible for people to abide by principles of political cooperation. In Rawls' view it is in this ideal state that the fundamental principles of justice that govern the basic institutions of society can be revealed. He maintains that the conception of the ideal of a just society needs to proceed prior to moving towards justice in the non-ideal circumstances because otherwise we would be lacking fundamental ideals.[28]

Rawls then poses an intriguing question that inquires into the principles of cooperation that free and equal citizens would ultimately agree to under fair conditions. By employing the original position argument principles of justice emerge with unanimous agreement. The original position is a thought experiment, an imaginary situation where independent citizens come together to select and agree upon the principles of justice that would govern the entire society. The move to agreement is instigated through the social contract device. In the original position everyone is under a *veil of ignorance*. Behind this *veil of ignorance* participants are deprived of any information concerning race, gender, class position, natural endowments, educational attainment, religious beliefs, and so on. As such, participants are placed fairly with respect to one another, and prevented from being influenced by arbitrary factors. In the original position, according to Rawls, all relevant conceptions of the citizen[29] and society[30] are embodied – making it possible for judgements about justice to be made.

The selection of principles from the argument in the original position is derived by following a two-stage process. First, participants agree on the selected principles which, in effect, are principles that are perceived to work in favour of the citizens they represent. Then participants check that a society that is ordered by these selected principles remains stable over time. Consequently, the following two principles of justice are proposed:

1. Each person has an equal right to a fully adequate scheme of equal basic liberties which is compatible with a similar scheme of liberties for all.
2. Social and economic inequalities are to satisfy two conditions: first, they must be attached to offices and positions open to all under conditions of fair equality of opportunity; and second, they must be to the greatest benefit of the least advantaged members of society (Rawls 1993: 291).

Rawls claims that participants would prefer these principles over utilitarian principles (Rawls sees utilitarianism as the main competitor). Given that participants in this system could secure equal liberties for all their citizens, who would dare gamble their citizens' basic liberties by opting to favour an average utility system that might work to benefit minority groups? Furthermore, Rawls argues that offering equal basic liberties for all encourages mutual respect and cooperation, and as such increases social harmony. On the other hand, utilitarianism can be driven by various partisan policies that put forward speculative claims with respect to the relative average utility increase. This in turn creates a utilitarian society that is driven by mutual suspicion. In essence, Rawls argues that his principles provide a better basis for fostering cooperation and mutual trust among the citizenry. When it comes to *The Check for Stability* Rawls maintains that the argument from the original position will hold that the two principles are congruent with the citizen's best interests because they affirm the freedom and equality of each citizen. This provides sufficient reason for citizens to develop an *enduring overlapping* consensus, which in turn provides the basis for reasonable expectation that citizens will abide by the principles. 'The most stable conception of justice is one that is perspicuous to our reason, congruent with our good, and rooted not in abnegation but in affirmation of the self' (Rawls 1971: 261).

Rawls assigns absolute or *lexical priority* to the first principle, the *liberty principle*. That is to say, in cases of conflict between the principles – for instance if one had to advance the economic interests of the worst off at the expense of restricting individual liberties – the liberty principle takes precedence. The second principle, the *equality principle*, focuses on two particular aspects of justice. The first part relates to the *principal of fair equality of opportunity*, while the second part – which is referred to as the *difference principle* – advocates that social and economic inequalities between citizens are to be limited as long as they favour the least well-off members of society. In cases of conflict the *principal of fair equality of opportunity* takes priority over the *difference principle*.

When it comes to translating these principles into the specifications of a socio-political economy, Rawls emphasises that the State must fund high-quality education for the least well-off because the enactment of laws and policies aimed solely at preventing discrimination do not suffice in ensuring equal opportunities for all citizens. Rawls also advocates that the State must guarantee a basic minimum income and healthcare for all. In Rawls' view 'The least advantaged are not, if all goes well, the unfortunate and unlucky – objects of our charity and compassion, much less our pity – but those to whom reciprocity is owed as a matter of basic justice' (Kelly 2001: 139). However, Rawls explicitly rejects the welfare state (Kelly 2001: 137–40), arguing that it tends to create a demoralised underclass similar to that created by laissez-faire capitalism. In the case of a socialist command economy the State is afforded too much power, a situation that can threaten basic liberties.

In *A Theory of Justice: Revised Edition*, published in 1999, Rawls claims that if he were to rewrite *A Theory of Justice* there would be two things he would handle differently. The first would be the way he presented his argument of the two principles of justice from the original position; and the second would be 'to distinguish more sharply the idea of a property-owning democracy ... from the idea of a welfare state' (Rawls 1999: xiv). Indeed, owing to the fact that the notion of property-owning democracy was not discussed in any detail, various left wing critics were led to believe that Rawls was advocating welfare state policies in which capitalists would produce as much wealth as possible, while the State would act to protect the 'least well-off' through redistributive policies. The notion of a capitalist welfare state was considered implausible by critics on the left.

Rawls claims that the term 'property-owning democracy', as well as certain features of the idea, were borrowed from Meade (1964). Unlike the welfare state, whose basic institutions are designed to 'assist those who lose out through accident or misfortune', the basic institutions of a property-owning democracy attempt to make use of progressive taxation and rely on competitive markets 'to disperse the ownership of wealth and capital, and thus to prevent a small part of society from controlling the economy and indirectly political life itself' (Rawls 1999: xiv–xv). Without going into details of the political economic regime of a property-owning democracy, Rawls indicates a general outline that may be consistent with the principles of justice as fairness. Broadly speaking, the institutional structure that Rawls envisions in a property-owning democracy is familiar to citizens living under welfare state capitalism. Welfare state capitalism aims to provide – through redistributive taxation – an economic baseline to the *least well-off*, including the provision of public services such as healthcare, education and social housing. A property-owning democracy also aims to provide this economic baseline, but has an additional goal: that of seeking the wide dispersion of capital.[31] Therefore, property-owning democracy not only seeks to secure a social baseline – as is the case with State capitalism – it also seeks to set limits on the accumulation of wealth across a concentrated and narrow band of citizens by dispersing capital holdings across the population. As such, property-owning democracy seeks to narrow the margins of inequalities from two different levels – from the uppermost level of society's strata and the lowest level (Williamson and O'Neil 2009).[32]

Rawls' theory of justice has been, and remains, the subject of huge debate and major criticism. Dworkin highlights the importance of factoring in an element of *responsibility* when discussing inequalities (Dworkin 1981 (Part 1 and Part 2), 2000). It is argued that inequalities, on the one hand, may arise out of misfortunes that are beyond an individual's control; but on the other hand they may also arise as a consequence of individual preferences and choices. Dworkin argues that Rawls' principles of distributional justice fail to make such a distinction, therefore enabling scroungers to be subsidised. Other challenges to Rawls, as raised by Dworkin, take issue with his account of *primary goods* – in particular income and wealth – which fail to recognise the more expensive needs that certain groups of people require, such as the disabled. According to Sen, there is a strong case for shifting the focus from primary goods to an assessment of actual freedoms and capabilities (Sen 2009: 66). In addition, Sen views the absolute priority of liberty as too extreme: he cannot see why, for instance, starvation or medical neglect need be regarded as invariably less important than the violation of any kind of liberty.

1.4 On Europe's social model

The end of 2012 marked the twentieth anniversary of the Single Market. However, it has been claimed that Europe is still yet to reap its full potential (COM (2010) 608 final:4). Indeed, since the inception of the Single Market on 1 January 1993, the world has changed. Globalisation and technological changes have created new challenges and new competitors, and the EU has enlarged. Furthermore, the economic crisis has taken its toll. To this end, in the relaunch of Europe's Single Market, Professor Mario Monti (2010) in his report to the European Commission's President advocated a new strategy – 'a social market economy approach' that puts 'Europeans at the heart of the market once again' so as 'to safeguard the single market from the risk of economic nationalism' (Monti 2010). The 'success of the European model depends on its ability to combine economic performance with social justice and to involve economic operators and the social partners in achieving this goal' (Monti 2010: 4). Fifty measures have been proposed. In effect, the relaunch of the Single Market strategy has been considered as imperative for enabling the successful implementation of Europe's 2020 strategy – which envisages growth of $c.4$ per cent of GDP over a ten-year period (COM (2010) 2020). This estimate takes into particular account measures to reduce administrative and regulatory burdens, and not least the promotion of open public procurement.

But what is actually meant by a *social market economy*? Is it synonymous with Europe's social model? In the following sections we will first attempt to derive an idea of what might be understood by Europe's social model, and then proceed to take a reality snapshot of how Europe's social features unfold. The case for furthering public procurement's social dimension is then presented, followed by some concluding remarks.

1.4.1 Ordoliberalism

Following various contested debates (Joerges and Rödl 2004)[33] the term *social market economy* finds its place in the Lisbon Treaty, more specifically in Article 3 (3) TEU.[34] There are those who speculate that the inclusion of such a term is intended to reflect the desired character of Europe's new constitutional order (Joerges and Rödl 2004: 10). Despite the ambiguity, the term 'social market economy' conjures up a clear and specific meaning for the Germans since it carries a long-standing history that extends over the past 50 years.

For the Germans a clear distinction needs to be made between a *social market economy* and a *social State*. According to German constitutional literature a social market economy is an approach that enables the State to perform as a social State (Joerges and Rödl 2004: 11). Simply put, though State[35] and society[36] are considered as having diametrically different functions they concurrently influence each other to strike a balance that preserves the democratic order of society. A social market economy is conceived within this diametric function.

The notion of a social market economy – as employed in the Communication (COM (2010) 608 final) for the relaunch of the EU's Single Market Strategy – appears to draw largely on Müller-Armack's (1966) social market economy, which is deeply ingrained in the concept of ordoliberalism. Ordoliberalism is primarily concerned with the protection of the free market economy in which the role of law is to maintain a healthy level of competition through measures that adhere to market principles and the prevention of over-concentration of both public and private power (corporatism, cartelisation and monopolies). As such, ordoliberlism seeks to impose a stable legal framework on the economy, while the political system is required to respect it.

According to Müller-Armack, when a social market economy is realised the market economy becomes infused with the social dimension (Joerges and Rödl 2004). As long as one remains faithful to ordoliberal principles, social effects are generated automatically and directly. Müller-Armack's social market economy takes into account redistributive policies via taxation and subsidies, and measures to combat economic fluctuations in order to safeguard employment and laws on minimum wages and welfare aid. However, social policies in a social market economy are subordinated to market principles. Müller-Armack also elucidates the need to focus on societal problems. It is argued that such problems can lead to individual isolation and feelings of uncertainty, with the eventual possibility of triggering anti-liberal or totalitarian movements. Müller-Armack therefore advocates the expansion of public services, including increased public investment in higher education, the advancement of career opportunities, and regional and urban planning. However, none of these measures should interfere with the functioning of market mechanisms.

Has Müller-Armack's model been successful? In the case of Germany the principles were never really followed – according to Joerges and Rödl. They contend that the model's 'theoretical weakness ensures its political survival.'[37] It presupposes a social balance but the opposite has been claimed to be true since it 'consists of a clear restriction of instruments to achieve any social objective at all' (Joerges and Rödl 2004: 20).

1.5 Social Europe on the move

> Social policies have played a central role in building Europe's economic strength, through the development of a unique social model. This has proven to be both flexible and dynamic in responding to rapid changes in Europe's economy and society over the past decades.
>
> (COM (2000) 379 final)

In 2000 the European Union was described as 'experiencing its best macroeconomic outlook for a generation' (European Council 2000). The internal market was at the time considered 'largely complete and is yielding tangible benefits' (European Council 2000). European governments therefore set out to commit themselves to a new strategic goal: 'to become the most competitive and dynamic knowledge-based economy in the world, capable of sustainable economic growth with more and better jobs and greater social cohesion' (European Council 2000). To this end, the modernisation of 'the European social model, investing in people and combating social exclusion' (European Council 2000) constituted one of the strategic measures in pursuit of its goal. European governments clearly acknowledged the essential link between sustainable economic growth and Europe's social dimension. Indeed, the link between social expenditure and its *consequent* economic benefits' (COM (2000) 379 final) was highlighted in the European Commission's Social Policy Agenda.

In the Council Conclusions of June 2009, European governments stressed

> the increased need for social services in the current economic crisis, as these services may help to mitigate the social impact of the crisis and could act both as a safety net and an additional support for active inclusion and employment for people affected by the crises.
>
> (European Council 2009)

The Council Conclusions of December 2010 underlined the fact that social services of general interest

> are *person-oriented* services, designed to respond to human vital needs, generally driven by the principle of solidarity and *often rooted in (local) cultural traditions* and contribute to the safeguard of fundamental rights and human dignity, to non-discrimination and to ensuring the creation of equal opportunities for all, therefore *enabling individuals* to play a significant part in the economic and social life of the society.
>
> (European Council 2010)

Notwithstanding the refined oratory and orchestrated rhetoric, social reality is always obliged to appear – unfolding and exposing itself at some point in time. The following snapshot attempts to depict a few of the 'welfare reform measures' that some Member States adopted in response to a background of growing national debt and the global financial and economic crisis.

Denmark's national debt amounts to 38.1 per cent of its GDP (2009 estimates). Well-known for its very generous cradle-to-grave social welfare system, in May 2010 Denmark launched an austerity plan in an attempt to avoid the fate of Greece. Measures included slashing its unemployment benefits in half, cutting ministers' salaries by 5 per cent, capping family welfare payments, and abolishing tax breaks. Its public deficit is expected to come in below the EU limit of 3 per cent of GDP by 2013 (Lanka Business Online 2010; Economics 2010).

France's national debt amounts to 79.7 per cent of its GDP (2009 estimates). Government plans to raise the retirement age from 60 to 62 spurred strong protests and nationwide strikes. The French healthcare system is gradually increasing its co-payments' systems (Beardsley 2010; Tanner 2010; Economics 2010).

Germany's national debt amounts to 77.2 per cent of its GDP (2009 estimates). Its national debt was forecast to rise beyond €2 trillion by 2013. Measures to slash €80 billion from its government budget by 2014 included modest cuts in parental benefits and unemployment benefits. State-run universities, previously free to attend, have begun to charge tuition fees. The retirement age will be raised from 65 to 67 by 2029 (*E-commerce Journal* 2013; The Local – Germany's News in English 2010; Tanner 2010; Economics 2010).

Greece's national debt amounts to 108.1 per cent of GDP (2009 estimates). Its welfare system, established in the early 1980s, is relatively new. The austerity measures have been described by unions as 'savage', and include second round wage cuts for public workers and a three-year pension freeze. As of May 2010 Greece had experienced three general strikes, and protests were expected to escalate (Petrakis 2010; Economics 2010).

Ireland's national debt amounts to 63.7 per cent of its GDP (2009 estimates). After receiving a bailout package in the region of €85 billion, in November 2010, the Irish government outlined its four-year austerity plan. Measures included a reduction in the minimum wage, a new property tax, and the axing of 25,000 public sector jobs (Murchie 2010; Economics 2010).

Italy's national debt amounts to 115.2 per cent of GDP (2009 estimates). A total of €30 billion worth of budget cuts, over a period of two years, were proposed. The austerity measures have included a €1 billion cut to the national healthcare system, a crackdown on fraudulent disability benefit claims, and a three-year pay freeze for all government workers (Tanner 2010; Economics 2010).

Portugal's national debt amounts to 75.2 per cent of GDP (2009 estimates). Considered as a potential candidate for a bailout, in November 2010 the Portuguese Parliament voted to adopt the 2011 austerity budget. The government is focusing on budget savings of around five billion euros through a combination of tax hikes and a reduction in public sector wages. Although drastic changes to welfare benefits are being avoided, unemployment benefits will be slashed. The austerity measures triggered the largest general strike seen in the last two decades (stuff.co.nz.Business Day 2010; Economics 2010).

Spain's national debt amounts to 59.5 per cent of GDP (2009 estimates). Faced with its worst economic crisis in decades, Spain has slashed government spending by €15 billion, abolished payments to parents of newborn children, and cut disability payments. The retirement age for men is expected to rise from 65 to 67 (Tanner 2010; Economics 2010).

The *United Kingdom*'s national debt amounts to 68.5 per cent of GDP (2009 estimates). It plans to raise the retirement age to 66 and bring an end to payments to parents of newborn children. Spending cuts are expected to lead to the loss of about 490,000 jobs in the public sector over a four-year period. Education spending is expected to be cut by 25 per cent over the next four years (UK economy 2010; Underhill 2010; Richardson 2010; Economics 2010).

In general, fiscal austerity measures have depressed growth in those countries most affected by the crisis. A reduction in tax revenues made the restoration of fiscal sustainability and market confidence more difficult (Armstrong *et al.* 2012). In Europe, the financial crisis – which later developed into a sovereign debt crisis – bore heavily on the EU economy. Between 2008–12 European governments provided state aid amounting to €1.5 trillion in order to prevent the collapse of the financial system (SWD (2014) 158 final). Central banks had to provide significant liquidity support; for instance, the European Central Bank lent about one trillion euros to banks in the Eurozone (SWD (2014) 158 final).

Growth in the EU27 GDP declined sharply in 2008, and contracted considerably in 2009. Five years after the crisis GDP levels for some Member States have remained below pre-crisis levels. The EU unemployment rate increased from a pre-crisis low of 7.2 per cent in 2007 (16.9 million people) to a record high of 10.8 per cent in 2013 (26.2 million people) – an increase of 9.3 million. These are some of the factual realities that shed light on Europe's socio-economic status. Worth noting are the disparities across Member States. In 2013, the unemployment rate ranged from 4.9 per cent in Austria, 5.3 per cent in Germany, 5.9 per cent in Luxembourg, 6.5 per cent in Malta and 6.7 per cent in the Netherlands to 27.3 per cent in Greece, 26.4 per cent in Spain, 17.2 per cent in Croatia and 16.5 per cent in Portugal. Youth unemployment during the crisis period rose considerably (see Table 1.1).

In May 2014 EU citizens elected a new European Parliament. Far right and populist parties made large gains. The European People's Party managed to maintain the largest number of parliamentary seats (28 per cent), though this was down from the 36 per cent they had held.

The message relayed is loud and clear – European priorities need reordering.

1.6 On the power of social protection expenditure

Member States are responsible for the organisation and financing of their social protection systems. The following figures are worth noting when it comes to

Table 1.1 Youth unemployment rate – annual average percentage

Youth unemployment rate – Annual average % (not seasonally adjusted)

	2004	2007	2008	2009	2010	2011	2012	2013
European Union (28 countries)	9.3	7.2	7.0	9.0	9.6	9.6	10.4	10.8
Euro area (17 countries)	9.2	7.5	7.6	9.5	10.1	10.1	11.3	12.0
Belgium	8.4	7.5	7.0	7.9	8.3	7.2	7.6	8.4
Bulgaria	12.1	6.9	5.6	6.8	10.3	11.3	12.3	13.0
Czech Republic	8.3	5.3	4.4	6.7	7.3	6.7	7.0	7.0
Denmark	5.5	3.8	3.5	6.0	7.5	7.6	7.5	7.0
Germany (until 1990 former territory of the FRG)	10.5	8.7	7.5	7.8	7.1	5.9	5.5	5.3
Estonia	10.1	4.6	5.5	13.5	16.7	12.3	10.0	8.6
Ireland	4.5	4.7	6.4	12.0	13.9	14.7	14.7	13.1
Greece	10.5	8.3	7.7	9.5	12.6	17.7	24.3	27.3
Spain	11.0	8.2	11.3	17.9	19.9	21.4	24.8	26.1
France	8.9	8.0	7.5	9.1	9.3	9.2	9.8	10.3
Croatia	13.8	9.6	8.4	9.1	11.8	13.5	15.9	17.2
Italy	8.0	6.1	6.7	7.8	8.4	8.4	10.7	12.2
Cyprus	4.6	3.9	3.7	5.4	6.3	7.9	11.9	15.9
Latvia	11.7	6.1	7.7	17.5	19.5	16.2	15.0	11.9
Lithuania	11.6	4.3	5.8	13.8	17.8	15.4	13.4	11.8
Luxembourg	5.0	4.2	4.9	5.1	4.6	4.8	5.1	5.8
Hungary	6.1	7.4	7.8	10.0	11.2	10.9	10.9	10.2
Malta	7.2	6.5	6.0	6.9	6.9	6.5	6.4	6.5
Netherlands	5.1	3.6	3.1	3.7	4.5	4.4	5.3	6.7
Austria	4.9	4.4	3.8	4.8	4.4	4.2	4.3	4.9
Poland	19.1	9.6	7.1	8.1	9.7	9.7	10.1	10.3
Portugal	7.5	8.9	8.5	10.6	12.0	12.9	15.9	16.5
Romania	8.0	6.4	5.8	6.9	7.3	7.4	7.0	7.3
Slovenia	6.3	4.9	4.4	5.9	7.3	8.2	8.9	10.1
Slovakia	18.4	11.2	9.6	12.1	14.5	13.7	14.0	14.2
Finland	8.8	6.9	6.4	8.2	8.4	7.8	7.7	8.2
Sweden	7.4	6.1	6.2	8.3	8.6	7.8	8.0	8.0
United Kingdom	4.7	5.3	5.6	7.6	7.8	8.0	7.9	7.5

Source: Eurostat.

social protection expenditure. In 2005 it amounted to 27 per cent of GDP across the 27 EU Member States; in 2006 it accounted for 26.6 per cent of GDP; and 26 per cent, 26.7 per cent, 29.5 per cent, 29.4 per cent and 29.1 per cent of GDP for years 2007, 2008, 2009, 2010 and 2011 respectively (Eurostat 2014b).[38] However, in view of the significant differences in the way social protection is financed the percentage share of expenditure varies across Member States. This depends on whether a social security contributions system is utilised, or whether general government funding is preferred. In 2005 social protection expenditure as a percentage of GDP was highest in Sweden (31.1 per cent) and lowest in Latvia (12.8 per cent). In 2011 social protection expenditure as a percentage of GDP amongst the EU Member States was highest in Denmark (34.2 per cent) followed by France (33.4 per cent) Belgium (30.4 per cent) and Greece (30.2 per cent). By contrast Bulgaria, Estonia, Latvia, Lithuania, Malta, Poland and Spain spent less than 20 per cent of their GDP on social protection measures. In 2009 social protection expenditure made it possible for 35 per cent of the EU population to be lifted above the poverty line (Eurostat 2011a).

Apart from the crucial direct support that social protection expenditure provides – for example protection against risks linked to unemployment, sickness, old age and social exclusion – there is another dimension to it that is worth noting. The level of social protection expenditure correlates strongly with the proportion of employees working in the health and social services sector (SEC (2010) 1284 final). Employment in this sector has grown much faster than in other sectors, with a net increase of 4.2 million jobs between 2000–09 (this increase represents more than a quarter of the net total employment growth in the EU).[39] Some 81 per cent (equivalent to 3.4 million jobs) of this net increase is attributable to female employees. Indeed, the workforce in the health and social services sector is predominately female, capturing 78 per cent (16.8 million) of total female employment across the EU27 (SEC (2010) 1284 final: 12). Work in this sector is highly intensive, and the prevalence of part-time work is higher here than it is across the EU27 economy more generally.[40] Furthermore, and in addition to its significant contribution in terms of job creation, the health and social services sector generates around 5 per cent of the total EU economic output across the whole of the EU27 (SEC (2010) 1284: 9). Another interesting finding is that according to the competitiveness ranking among the OECD countries, countries such as Finland, Germany and the Netherlands – which have a relatively high rate of social protection expenditure – all featured high in the global competitive index of the World Economic Forum (Vandenbroucke and Vanhercke 2014).

Trends indicate the demand for health and social services are expected to grow. The aging of the European population,[41] coupled with changing family structures,[42] will no doubt present new challenges that will exert even more pressure on this sector. Notwithstanding the dynamic nature of the health and social services sector, most Member States are attempting to balance their budgets by implementing financial cutbacks that are aimed largely at the public sector, the health and education sector, and the social sector. Such measures are therefore likely to trigger a whole chain of undesirable effects since changes in working conditions bring about added work pressures, employee discontent, decreasing levels of employee motivation, lower service quality outcomes, and customer dissatisfaction. Furthermore, when it comes to unemployment, women are most likely to suffer the brunt of any cuts since they are proportionally over-represented in the most-affected sectors. Women are more vulnerable than men on the open labour market in view of their relative lack of experience and the fact that their work is more often based on part-time or short-term contracts (Governatori et al. 2010: 54).

1.7 The case for a reordered public procurement regime

In December 2011 a proposal was presented for a Directive of the European Parliament and of the Council on public procurement (COM (2011) 896).[43] This built on the Europe 2020 strategy for smart, sustainable and inclusive growth (COM (2010) 2020). The case for retaining public procurement at EU level was made on the basis that this was neccessary in order to attain two complementary objectives:

> Increase the efficiency of public spending to ensure the best possible procurement outcomes in terms of value for money. This implies in particular a simplification and flexibilisation of the existing public procurement rules. Streamlined, more efficient procedures will benefit all economic operators and facilitate the participation of SMEs and cross-border bidders.
> Allow procurers to make better use of public procurement in support of common societal goals such as protection of the environment, higher resource and energy efficiency, combating climate change, promoting innovation, employment and social inclusion and ensuring the best possible conditions for the provision of high quality social services.
> (COM (2011) 896: 2)

As such, the Subsidiarity Principle was invoked – because it was claimed that the proposal could not be sufficiently achieved by Member States for the following reasons:

> The coordination of procedures for public procurement above certain thresholds has proven an important tool for the achievement of the Internal Market in the field of public purchasing by ensuring effective and equal access to public contracts for economic operators across the Single Market. Experience with Directives 2004/17/EC and 2004/18/EC and the earlier generations of public procurement Directives has shown that European-wide procurement procedures provide transparency and objectivity in public procurement resulting in considerable savings and improved procurement outcomes that benefit Member States' authorities and, ultimately, the European taxpayer.
> (COM (2011) 896 final: 6)

The above claims are very difficult to substantiate, especially in light of the various issues that this book raises. For instance, the following examples reflect upon the lack of transparency in European-wide procurement: (1) Over the past 20 years cross border public procurement has remained relatively low – over 98 per cent of contracts awarded according to EU rules are won by national bidders; (2) The European Commission's Director General (DG) for Regional Policy has repeatedly expressed reservations in its declaration of assurance concerning the regularity and legality of the applicable EU budget in view of the serious lack of compliance with the EU public procurement rules (3) Statistical public procurement reports are heavily based on estimates because a large proportion of public procurement data is unavailable. In essence, this indicates that preferential public procurement (in some form or other, and for some reason is still taking place across the EU – despite the fact that this runs counter to EU public procurement legislation.

Notwithstanding all of this, and in a scenario in which the EU economy is still growing slowly following the financial and economic crisis that began in late 2007, due consideration needs to be given to the EU's social dimension. Indeed, the impact of the financial and economic crisis goes beyond the economic dimension because it tears at the very heart of the EU's social fabric. Eurostat, for example, concludes that current (high) levels of poverty and social exclusion are jeopardising the liklihood of hitting the Europe 2020 target of lifting 20 million people out of being at risk of poverty and social exclusion (COM (2011) 896 final: 15). In 2012 there were 124.4 million people at risk of poverty or social exclusion, a growth of 8.7 million since 2008. Put differently, one quarter of the EU population in 2012 experienced at least one form of poverty. Such measures of poverty include monetary poverty (being at risk of poverty after social transfers – covering, for example, retirement pensions, widows' and widowers' pensions, unemployment benefits, sickness and invalidity benefits, education-related benefits, etc.) – is the most prevalent form of poverty in the EU and affected 17.1 per cent of the 2012 population); severe material deprivation (this has grown considerably from 41.4 million in 2008 to 51 million in 2012); and a lack of access to jobs. Regional disparities in employment within the EU were reduced by 2.1 percentage points between 2000–07. However, the economic crisis brought regional disparities in employment back to 2000 levels (13.3 per cent in 2012) (European Commission 2013: 12). An EU employment rate of just 68.5 per cent in 2012 has pushed it off course to meet the Europe 2020 target of 75 per cent (European Commission 2013: 12). Following a continuous fall in the EU's unemployment rate during the period 2005–08 – reaching a low of 7.1 per cent in 2008 – a sharp increase to a record high of 10.5 per cent in 2012 was reported (European Commission 2013: 12). The EU's long-term unemployment rate reached a historical high of 4.6 per cent in 2012.

Social failure disrupts economies and comes at major cost. Public procurement can accommodate and serve the particular and diverse socio-economic needs of Member States. It is capable of providing much-needed breathing space at the domestic level, one that allows Member States space to manoeuvre, to innovate and to cooperate. Nonetheless, this need not come at the expense of inhibiting the multi-dynamic uses of public procurement as a policy tool that can also serve at EU level in support of common EU goals by way of reinforcing transparency, objectivity and non-discrimination between competing participants in tenders; increasing efficiency in public procurement; and supporting common goals such as protection of the environment, higher resource and energy efficiency, combating climate change, and promoting innovation, etc. The main argument here is that the EU should seek to capitalise and make best use of public procurement's potential as a policy instrument that is capable of acting as a highly powerful and dynamic socio-economic lever in a way that is aligned to the needs of the EU citizen. Hence, the ultimate motivations underpinning EU actions need to be guided by a *public interest* function that recognises the full dignity of the human person as an end in itself, and that its flourishing can only be brought about through interdependent cooperation and coordination within the community. Indeed, deriving a balance between the social and economic uses of public procurement at EU level and at Member State level is possible through a politics of cooperation and coordination.

European economic development relies heavily on the diverse socio-political building capacities of the EU Member States. But why should the European citizen serve as the means for the 'achievement of the *internal market*' (COM (2011) 896: 6, emphasis added) at the expense of public purchasing autonomy? The extent to which the EU public procurement regime is contributing towards the internal market, and its subsequent perceived contribution towards European integration, are not at all convincing. Public procurement as a highly powerful and dynamic policy instrument has the power to steer a country's socio-economic policies. Given the different socio-economic scenarios that Member States continuously experience – not only during times of crisis – there will always be Member States with relatively more advanced economies, others that are standing still, others that are going slightly backwards, and yet others that are going more quickly backwards. In such a scenario – one that is never fixed but in a state of continuous flux – 'how could there ever be a set of universal trade rules that would serve the interests of all?' (Unger 2007: 118). Free trade, it is argued, may be more attractive for some while simultaneously less so for others, since completely different scenarios prevail at different points in time. It is within this context that public procurement as a highly dynamic and powerful socio-economic lever needs to be regarded. It presents and justifies the case for the incorporation of a reordered regime, one that also has the potential to realise a social model of integration in the European Union in which the European citizen is the key actor in the integration process. The chapters that follow will elaborate further on this vision – one that explicates a socially just model of integration in the European Union.

1.8 Concluding remarks

European challenges need not rely solely upon European economic efficiency logic. 'Europe', Schuman proposed 'will not be made all at once, or according to a single plan. It will be built through concrete achievements which first create a *de facto* solidarity' (European Commission 2014). What Schuman proposed more than 60 years ago remains highly relevant today.

The ratification of the Treaty of Lisbon, which came into force in 2009, has been looked upon by some as shifting towards a more social market stance (Spiegel Online 2007; Ross 2009). It is worth noting that the new Articles 2 and 3 of the Treaty of the European Union (TEU) appear more inclined towards upholding social values and aims, rather than addressing purely economic objectives (Jones and Sufrin 2010: 41). Article 2 (TEU) holds:

> The Union is founded on the values of respect for human dignity, freedom, democracy, equality, the rule of law and respect for human rights, including the rights of persons belonging to minorities. These values are common to the Member States as a society in which pluralism, non-discrimination, tolerance, justice, solidarity and equality between women and men prevail.

Article 3 (3) of the TEU describes the internal market as working for 'the sustainable development of Europe based on balanced economic growth ... a highly competitive social market economy, aiming at full employment and social progress'. In addition, this Article describes the internal market as combating 'social exclusion and discrimination, and shall promote social justice and protection, equality between women and men, solidarity between generations and protection of the rights of the child'. Article 9 of the TFEU stipulates that the Union shall 'take into account requirements linked to ... the guarantee of adequate social protection' and 'the fight against social exclusion'. Pursuant to Article 1 of the Charter of Fundamental Rights, human dignity is inviolable: it must be respected and protected. Article 6 (1) of the Treaty confers on the Charter of Fundamental Rights the same legal value as the Treaties. Indeed, the dignity of the human person is not only a fundamental right in itself, but constitutes the real basis of fundamental rights.

Furthermore, social policies rest with Member States' sovereignty and are immune from supranational intervention.

All in all, the Treaty of Lisbon is perfectly balanced in allowing a reordered EU public procurement regime that has the potential to realise a social model of integration in the European Union in which the European citizen features as the key actor in the integration process. Such reorganisation entails an EU public procurement regime which, on the one hand, seeks open market access opportunities by way of reinforcing transparency, objectivity and non-discrimination between competing participants in tenders at EU-wide level; and on the other hand takes into account domestic distributive objectives of societal welfare – albeit in a limited manner as far as public procurement contracts are concerned. The balance between EU and domestic State public purchasing occurs through various processes of exchange. Consequently, European integration is furthered as it becomes deepened with the European social space.

Notes

1 It is worth noting that the Maastricht Treaty, formally known as the Treaty on the European Union (TEU) and put into force in 1993, established the three pillars of the European Union; namely, the European Community, the Common Foreign and Security Policy, and the Justice and Home Affairs pillar. In the first pillar, the European Community – a continuation of the European Economic Community – had the term 'Economic' dropped in order to reflect its wider policy base.
2 Chapter 2, section 2.3, provides a more detailed account of the Directives that were issued at the time.
3 Council Directive 77/62/EEC of 21 December 1976.
4 It is worth noting that the adoption of a new legislative package for the modernisation of EU public procurement was agreed upon by the Council in June 2013, and by the European Parliament in January 2014. For this purpose:

> Directive 2004/18/EC of the European Parliament and of the Council of 31 March 2004 on the coordination of procedures for the award of public works contracts, public supply contracts and public service contracts (30.04.2004) will be repealed with effect from 18 April 2016 and replaced by Directive 2014/24/EU of the European Parliament and of the Council of 26 February 2014 on public procurement.
>
> Directive 2004/17/EC of the European Parliament and of the Council of 31 March 2004 coordinating the procurement procedures of entities operating in the water, energy, transport and postal services sectors (30.04.2004) will be repealed with effect from 18 April 2016 and replaced by Directive 2014/25/EU of the European Parliament and of the Council of 26 February 2014 on procurement by entities operating in the water, energy, transport and postal services sectors.

A new Directive, 2014/23/EU of the European Parliament and of the Council of 26 February 2014, has been issued concerning the award of concession contracts. Member States are to take the necessary measures to impose this Directive and comply with its provisions by 18 April 2016.

5 For a more detailed account see Chapter 3.
6 For a more detailed account see Chapter 3, section 3.3.
7 For a more detailed account see Chapter 3, section 3.5.
8 The calculation of error rates is based on representative statistical samples with a 95 per cent confidence level. See, for example, Court of Auditors (2010).
9 For a more detailed account see Chapter 3, section 3.2.
10 See for example Article 67 of Directive 2004/17/EC, and Article 75 of Directive 2004/18/EC.
11 According to Peterson, 'Conventional accounts in international relations separate political activities associated with states from economic activities associated with markets' (p. 19).
12 According to Eurostat, people at risk of poverty are defined as follows:

> This indicator reflects the percentage of people with an equivalised disposable income below the 'at-risk-of-poverty threshold'. The at-risk-of-poverty threshold is set for each country at 60% of the national median equivalised disposable income.

13 This draws on natural law theory, see Currie 2008: 155. See also Chapter 5, in particular section 5.4.
14 The author also notes that this is very much in line with James Meade's opinion about policies concerning a property-owning democracy, and quotes his view in this respect: 'These measures are needed, for the most part, to supplement rather than to replace the existing Welfare-State policies' (Smith 1776: 75).

Introduction 33

15 This is consistent with the enactment of type (1) policies, as referred to in a property-owning democracy. For a more detailed discussion refer to Chapter 8, section 8.4.1.
16 This is consistent with the enactment of type (2) policies, as referred to in a property-owning democracy. For a more detailed discussion refer to Chapter 8, section 8.4.1.
17 This is consistent with the enactment of type (3) policies, as referred to in a property-owning democracy. For a more detailed discussion refer to Chapter 8, section 8.4.1.
18 On the value of respect for human dignity – each and every person as a rational human being, has dignity. Human dignity is inviolable. It is 'superior to human rights and fundamental freedoms who owe their origin and existence to the dignity of the human person' (Directive 2003/55/EC). See also the discussion in Chapter 5, in particular section 5.4.3 and section 5.5.
19 On the value of equality – what we are concerned with here is an equality vis-à-vis the person in their totality. This totality recognises the individual not just as a physical being, but also as a social being at whose very core lies human dignity. It calls for the recognition of the human being as an end in itself, and not as a means to an end. More specifically, we need to refer to an equality that takes into account the *capability to function*. Capabilities to function assert freedom. The notion of capability to function refers to that conceived by Professor Amartya Sen, as discussed in Chapter 5, section 5.3.
20 On the value of freedom of participatory action – what we are concerned with here is a freedom that enables the full participation of the individual in society; a freedom that defines and serves the ends of its citizens, liberates the individual, and provides space for initiative and action. Such space for initiative and action unleashes the individual's capability to function, which in itself asserts freedom. This is the freedom that finds its epitome when expressed through the flourishing of the individual.
21 In its very simplistic form the political community here refers to the community that is living within a framework of law.
22 Friedrich Hayek (1899–1992), an influential Austrian economist and political philosopher, was a stout believer in individualism and market order – and a critic of socialism.
23 It has been argued that it is impossible for a theory to have a double maxim; that is, in this case, one cannot produce simultaneously the greatest happiness and the happiness of the greatest number. See Doucet 2002, cited in Dahringer 1991: 1868.
24 Wright, Finnis and Kant have noted that such impartiality of interest leads to 'complete self-abnegation and to the destruction of personhood, rather than to its complete fulfilment, and thus is not a principle that any rational person would adopt as the supreme principle of morality'.
25 'The basic formula is this: if a person would choose an alternative x over another, y, then and only then that person has more utility from x than from y.' See Dworkin 1981: 59).
26 John Rawls (1921–2002), an American political philosopher, continued throughout his life to work further on his theory of justice as fairness. Subsequent publications include *Political Liberalism* (1993), *The Law of Peoples* (1999) and *Justice as Fairness* (2001).
27 The notion of the social contract implies that for the maintenance of social order through the rule of law, people give up their sovereignty.
28 Critics of ideal theory have questioned the usefulness of deriving principles that are applicable in ideal circumstances when these need to be applied in a non-ideal world that is overshadowed by various forms of injustice and oppression. One of Rawls' well-known critics is Amartya Sen, who argues that ideal theory – which he refers to as *transcendental theory* – is redundant because: 'If a theory of justice is to guide reasoned choice of policies, strategies or institutions, then the identification of fully just social arrangements is neither necessary nor sufficient.' Sen argues in favour of a comparative theory of justice. See Dworkin 1977.

29 For Rawls, citizens are not only free and equal, but also reasonable and rational. Citizens are reasonable because of their capacity for a sense of justice; and they are rational because of their capacity for a conception of the common good. In effect, these capacities give citizens moral powers. In order to develop and exercise these moral powers – which are needed in the pursuit of a good life – citizens are driven by fundamental interests, which Rawls refers to as primary goods. Primary goods include: basic rights and liberties; freedom of movement and free choice among a wide range of occupations; the power of offices and responsibility; income and wealth.
30 Rawls' conception of society draws on social institutions which he maintains need to be fair for all cooperating members of society – irrespective of their race, gender, religion, class of origin, and so on. Social institutions need to stand up to public scrutiny. Publicity, for Rawls, is an integral aspect of fairness because for 'public political life, nothing need be hidden' (Rawls 1993: 68).
31 Here the notion of capital, as well as income, includes capital assets and the equitable distribution of human capital.
32 The concept of property-owning democracy, and its relevance to public-private partnerships, will be further explored and discussed in Chapter 8.
33 See in particular their footnote 38 (Joerges and Rödl 2004).
34 Article 3 (3) TEU states:

> The Union shall establish an internal market. It shall work for the sustainable development of Europe based on balanced economic growth and price stability, a highly competitive social market economy, aiming at full employment and social progress, and a high level of protection and improvement of the quality of the environment. It shall promote scientific and technological advance. It shall combat social exclusion and discrimination, and shall promote social justice and protection, equality between women and men, solidarity between generations and protection of the rights of the child. It shall promote economic, social and territorial cohesion, and solidarity among Member States. It shall respect its rich cultural and linguistic diversity, and shall ensure that Europe's cultural heritage is safeguarded and enhanced.

35 '[T]he possibility of the state to influence the sphere of society should establish and secure the democratic character of society, shaped and guided according to the classical liberal imperatives' (Joerges and Rödl 2004: 11).
36 '[T]he influence of the society upon the state should guarantee the liberality (*Freiheitlichkeit*) of the democratic order as a whole against a totalitarian threat and danger of state usurpation of society' (Joerges and Rödl 2004: 11).
37 '[T]he ordoliberal argument perpetually immunises itself: Its promises would be fulfilled if the political system, the law and economic actors would comply with the imperatives of ordoliberalism. They never fully complied' (Joerges and Rödl 2004: 14).
38 The figures for the years 2009, 2010 and 2011 are presented as provisional ones. Social protection expenditure contains: social benefits, which consist of transfers (in cash or in kind) to households and individuals to relieve them of the burden of a defined set of risks or needs; administration costs, which represent the costs charged to the scheme for its management and administration; other expenditure, which consists of miscellaneous expenditure by social protection schemes (payment of property income and others). It is calculated in current prices.
39 Total employment in the EU grew by 7.9 per cent (15.5 million new jobs) between years 2000–09 (SEC (2010) 2010: 9).
40 The proportion of part-time workers in the EU27 in year 2009 was 18.8 per cent. In the health and social services sector the share of part-time employment in the EU27 is 31.6 per cent (SEC (2010) 2010: 17).

41 In the EU27, between 2008–60, the population aged 65+ is projected to increase from 84.6 to 151.5 million, while the population aged 80+ is projected to increase from 21.8 to 61.4 million (SEC (2010) 2010: 20).
42 As life expectancy rises, fertility rates fall. European fertility in 2003 was on average 1.5 children per couple. This is below the replacement fertility rate of 2.1 children. Single parent households are on the increase. Same sex parents can adopt children in some countries. Marriage is on the decline, while divorce is on the increase (Thiry 2006).
43 The adoption of a new legislative package for the modernisation of EU public procurement was agreed by the Council in June 2013, and by the European Parliament in January 2014. Member States are to take the necessary measures to operationalise the relative Directives – namely Directive 2014/23/EU, Directive 2014/24/EU, Directive 2014/25/EU – and comply with their provisions by 18 April 2016.

References

Althusser, L., 1977. *For Marx*. London: New Left Books.
Antuofermo, A. and Di Meglio, E., 2012. *Eurostat statistics in focus 9/2012 – Population and social conditions*. Luxembourg: Eurostat.
Armstrong, A., Delannoy, A., Fic, T., Holland, D., Hurst, I., Liadze, I., Lisenkova, K., Orazgani, A. and Paluchowski, P., 2012. 'At A Glance ... The world economy' in *National Institute Economic Review*, vol. 222, p. F2.
Atkins, W.S. Management Consultants, 1988. *The Costs of Non-Europe in Public Sector Procurement. Basic Findings Vol 5, Part A and B*. Luxembourg: Office for Publications of the EC.
Bach, M., 2000. 'Die Europäisierung der nationalen Gesellschaft? Problemstellungen und Perspektiven einer Soziologie der europäischen Integration' in *Kölner Zeitschrift für Soziologie und Sozialpsychologie*, pp. 11–35.
Barr, N., 2004. *Economics of the welfare state*. New York: Oxford University Press.
Beardsley, E., 2010. 'Can the European Welfare State Survive?' Available at: www.npr.org/templates/story/story.php?storyId=128485416 [accessed November 2010].
Bentham, J., 1907. *An Introduction to the Principles of Morals and Legislation*. Oxford: Clarendon Press.
Bovis, C., 2006. *EC Public Procurement Case Law and Regulation*. Oxford: Oxford University Press.
Cecchini, P., 1988. *The European Challenge, 1992: The benefits of a Single Market*. Aldershot, Hants: Wildwood House Limited.
Centre for Economic and Social Justice, 2010. 'Defining Economic Justice and Social Justice'. Available at: www.cesj.org/thirdway/economicjustice-defined.htm18 [accessed November 2010].
Cox, A., 1993. *The Single Market Rules and the Enforcement Regime After 1992*. Great Britain: Earlsgate Press.
Craig, P. and De Búrca, G., 2011. *EU Law – Text, cases and materials*. Oxford: Oxford University Press.
Currie, C., 2008. *Inequalities in young people's health: HBSC international report from 2005*. Copenhagen: WHO Regional Office for Europe.
Dahringer, L.D., 1991. *Marketing Services Internationally: Barriers and Management*. United Kingdom, Santa Barbara: Emerald Group Publishing Limited.
Delhey, J., 2004. 'European social integration: From convergence of countries to transnational relations between peoples'. Inequality and Social Integration, Berlin Social Science Centre. Available at: www.wz-berlin.de.

36 The status quo

Doucet, A. and Mauthner, N., 2002. 'Knowing responsibly: linking ethics, research practice and epistemology' in M. Mauthner, M. Birch, J. Jessop and T. Miller (eds), *Ethics in qualitative research*. London: Sage Publications, pp. 123–45.

Dworkin, R., 1977. *Taking Rights Seriously*. Cambridge: Harvard University Press.

Dworkin, R., 1981. 'What is equality? Part 1: equality of welfare' in *Philosophy and Public Affairs*, vol. 10, pp. 185–246.

Dworkin, R., 1981. 'What is equality? Part 2: equality of welfare' in *Philosophy and Public Affairs*, vol. 10, pp. 283–345.

Dworkin, R., 2000. *Sovereign virtue: The theory and practice of equality*. Cambridge, MA: Harvard University Press.

E-commerce Journal, 2010. 'German debt may top 2 trillion euros by 2013'. Available at: http://ecommerce-journal.com/news/16736_german_debt_may_top_2_trillion_euros_by_2013.

Economics, 2010. 'List of national debt by Country'. Economics. Available at: www.economicshelp.org/blog/economics/list-of-national-debt-by-country/.

Finnis, J., 2011. *Natural Law and Natural Rights*, 2nd edition. Oxford: Oxford University Press.

Frankena, W.K., 2003. 'The Concept of Social Justice' in L.C. Becker (ed.), Equality and Justice: Justice in General. London: Routledge, p. 63.

Frazer, H., 2009. *Poverty and Inequality in the EU*. Brussels: European Anti Poverty Network Social Inclusion.

GHK, 2010. *Evaluation of SMES' Access To Public Procurement Markets In The EU*. Brussels: DG Enterprise and Industry.

Giddens, A., 1976. *New Rules of the Sociological Method*. London: Hutchinson.

Governatori, M., Grzegorzewska, M., Medeiros, J., Meyermans, E., Minty, P., Peschner, J. and Van der Valk, J., 2010. *Employment in Europe 2010*. Brussels: European Commission.

Heywood, A., 2004. *Political Theory, An Introduction*. Third edition. New York: Palgrave Macmillan.

Hyun Woong Park., 2013. 'Overdetermination: Althusser versus Resnick and Wolff, Rethinking Marxism' in *A Journal of Economics, Culture & Society*, vol. 25, no. 3.

Joerges, C. and Rödl, F., 2004. *'Social Market Economy' as Europe's Social Model?* Florence: European University Institute.

Jones, A. and Sufrin, B., 2010. *EU Competition Law: Text, Cases & Materials*. Oxford: Oxford University Press.

Kelly, E., 2001. *Justice as Fairness: A Restatement*. Cambridge, MA: Harvard University Press.

Kymlicka, W., 1990. *Contemporary Political Philosophy: an Introduction*. New York: Oxford University Press, in Wright, R.W., 2000, 'The Principles of Justice', *Notre Dame Law Review*, vol. 75, p. 1868.

Lamont, J. and Favor, C., 2007. *Distributive Justice*. Stanford Encyclopedia of Philosophy. Available at: http://plato.stanford.edu/entries/justice-distributive/.

Lanka Business Online, 2010. 'Debt Crisis – Denmark launches austerity plan, slashes benefits'. Available at: www.lankabusinessonline.com/fullstory.php?nid=1629811302 [accessed November 2010].

Lister, R., 2007. 'Social Justice meanings and politics' in *Benefits*, vol. 15, no. 2, pp. 113–25.

McCrudden, C., 2007. *Buying social justice: Equality, government procurement, & legal change*. Oxford: Oxford University Press.

Meade, J.E., 1964. *Efficiency, Equality and the Ownership of Property*. London: G. Allen and Unwin.

Mill, J.S., 1962. Utilitarianism [1861], ed. M. Warnock. Glasgow: William Collins, pp. 251–321.

Mill, J.S., 1963. Utilitarianism [1861], ed. J.M. Robson. Toronto: University of Toronto Press.

Monti, M., 2010. *A new strategy for the single market: At the service of Europe's economy and society – Report to the President of the European Commission*. Brussels.

Müller-Armack, A. (reprinted in 1966). 'Wirtschaftslenkung und Marrktwirtschaft (1946)' in *Wirtschatsordnung und Wirtschaftspoliik. Studien und Konzepte zur sozialem Maktwirtschaft und zur europäischen Integration*, Freiburg i. Br., Verlag Rombach.

Murchie, K., 2010. 'Ireland unveils tough austerity measures', *Finance Markets*. Available at: www.financemarkets.co.uk/2010/11/24/ireland-unveils-tough-austerity-measures/.

Myrdal, G., 1956. *An International Economy: Problems and Prospects*. London: Routledge & Kegan Paul.

O'Neill, M., 2009. *Liberty, Equality and Property-Owning Democracy*. London: Blackwell Publishing Inc.

Peterson, J., 2001. 'Integration: European' in Smelser, N.J. and Baltes, P.B. (eds), *International Encyclopedia of the Social & Behavioral Sciences*, Volume 11. Amsterdam: Elsevier.

Peterson, V.S., 1998. 'Shifting Ground(s): Epistemological and Territorial Remapping in the Context of Globalisation(s)' in E. Koffman and G. Youngs (eds), *Globalisation Theory and Practice*. London: Pinter, pp. 11–28.

Petrakis, M., 2010. 'Greek State Workers Escalate Protests at Budget Cuts (Update 1)'. *Bloomberg Businessweek*. Availalble at: www.businessweek.com/news/2010-05-04/greek-state-workers-escalate-protests-at-budget-cuts-update1-.html.

PWC, ICF, GHK and ECORYS, 2014. *SMEs' access to public procurement markets and aggregation of demand in the EU*. DG Internal Market and Services, Brussels.

Rawls, J., 1971. *A Theory of Justice*. Oxford: Oxford University Press.

Rawls, J., 1993. *Political Liberalism*. New York: Columbia University Press.

Rawls, J., 1999. *A Theory of Justice: Revised Edition*. Cambridge, MA; Harvard University Press.

Rawls, J., 2001. *Justice as Fairness: A Restatement*. Cambridge, MA: Harvard University Press.

Resnick, S.A. and Wolff, R.D., 1987. *Knowledge and Class: A Marxian Critique of Political Economy*. Chicago: University of Chicago Press.

Richardson, H., 2010. 'Budget: Education spending faces 25% cut'. BBC News. Available at: www.bbc.co.uk/news/10378384 [accessed November 2010].

Robbins, L., 1938. 'Interpersonal Comparisons of Utility: A Comment' in *Economic Journal*, vol. 48.

Roberts, D., 1960. *Victorian Origins of the British Welfare State*. New Haven: Yale University Press.

Ross, M., 2009. *A healthy approach to services of general economic interest? The BUPA judgement of the Court of First Instance (2009)*. 34 E.L. Rev. 134.

Scharpf, F.W., 1997. 'Economic integration, democracy and the welfare state' in *Journal of European public policy*, vol. 4 no. 1, pp. 18–36.

Sen, A., 1993. 'Markets and freedom: Achievements and limitations of the market mechanism in promoting individual freedoms' in *Oxford Economic Papers*, vol. 45, no. 4, pp. 519–41.

Sen, A., 1999. *Development as Freedom*. New York: Anchor Books.
Sen, A., 2009. *The Idea of Justice*. Massachusetts: The Belknap Press of Harvard University Press Cambridge.
Smith, A., 1776. *The Wealth of Nations, Books I-III*. London: Penguin Books.
Spiegel Online, 2007. 'A Less "Anglo-Saxon" EU: Sarkozy Scraps Competition Clause from New Treaty'. Available at: www.spiegel.de/international/europe/0,1518,490136,00.html.
Stuff.co.nz.Business Day, 2010. 'Europe's welfare system under threat'. Available at: www.stuff.co.nz/business/world/3730479/Europes-welfare-system-under-threat [accessed November 2010].
Tanner, M.D., 2010 'As Europe laments welfare state, U.S. turns to it' in *USA Today*. Available at: www.usatoday.com/news/opinion/forum/2010-06-26-tanner25_ST_NO.htm.
The Local – Germany's News in English, 2010. 'Where the axe has fallen: a budget cut breakdown'. Available at: www.thelocal.de/money/20100608-27715.html [accessed November 2010].
Thiry, F., 2006. *Demography and family – The changing face of the family*. Brussels: European Commission.
UK Economy, 2010. 'UK National Debt'. Available at: www.economicshelp.org/blog/uk-economy/uk-national-debt/ [accessed November 2010].
Underhill, W., 2010. 'Britain's Unions cautious about austerity measures' in *Newsweek*. Available at: www.newsweek.com/2010/10/22/britain-s-unions-cautious-about-austerity-measures.html.
Unger, R., 2004. *False Necessity: Anti-Necessitarian Social Theory in the Service of Radical Democracy*. London: Verso.
Unger, M.R., 2007. *Free trade reimagined: the world division of labor and the method of economics*. Princeton, NJ: Princeton University Press.
United Nations., 1948. Universal Declaration of Human Rights, Article 1. United Nations General Assembly.
Van Hamme, A., 1990. 'EC Public Procurement Rules in the Wake of the Single European Market: A Survey of Recent Changes' in *Studia Diplomatica*, vol. 43, no. 3, p. 6.
Vandenbroucke, F. and Vanhercke, B., 2014. *A European Social Union: 10 Tough Nuts to Crack*. Brussels: Friends of Europe.
Warnock, M., 1962. *Introduction to John Stuart Mill, Utilitarianism* (ed. by Mary Warnock). Fontana Press.
White, S., 2004. 'Social Minimum' in *Stanford Encyclopedia of Philosophy*. Available at: http://plato.stanford.edu/entries/social-minimum/ [accessed October 2010].
Williamson, T. and O'Neil, M., 2009. *Property Owning Democracy and the Demands of Justice. Living Reviews in Democracy*, Volume 1. Available at: http://democracy.livingreviews.org/index.php/lrd/article/viewArticle/lrd-2009-5/15.
Wright, R.W., 2000. 'The Principles of Justice' in *Notre Dame Law Review*, vol. 75, pp. 1859–93.

Official documents

Cases before the Court of Justice of the European Union

Case C-320/91, *Paul Corbeau, 1993*. ECR I-02533.
Case C-360/96, *Gemeente Arnhem and Gemeente Rheden* v. *BFI Holding BV, 1998*. ECR I-06821.

Court of Auditors

Court of Auditors, 2010. 'Annual report concerning the financial year 2009 (2010/C 303/01)'. *Official Journal of the European Union*.

Directives

Council Directive 71/305/EEC of 26 July 1971, *Concerning the coordination of procedures for the award of public works contracts*, OJ No L 185, 16 August 1971, p. 5.

Council Directive 77/62/EEC of 21 December 1976, *Coordinating procedures for the award of public supply contracts*, OJ No L 13, 15. 1. 1977, p. 1.

Council Directive 2003/55/EC, *Directive of the European Parliament and of the Council of 26 June 2003 concerning common rules for the internal market in natural gas and repealing Directive 98/30/EC*.

European Council

European Council, 23 and 24 March 2000, Presidency Conclusions. Lisbon.

European Council 2009. *Council Conclusions on Social Services as a Tool for Active Inclusion, Strengthening Social Cohesion and an Area for Job Opportunities*, 2,947th Employment, Social Policy, Health and Consumer Affairs Council meeting. Luxembourg.

European Council, 2010. *Council Conclusions, Social Services of General Interest: at the Heart of the European Social Model*, 3,053rd Employment, Social Policy Health and Consumer Affairs Council meeting, Brussels.

European Commission

COM 85 (310) final, 1985. *Completing the Internal Market. White Paper from the Commission to the European Council*. Milan: Commission of the European Communities.

COM (1989) 400 final, 1989. *Public Procurement Regional and Social Aspects (Communication from the Commission)*. Brussels: European Commission.

COM (2000) 379 final, 28 June 2000. *Communication from the Commission to the Council, the European Parliament, the Economy and Social Committee and the Committee of the Regions – Social Policy Agenda*. Brussels: European Commission.

COM (2009) 592 final, 28 October 2009. *Report from the Commission Concerning Negotiations Regarding Access of Community Undertakings to the Markets of Third Countries in Fields Covered by the Directive 2004/17/EC*. Brussels: European Commission.

COM (2010) 2020 final, 3 March 2010. *Communication from the Commission, Europe 2020: A strategy for smart, sustainable and inclusive growth*. Brussels: European Commission.

COM (2010), 608 final, 27 October 2010. *Towards a Single Market Act for a Highly Competitive Social Market Economy*. Brussels: European Commission.

COM (2011) 896 final, 20 December 2011. *Proposal for a Directive of the European Parliament and of the Council on Public Procurement*. Brussels: European Commission.

European Commission, 2004. *A report on the Functioning of Public Procurement Markets in the EU: Benefits from Application of EU Directives and Challenges for the Future*. Brussels.

European Commission, 2010. *Working Document – Public Procurement Indicators 2008*. Brussels.
European Commission, 2012. *2011 Annual Activity Report – Directorate General Regional Policy*. Brussels.
European Commission, 2013. *Sustainable Development in the European Union*, Eurostat Statistical Books. Luxembourg.
European Commission, 2014. *Robert Schuman: the Architect of the European Integration Project*. Available at: http://europa.eu/about-eu/eu-history/founding-fathers/pdf/robert_schuman_en.pdf [accessed 20 November 2014].
SEC (2010) 1284 final, 22 October 2010. *Commission Staff Working Document – Second Biennial Report on Social Services of General Interest*. Brussels: European Commission.
SEC (2011) 1586 final, 20 December 2011. *Commission staff working paper executive summary of the impact assessment accompanying the document proposal for a Directive of the European Parliament and of the Council on Public Procurement and the Proposal for a Directive of the European Parliament and of the Council on procurement by entities operating in the water, energy, transport and postal sectors*. Brussels: European Commission.
SWD (2014) 158 final, 15 May 2014. *Commission Staff Working Document – Economic Review of the Financial Regulation Agenda*. Brussels: European Commission.

European Commission – press releases

IP/11/785, 2011. 'Single Market Act: EU public procurement framework has saved around 20 billions euros', Brussels: European Commission.

Eurostat

Eurostat, 2011a. 'Living conditions statistics'. Available at: http://epp.eurostat.ec.europa.eu/statistics_explained/index.php/Living_conditions_statistics [accessed 25 April 2011].
Eurostat, 2014b. 'Total expenditure on social protection'. Available at: http://epp.eurostat.ec.europa.eu/tgm/table.do?tab=table&init=1&language=en&pcode=tps00098&plugin=0 [accessed 17 Ocotber 2014].
Eurostat, 2014c, 'Total population, candidate countries and potential candidates'. Available at: http://epp.eurostat.ec.europa.eu/tgm/table.do?tab=table&init=1&language=en&pcode=tgs00027&plugin=1 [accessed October 2014].

2 European integration and the interplay with public procurement

2.1 Introduction

Visions of a unified Europe go back to ancient Rome and medieval Christendom (Nelson and Stubb 2014). If one were to refer to the history of European economic integration since 1815 two major forces shaping European economic integration come to the fore – technological innovations and political forces (Milward 1981).[1] Technological innovations have made it necessary that structures and systems be adapted in order to be able to catch up with the new demands. Hence, from this line of advance, the drive towards economic integration has come about as a seemingly natural process. Thus, as railways (for instance) became more efficient, natural logic forced European countries to give up some of their decision-making power so as to enable such railways to cut across the whole continent rather than stop at frontiers. The second line of advance comes from a political plane that has been in existence since the Middle Ages: an idealised concept of a European continent with a common Christian cultural heritage. Whether because of the support of the Christian religion, or under the plight of common humanity of the Enlightenment, calls for a unified Europe increased in frequency during the late eighteenth and nineteenth centuries. The drive towards economic integration, then, was never the main motive, but rather it emerged as a by-product: a gradual and piecemeal process that took place as other interests were being pursued. And yet, European economic integration stood out for its significant development.

The harsh realities of the Second World War reignited visions of a united Europe. In June 1941 Altiero Spinelli and Ernesto Rossi wrote, while in prison, what came to be known the Ventotene Manifesto (Nelson and Stubb 2014). It was published later that year, and in August 1943 Spinelli founded the European Federalist Movement – adopting the manifesto as its political programme. Today, the manifesto is widely recognised as the birth of European federalism. The manifesto called for a new political system through the establishment of a 'European Federation' that sought security and social justice for all Europeans (Nelson and Stubb 2014: 4).

Calls for a 'United States of Europe' were reiterated by Winston Churchill in his influential 'The Tragedy of Europe' speech at Zurich University in September

1946. He envisioned a united Europe led by former antagonists France and Germany. Although he did not outline how Europe could achieve unity, his efforts led to the Hague Congress of May 1948 and the creation of the Council of Europe in 1949 (Nelson and Stubb 2014: 11–14). In May 1950 Robert Schuman outlined a plan that sought to unite – under a single authority – Europe's coal and steel industries, the two industries that were essential for the making of war. Jean Monnet, who developed the purpose of the plan, sought to build of a united, peaceful, Europe one step at a time, gradually proceeding to other economic and political sectors. The underpinning logic, as Schuman put it, was the creation of '*de facto* solidarity' – one where war between France and Germany would be 'materially impossible' (Nelson and Stubb 2014: 15). In 1952, France, West Germany, Italy and the Benelux countries (Belgium, Netherlands and Luxembourg) united to create the European Coal and Steel Community (ECSC).

On 25 March 1957 the Treaty of Rome established the European Atomic Energy Community (EURATOM), and the European Economic Community (EEC) was established by the six founding member countries of the European Coal and Steel Community. The Treaty laid down the visions of its predecessors for an 'ever closer union among the peoples of Europe' (Nelson and Stubb 2014: 17). While the deep desire for peace runs through the Preambles, a subtle shift for unity brought about by economic and social progress could be noted in the Schuman Declaration, the Preamble to the ECSC Treaty, and the EEC Treaty (Nelson and Stubb 2014: 17).

The European Economic Community (EEC) came after a major setback following the lack of progress in ratifying the treaty concerning the European Defence Community (EDC), which was signed in 1952 by the six European Coal and Steel Community (ECSC) states and following the shelving of plans for a European Political Cooperation (EPC) treaty. Replacing earlier moves towards integration that sought to bring about explicit political cooperation, the Treaty of Rome – although politically motivated – has primarily an economic focus with anticipated spillover effects. In this respect, neofunctionalist theory attempts to explain the intellectual rationale behind the development of the European integration process. Accordingly, neofunctional integration sees initial cooperation on non-controversial technical sectors as bringing about a gradual spillover effect to other sectors, with the possibility of the sort of greater political cooperation that necessitates a gradual reduction in the power of national government and the concurrent centralisation of powers for dealing with sensitive and politically charged issues (Craig and De Búrca 2011).[2]

Therefore, having as its primary focus economic objectives with anticipated spillover effects, the Treaty of Rome provided for the creation and functioning of a common market[3] that would oversee economic policies within the EEC's member states, and their harmonious development over successive stages. Obstacles to the free movement of goods, workers, services and capital were to be eliminated. Tariff barriers were to be abolished and a common external customs tariff set up. Undistorted competition was to be ensured. The creation of a single currency and the adoption of a common economic and monetary policy were to be progressively coordinated. The treaty also provided for the creation of common transportation and agricultural policies, as well as a European Social Fund and an investment bank to give loans and guarantees and to help less developed regions or sectors.

The European integration project is a momentous one, one that continues to evolve and bear its mark throughout history. The following section examines further the evolution of the EU following the signing of the Treay of Rome: from both social and economic perpectives.

2.2 The relationship between the EU's social and economic dimensions

The Community's task of establishing a common market, and its progressive approximation of economic policies, was aimed at raising the standard of living and bringing about closer relations – including a continuous and balanced expansion of the Community and an increase in stability.[4] In view of Member States' reluctance to allow for the development of more general social policies[5] at EU level, social policy was restricted to easing the transition to the common market. Various treaty provisions allowed for a balance between market concerns and social concerns.

Article 90 (2)[6] of the Treaty of Rome Establishing the European Economic Community held that undertakings entrusted with the operation of services of general economic interest were subject to the treaty rules on competition: insofar as the application of such rules did not obstruct their performance when conducting the tasks assigned to them. Special provisions for agriculture and transport also provided for certain safeguards against the rules on competition. For instance, Article 77[7] headed within the framework of a common transport policy in the areas of road, rail, inland waterways, sea and air transport sectors, recognised aid as being compatable with the treaty, 'if they meet the needs of co-ordination of transport or if they represent reimbursement for the discharge of certain obligations inherent in the concept of a public service'. Article 92 (2)[8] held that aid of a social character granted by States was compatible with the treaty when it was provided to mitigate damage caused by natural disasters or exceptional occurrences, or when it was granted to the economy of certain areas of the Federal Republic of Germany that had been affected by the division of Germany – in order to compensate them for the economic disadvantages caused by that division. Article 92 (3)[9] allowed for the consideration of aid to promote economic development in areas with abnormally low standards of living; or where serious underemployment existed; or to promote an important project of common European interest; or to remedy serious disturbances in the economy of a Member State; or to facilitate the development of certain economic activities.

Article 117 – headed under Title III, Social Policy[10] of the Treaty of Rome Establishing the European Economic Community – recognised the need for promoting working conditions and workers' living standards. Article 118 assigned to the Commission the task of promoting close cooperation between Member States in the social field. Particular mention is made of the following areas: 'Employment; labour law and working conditions; basic and advanced vocational training; social security; prevention of occupational accident, and diseases; occupational hygiene; the right of association, and collective bargaining between employers and workers.' Article 119 dealt with the application of the principle of equal pay for men and women. Articles 123–8 provided for the establishment of the European Social Fund with the aim of improving employment opportunities in the common market and contributing towards the raising of standards of living.

The founding fathers of the Treaty of Rome Establishing the European Economic Community acknowledged the fact that in order to ensure a well functioning and socially just economy, government interventions were necessary. It has been argued that the social and economic dimensions of integration were meant to interrelate normatively (Schiek et al. 2011). Nonetheless, the treaty's predominant economic focus, with anticipated spillover effects, constitutionalises the EU's economic dimension. By contrast, social welfare policy remains within the sovereign competence of Member States. According to neofunctionalists economic issues allowed for the integration of primary areas, with social issues expected to follow. Such an arrangement may not necessrily be interpreted as a choice in favour of economic liberalism: it can also be interpreted as a fundamental decision favouring 'domestic welfare states under direct democratic control' (Sauter 2009: 3). The Court of Justice of the European Union has played a major role in maintaining, more or less, such a compromise (Sauter 2009).

For de Gaulle[11] visions of Europe as a supernational state were unrealistic and undesirable. Instead, de Gaulle envisioned a 'concert of European states' (Nelson and Stubb 2014: 29) in which governments coordinated extensively their policies but did not give up their sovereign rights to the European superstate (Nelson and Stubb 2014). This position led to the 'Empty Chair Crisis'. In 1965 de Gaulle boycotted European institutions in response to the Commission's attempt to create a shift towards supranationalism. This eventually led to the Luxembourg Compromise (1966), where, in essence, every Member State had the right to veto Community decisions. Hence, by mid-1960, neofunctionalists' anticipated spillover was cut short by de Gaulle's 'empty chair' policy, making the European Community more intergovernmental than a supranational state. For intergovermentalists, social policy could develop insofar as it did not interfere with the more important 'high politics' (Geyer 2000: 248). At the time, economic policy integration was very slow and social policy development non-existent. However, this all changed with the December 1969 Hague Summit. This summit opened the floor to the Social Action Programme covering the period 1974–76, and described as the first major advance for EU social policy since the Treaties of Paris and Rome (Geyer 2000). The European Monetary Union (EMU) was expected to pursue further the object of economic integration, while social policy was recognised as a necessary complement. Three areas for furthering social policy actions targeted full and better employment, improvement of living standards and working conditions, and the increased involvement of management and labour in economic and social decisions of the Community. However, during the early 1970s, and following the oil shocks and massive currency fluctuations, the European Community was faced with another period of stagnation and uncertainty. Attempts to create the EMU were abandoned and there was very limited progress on the Social Action Programme. However, it appears that the lack of progress on the Social Action Programme may not only be attributed to prevailing international circumstances but also to other factors such as the internal structure and dynamics of the EC itself (Geyer 2000).

> The general strategy of policy 'harmonisation' undercut the ability of the EC to reach any agreements on social policy issues. The institutional weakness of the European Parliament (not even directly elected until 1979) and the Economic and Social Committee meant that social actors, such as the ETUC and European socialists, were less capable of promoting social policies within the EC. The power of the Council and the demands of unanimous voting on all major social policy questions clearly limited their development. Finally, with the rise of Margaret Thatcher in Britain in 1979, all EC social policy initiatives had to pass the barrier of militant free market ideology.
>
> (Geyer 2000: 249)

By the mid-1980s the European Community had grown to 12 Member States, but the veto power of Member States was proving an obstacle to moving the Single Market project forward. This all changed with the adoption of the Single European Act (SEA). The SEA increased the number of areas that required Qualified Majority Voting, thus making it very difficult for a single Member State to veto proposed legislation. The SEA enhanced the power of the European Parliament in the legislative process, giving it veto power over the accession of new Member States and the conclusion of agreements with associate states. It provided for the establishment of the Court of First Instance, it formally recognised the European Council, and it included the comitology procedure. The SEA gave a legal basis for the European Communities and European Political Cooperation to have as their objective concrete progress towards European unity.

The adoption of the Single European Act in 1986 revived Community momentum towards the integration process. Member States gave a clear signal in favour of economic liberalism.

> The adoption of the Single European Act was a choice for the market, a judgement on the part of the Member States to shift decision-making authority away from national political institutions as well as government-regulated economies and toward that abstraction, buyers and sellers. It represented an acknowledgement that the model of the national mixed-economy had had its day.
>
> (Gillingham 2003: 294)

In view of rising concerns relating to the creation of a Single European Market and the possible repurcussions that this might have on the social aspect, provisions within the SEA laid out the foundations for an EU social dimension. The social dimension comprised of the Community Charter of the Fundamental Social Rights of Workers,[12] which was adopted on 9 December 1989 by a solemn declaration of all Member States except for the United Kingdom. The Community Charter of the Fundamental Social Rights of Workers established the principles upon which the European labour law model is based. The charter led to the development of a Social Action Programme (COM (89) 568 final, 29 November 1989). Other additions to the SEA included provisions on the establishment of a European Investment Bank, research and development, environmental policy and provisions for economic and social cohesion that aimed at harmonous development and the reduction of disparities between the various regions.

The revival of the European integration project generated an 'explosion of new European integration work' (Geyer 2000: 251) although it managed to come up with a limited amount of innovation (Geyer 2000). To neofunctionalists it appeared that the neofunctionalist dynamic had returned. The prevaling assumption was that Member States were losing their sovereignty to the supranational state. However, this was not how Andrew Moravcsik interpreted the situation (Moravcsik 1991, 1993). For Moravcsik, European governments were still very much in control of the integration process and were responding rationally to their changing environment rather than exhibiting some extraordinary behaviour (Nelson and Stubb 2014: 215–18). Reliance on supranational institutions made it possible for Member States to enforce their own commitments. Other scholars were of the view that the European Community's success came as a result of a combination of various factors which included neofunctionalists' spillover arguments, intergovernmental bargains, the international context, and the Community's institutional efforts (Keohane and Hofmann 1991). Nevertheless, despite efforts to drive the EU social policy agenda forward progress during the late 1980s and early 1990s was limited. In this respect most of the related legislation was rejected, put on hold, or watered down (Geyer 2000: 251).

According to Scharpf (1997), competitive pressures upon European welfare states cannot be avoided in view of deeply ingrained structural problems resulting from EU competition rules and the frustrations of democratic governance.[13] The separation of the market from social and political life has been described as artificial (Sauter 2009: 5). This, together with attempts to rectify what Scharpf refers to as 'constitutional asymmetry', led to the 'demise of embedded liberalism' that took place during the 35 years separating the Rome and Masstricht treaties (Sauter 2009).

> At the national level, economic policy and social-protection policy had and still have the same constitutional status – with the consequence that any conflict between these two types of interest could only be resolved politically, by majority vote or by compromise. However, once the ECJ had

established the doctrines of 'direct effect' and 'supremacy', any rules of primary and secondary European law, as interpreted by the Commission and the Court would take precedence over all rules and practices based on national law, whether earlier or later, statutory or constitutional. When that was ensured, all employment and welfare-state policies at the national level had to be designed in the shadow of 'constitutionalised' European law.

(Scharpf 1999: 43)

The Maastricht Treaty[14] has been considered as the means of rectifying such a state of affairs (Sauter 2009: 6). It sought to promote the integration project through the economic, political and social aspects. Its premise was to revive the European Monetary Union, and it introduced elements of citizenship, and common foreign and internal affairs policy. Regional policy was given a boost through the expansion of structural funds. A Protocol on Social Policy was annexed to the Maastricht Treaty, together with an agreement between 11 Member Sates – the UK made use of the 'opt-out' clause. As a consequence the implementation of EU social policies proved highly complicated. However, the election of a UK Labour government in May 1997, the UK's subsequent 'opt in', and the Treaty of Amsterdam,[15] led to a revised 'Social Chapter'. It replaced the Social Policy Protocol since provisions were now contained in the basic text. A new task assigned to the Community – by way of Article 2 – included equality between women and men. Article 13 introduced a new non-discrimination provision conferring competence upon the Community to combat discrimintion on grounds of sex, racial or ethnic origin, religion or belief, disability, age, or sexual orientation. Articles 125–30, headed under a new Title on Employment, provided for the establishment of a new Employment Committee with an advisory role. The Treaty of Nice[16] was a vital prerequisite to ensure the efficient functioning of the prospective enlargement. It brought about a reform of the institutions, including a redefinition of the voting system within the Council. For instance, in 2007, the use of qualified majority voting included economic and social cohesion policy.

The Lisbon Treaty[17] has been regarded by some as serving more the social sphere, and possibly capable of halting the tendency whereby the economic dimension takes precedence. Nonetheless, it remains first and foremost an economic constitution. Social issues fall mainly under the prerogative of the Member States. At the European level, actions in this respect remain constrained by the subsidiarity principle and the European treaties. Shared competences between the Union and the Member States include, amongst other things, the internal market, social policy for aspects defined in the treaty, economic, social and territorial cohesion, and environmental and consumer protection (Article 4 TFEU). Article 6 TFEU holds that the Union has the competence to support, coordinate or supplement actions of the Member States in the protection and improvement of human health, industry, culture, tourism, education, vocational training, youth and sport, civil protection and administrative cooperation (Article 6 TFEU).

48   The status quo

The Treaty Establishing a Constitution for Europe recalls the Union's objectives: 'a highly competitive social market economy, aiming at full employment and social progress':

> It shall combat social exclusion and discrimination, and shall promote social justice and protection, equality between women and men, solidarity between generations and protection of the rights of the child.
>
> It shall promote economic, social and territorial cohesion, and solidarity among Member States.
>
> It shall respect its rich cultural and linguistic diversity, and shall ensure that Europe's cultural heritage is safeguarded and enhanced.[18]

Article 6 (1) TEU confers on the Charter of Fundamental Rights the same legal value as the treaties. It includes various provisions on social rights, and in particular Title IV on solidarity. However, it appears to lack binding specifications since rights are recognised pursuant to national legislation (Mathieu and Sterdyniak 2008). Article 6 (2) TEU grants the Union accession to the 'European Convention for the Protection of Human Rights and Fundamental Freedoms. Such accession shall not affect the Union's competences as defined in the Treaties'. The possible alignment of the jurisprudence of the European Court of Justice with the European Court of Human Rights has been seen as allowing for a potentially healthier balance between fundamental social rights and economic freedoms (Schömann 2010).

Worthy of note are the following articles enshrined in the constitution. Article 9 TFEU stipulates that the Union shall 'take into account requirements linked to ... the guarantee of adequate social protection' and 'the fight against social exclusion'. Article 14 TFEU and Protocol 26 highlight the important role of Services of General Interest in social and territorial cohesion. The European Union and Member States, both in accordance to their relative competencies and within the scope of application of the treaties, are to ensure that these services fulfil their mission. Under Title X, Social Policy, Article 152 TFEU refers to the facilitation of dialogue between the social partners and stipulates that 'The Tripartite Social Summit for Growth and Employment shall contribute to social dialogue'. The annual Tripartite Social Summit seeks to add impetus to the social dialogue at both national and EU level. The summit brings together the Presidency of the Council, the Presidency of the Commission and the European social partners. Article 153 TFEU lists a number of areas in which the Union is to support and complement the activities of Member States in the social field. Actions are subject to a unanimous vote when it comes to social security and social protection of workers; protection of workers where their employment contract is terminated; representation and collective defence of the interests of workers and employers; and conditions of employment for third country nationals (Articles 153 (c), (d), (f) and (g) respectively). Article 153 (5) TFEU explicitly excludes Union action with respect to pay, the right of association, the right to strike, or the right to impose a lock-out. Under Article 168 TFEU a high level of human health protection shall be ensured in the definition and implementation of all Union policies and activities; Union action should complement national policies and be directed towards improving public health; cooperation should be encouraged between the Member States in the field of public health and, if necessary, the Union should lend support to such actions and fully respect the responsibilities of Member States for the organisation and delivery of health services and medical care.

Serving as a vehicle for cooperative exchange between Member States and the European Commission, the Social Protection Committee established pursuant to Article 160 TFEU[19] seeks through the framework of the Open Method of Coordination (OMC) on social protection and social inclusion to monitor the social situation and the development of social protection policies across Member States. The OMC is a voluntary process for political cooperation. Initially the method was only applied to employment and economic policy.

The OMC on social inclusion was introduced by the European Council of Lisbon in March 2000. It was introduced as 'the means of spreading best practice and achieving greater convergence towards the main EU goals' (Presidency Conclusions 2000) – thus helping Member States progress jointly in their reforms in pursuit of the Lisbon goals. Hence, on the one hand, within the OMC framework Member States report upon their strategies, goals and policies to the EU; while on the other, the EU collates the national strategic reports and draws common policy conclusions that are jointly adopted by the European Commission and Member States. Most important is the fact that under the OMC framework, social policy remains under the competency of Member States.

As has been evidenced in this section, tensions between the EU's social and economic dimensions have emerged as a common thread ever since its inception. For Geyer, the central question for EU social policy research needs to shift from a stance that looks at how domestic social policy could be protected or replaced, to one that looks at how EU social policy can interact with distinctive national-level social policy regimes (Geyer 2000: 254). For Scharpf, a respecification of the EU's original goals and strategies is necessary in the light of what the Nation State is capable of doing and in terms of what the EU – in its present institutional format – is capable, or incapable, of achieving: 'I am fully convinced that the range of significant choices that are still available is much wider than is suggested by the political hysteria about cost-cutting and welfare cutbacks at present sweeping all European countries' (Scharpf 1997: 30). In line with such a rationale, this book calls for a reordering of Europe's economic and social dimensions in pursuit of the creation of a socially just model of European integration, and public procurement as a policy instrument is one of the significant choices available to the EU in this quest.

2.3 The beginnings of the development of EU public procurement regulation and its role in European integration – an overview

Although the Treaty of Rome does not provide for a general Community regime on public procurement[20] several of its provisions have been nonetheless applied and currently remain applicable; that is, the rules and principles instituting and guaranteeing the proper operation of the Single Market, namely,

- The rules prohibiting any discrimination on grounds of nationality (Article 18 TFEU); the rules on the free movement of goods (Article 34 TFEU et seq), freedom of establishment (Article 49 TFEU et seq), and freedom to provide services (Articles 56 TFEU et seq); and the exceptions to those rules provided for in Articles 36, 51 and 52 TFEU; Article 106 TFEU concerning public undertakings and undertakings to which Member States grant special or exclusive rights and state monopolies providing services of general economic interest may help to determine if the granting of such rights are legitimate.
- The principles emerging from the Court's case law; namely, the principles of non-discrimination, equality of treatment, transparency, mutual recognition and proportionality.

However, as it transpires, the treaty provisions were considered to be too general and imprecise to be easily applied to public procurement practices. The reasons for such poor performance were related to economic and political issues (Cox 1993). During the period from 1950 until early 1970s – economic growth was described as exceptional in historic terms (Cox 1993: 30).[21] Therefore, given such a healthy economic climate, Member States did not feel the need to address public sector preferential purchasing – the liberalisation of public procurement was not an issue (Cox 1993).[22] From the political aspect, by the end of the 1960s trade was essentially free from tariffs and quotas and only non-tariff barriers remained (Cox 1993: 34). So it was only by the end of that decade that the Community's attention focused on the eradication of non-tariff barriers, with national product and technical standards and protectionism in public procurement being identified as the most common and blatant examples (Cox 1993).

In 1971, and later in 1977, the first Community Directives providing a more specific framework enshrining the basic treaty rules applicable to public procurement procedures, were enacted (Council Directive 71/305/EEC of 26 July 1971; Council Directive 77/62/EEC of 21 December 1976). The Directives aimed at liberalising public procurement practices, thus instituting and guaranteeing the proper operation of the Single Market. This could be considered as a first step in the direction towards eliminating some of the means by which governments avoided open competition through the use of hidden non-tariff barriers. Thus, in the case of public works contracts, the Directives were applicable to all contracts above one million ECUs, and for public supplies all contracts over 200,000

ECUs. The introduction of measures seeking equal conditions for tendering in public procurement contracts aimed at encouraging a more transparent, open, competitive and efficient public procurement market. However, the Directives failed to have the desired impact. According to the Atkins Report (1988) only 2–5 per cent of public purchasing could be attributed to cross border trade. Member States did not comply with the public procurement rules and the lack of an effective enforcement and remedy regime did not prove to be helpful (COM 85 (310) 1985; Van Hamme 1990).

The period around the time when the Directives were introduced – that is, the years following 1973 – coincided with the start of the technical revolution and the setting in of the recession. Faced with difficult choices governments were more inclined to protect their domestic industries. The 1970s have been referred to as a period of political stagnation or malaise for the Community (Craig and De Búrca 2011). The European Commission experienced great difficulty in securing Council agreements to its proposals, and as a result there were significant delays in the attainment of treaty objectives (Craig and De Búrca 2011).

In the light of the economic threat posed by the US and Japan in high technology, and from the assembly industries of newly industrialising countries, the protected European firms operating in closed markets were unable to compete against such highly efficient and competitive firms. Despite this, and as noted above, governments remained unwilling to open up their markets: to do so opened up the risk of their national firms collapsing. Such firms could only survive if they continued to be protected by their own governments. The General Agreement on Tariffs and Trade rules (GATT) and European Community (EC) trade rules were mechanisms that national governments only paid lip service to. The 1970s and the early part of the 1980s were not conducive to the Commission embarking upon measures for the eradication of national protectionism in public procurement. But this would soon change.

The failure of state-led industrial policy to deal with major competition from highly efficient American and Japanese firms contrasted sharply with the apparent success of the economic policies enacted in the 1980s by the Reagan and Thatcher administrations. Such administrations embarked on policies which favoured market-based ideologies such as deregulation, supply-side tax cuts, privatisation and limiting social spending. At the time, such actions gave the necessary impetus for stimulating economic growth, and neoliberal intellectual ideas rose to prominence (Cox 1993). The shift to intellectual, political and economic thinking that favoured neoliberalism, deregulation and market integration was starting to see light in Europe. If European firms were to survive in the face of harsh competition, the restructuring of inefficient and overmanned public sector industries was inevitable. And the internal European market seemed to offer the right opportunities (Cox 1993).

In 1985 the EC Summit endorsed the European Commission's White Paper, 'Completing the Internal Market' (COM85 (310) 1985) – which argued for the elimination (by 1992) of a whole series of non-tariff barriers via 282 legislative measures that sought to free the costs of Europe's fragmented market in order for it to be able to enjoy what was referred to as a real European home market. At the time, liberal intergovernmental theory successfully challenged neofunctionalist arguments and provided the underpinning rationale for those actions that were taken to reinforce the Single European Market and that led to the signing of the Single European Act (SEA) in 1986 (and came into force in 1987 (Craig and De Búrca 2011)).[23] Liberal intergovernmental theory held that States rather than supranational institutions were the key actors in the integration process (Craig and De Búrca 2011). The White Paper acknowledged the apparent failure of the 1971 Public Works Directive and the 1977 Directive on the government procurement of supplies of goods and equipment, and also acknowledged that there had been minimal adherence by Member States to the legislation as contained within these Directives. The Single European Act (SEA) – which embodied the White Paper – represented Member States' willingness to accept treaty reform, as well as a political commitment to removing before the deadline of 1992 the long list of identified barriers to the Single European Market. It also reflected the shift in intellectual, political and economic thinking in favour of neoliberalism.

Although public procurement represented only one of the 282 legislative reforms proposed by the 1985 White Paper, this was enough for the European Commission to take its goals forward. It gave the Commission the opportunity to undertake studies in order to further sharpen policy formulation. To this end, in 1986, Lord Cockfield – Vice President of the European Commission – launched a study (herein referred to as the Cecchini Report) which revealed that by 1988 only a third to the journey towards accomplishing the 1992 programme had been completed (Cecchini 1988). What remained was described as a daunting and uphill task. The basic findings of the Cecchini Report further reinforced the White Paper by noting a whole series of barriers that needed to be eliminated; failure to achieve this had resulted in Europe's costly fragmented market – the so-called 'costs of non-Europe' (Cecchini 1988: 4).

The barriers identified (Cecchini 1988) were categorised under three main headings:

1 physical barriers – characterised mainly by frontier controls, delays and administrative burdens
2 fiscal barriers – characterised mainly by differing rates of VAT and excise duties
3 technical barriers – characterised mainly by differing technical standards and technical regulations, conflicting business laws and accessing nationally protecting public procurement markets.

Government protectionism in public procurement markets across the EU was identified as a significant non-tariff barrier, and described as a 'shot in the foot' (Cecchini 1988: 16). The reform in public procurement led to the introduction of new legislation that built on the structure of the previous Directives adopted in 1971[24] and 1977.[25] The reform aimed at assisting the process of creating the

Single European Market. This was clearly expressed in the Directives' Preamble, and additional safeguards designed to introduce transparency and to monitor compliance were introduced. The new Directives extended the scope of the rules concerning public services procurement and the previously excluded public utilities procurement (the utilities sector included entities operating in the water, energy, transportation and telecommunications sectors).[26] They aimed at coordinating the effective establishment of a competitive public procurement regime by instituting and guaranteeing the proper operation of the Single Market. As previously noted, the new set of European Directives built on the structure of the two previous ones. With the passage of time various modifications to the EU legislative public procurement framework took place. The following are some of the older rules governing EU public procurement contracts.[27]

- Directive 93/37/EEC coordinating the procedures for the award of public works contracts and consolidating Directives 71/305/EEC and 89/440/EEC (OJ No. L 199 of 9 August 1993).
- Directive 93/36/EEC coordinating procedures for the award of public supply contracts and consolidating Directives 80/767/EEC and 88/295/EEC (OJ No L 199 of 9 August 1993).

For public service contracts, a specific Directive – Directive 92/50/EEC relating to the coordination of procedures for the award of public service contracts (OJ No L 209 of 24 July 1992) – entered into force on 1 July 1993.

Directive 89/665/EEC harmonises review procedures for public supply, public works and public service contracts (OJ No L 395 of 30 December 1989).

With respect to utilities, a specific Directive was adopted – Directive 90/531/EEC (OJ No L 297 of 29 October 1990). This Directive was consolidated by Directive 93/38/EEC (OJ No L 199 of 9 August 1993). A specific Directive on review procedures for contracts in the water, energy, transport and telecommunications sectors was adopted – Directive 92/13/CEE (OJ No L 76 of 23 March 1992).

EU public procurement Directives are based on three underlying fundamental principles: Community-wide advertising of public contracts above certain value thresholds in order to ensure transparency; prohibition of technical specifications capable of discriminating against potential bidders; and application of objective criteria of participation in tendering and award procedures (Bovis 1998).

In essence, it could be argued that while the legislation on public procurement has sought to bring about a gradual reform of public procurement practices amongst Member States, its motives go beyond the eradication of discriminatory practices and protectionist behaviour. The White Paper on completing the internal market, the Single European Act, the Cecchini Report and the Atkins Report can all be said to have made crucial inroads into a journey that was conceived by the Treaty of Rome. They have played a vital role in building upon prevailing intellectual foundations in support of neoliberal economics (Cox 1993).

2.4 Advancing a socially just model of European integration through public procurement

Given the highly dynamic and multi-faceted nature of public procurement as a policy tool, its potential for significant strategic investments in the economic and social policy dimensions cannot and should not be ignored. Making utmost use of public procurement benefits both the EU and Member States. It is argued that in order to make utmost use of public procurement as a policy tool a paradigm shift that reorders how we conceptualise the public procurement regime is required. In a reordered public procurement regime the European citizen stands as the key actor. This section, in conjunction with the concluding remarks that follow, attempts to explain what is actually understood by a socially just model of European integration wherein the European citizen stands as the key actor; and how this can, in effect, be realised through a reordered public procurement regime.

The rationale behind the liberalisation of public procurement regulation in the European Union is based on neoliberal economics as it seeks to promulgate the EU's internal market. It draws upon utilitarian logic as the economic dimension superimposes upon the social dimension. In the proposed reordered regime, as far as public procurement is concerned the superimposition of the economic dimension upon the social dimension needs to be eliminated. Such reordering is essential as it seeks to correct, in part, the imbalance as manifested by the ever-increasing subordination of public policies to market forces. In doing so, a socially just model of European integration emerges as a by-product. It comes as a result of the implementing processes that are necessary to correct the imbalances and which consequently cause a ripple effect that reaches out towards the deepening of European integration. As noted earlier, such a process is only possible through a paradigm shift, one that reorders how we conceptualise the public procurement regime. While the logic and justifications for a reordered public procurement regime will be discussed in more detail in the chapters that follow, a very brief explanation follows on how a reordered regime can be manifested.

A reordered public procurement regime can be made possible by engaging in a public interest function, one that seeks to capitalise on Member States' diversity and operates on the basis of principles and conditions that enable the flourishing of its citizens. This public interest function mobilises a key umbrella concept that embraces three core values; namely, the respect for human dignity, equality, and freedom of participatory action. While such values correspond to the reduction of poverty, they instil content into the public interest function. Hence, simply put, a reordered public procurement regime mobilises a public interest function that treats the individual as an end in itself and hence eliminates the superimposition of the economic dimension upon the social dimesion. This is in contrast to what presently takes place. For as it transpires, and as the analysis in this book shows, as far as public procurement is concerned when it comes to promulgating the EU's internal market the individual is used as its means.

We will now proceed a step further in an effort to clarify what is meant by a socially just model of integration. In a reordered regime, public procurement is capable of serving as the medium wherein a balance between EU market needs and domestic social needs can be met in parallel. More specifically, the operational framework envisaged takes into account EU public procurement aims which seek open market access opportunities by way of reinforcing transparency, objectivity and non-discrimination between competing participants in tenders at EU-wide level. On the other hand, it also takes into account the domestic distributive objectives of societal welfare – albeit in a limited manner as far as public procurement contracts are concerned.

By engaging in politics of cooperation and coordination concerted efforts directed at accomodating the diverse domestic social welfare needs will in turn incentivise better political actors to succeed in attaining common EU-wide public procurement objectives. As a natural follower of political fashion, public procurement becomes more receptive and therefore more effective when held under the direct grip of the political actors. Hence, through a deep sense of solidarity, when political actors representing EU Member States engage in a discourse that seeks to strike a balance between EU economic needs and domestic social needs, the floor to deepening further European integration is opened. Such deepening occurs within the pan European social space. It is via this political interchange – and the eventual implementation of the reordered public procurement regime – that a socially just model of European integration can be realised. More specifically, it emanates as a by-product when the following two major processes occur.

First, by engaging in a clear public interest function that recognises the human person as an end in itself. In this respect the forum for cooperation and coordination by political actors is based on a public interest function that focuses on enabling members of the community to achieve reasonable objectives in life through the realisation of public procurement contracts. Since public procurement contracts are a special category of contracts, they represent complex exchanges that occur in social relationships and which, in the process, are separated in part by the passage of time. Rather than putting economic efficiency logic as the prevailing consideration when awarding public procurement contracts, social gains by way of upholding the respect for human dignity, equality and freedom of participatory action become the prime motivators. Such logic puts into motion a value-for-money concept wherein the grounds for the justification of awarding public procurement contracts is only acceptable when the most efficient mix of costs leads to cost-cutting with simultaneous increases in social welfare gains. On the grounds of practical reasonableness, the dynamic interchange between the political actors defining the balance between the fulfilment of EU market needs and the diverse socio-economic needs of Member States translates into a common good – the content of which will manifest itself through justice, authority and law.

Second, utilising public procurement as a countervailing mechanism helps defend and restore – to a certain extent – the EU's constitutional balance.

56 The status quo

A socially just model of European integration results when public procurement as a policy tool takes into consideration the domestic distributive objectives of societal welfare as an *ex ante* mechanism. The discussion in Chapter 8 demonstrates how this can, in effect, be realised when adopting the notion of a property-owning democracy – as advanced by John Rawls in *Justice as Fairness*. As the analysis in this book reveals, the notion of a 'decentred' state and the subordination of public policies to market forces are further accentuated within the EU. Therefore, the adoption of policies wherein public procurement takes into consideration domestic distributive objectives of societal welfare play a highly important role since they serve as a crucial safety valve that operates at the disposal of Member States. In doing so the insertion of a fair measure of socio-economic balance is enabled. To this end Scharpf's succint observations are worth noting:

> At the fundamental level, all constitutional democracies must try to balance 'republican' principles emphasizing political self-determination and 'liberal' principles providing constitutional and judicial protection for certain individual rights. If this balance is upset by the 'perpetual momentum' of ECJ case law that is consistently extending the domain of constitutionally protected individual rights – and hence the range of issues that are placed beyond the reach of democratic self-determination – the legitimacy of the multilevel European polity itself may be undermined (Scharpf 2009). The question is whether there are, or could be, countervailing mechanisms that would defend or restore the constitutional balance.
>
> (Scharpf 2012)

Indeed, when public procurement operates as a safety valve for the benefit, and at the disposal of, Member States, it also serves as a crucial countervailing mechanism that helps defend and restore – to a certain extent – the EU's constitutional balance. In this respect a socially just model of integration protects the legitimacy of the multi-level European polity.

It therefore follows that a socially just model of integration emerges within the pan European social space. It comes as a result of a reordered public procurement regime which intensifies the role of the citizen, both in its capacity as a national citizen and in its capacity as a European citizen.

2.5 Concluding remarks

It may be claimed that through fair competition and the preservation of the Single Market, enterprises are assured fair access to the competitive internal market. Consequently, as market efficiencies increase, consumers benefit from reduced prices, a wider choice and improved quality. In other words, fair competition and the Single Market enhance consumer welfare. Further, EU regional policy as a countervailing mechanism seeks to provide the necessary support to assist areas that may be lagging behind, support small- and medium-sized enterprises in becoming more innovative, and build a more inclusive society and improve the quality of life.

Indeed, the promotion of economic and social cohesion aiming at harmonous development and the reduction of disparities between the various regions (and the backwardness of the least favoured regions) was explicitly instituted as a key policy goal in the Single European Act, adopted in 1986. The key policy instruments for delivering this goal comprised the European Regional Development Fund, the European Agriculture Guidance and Guarantee Fund and the European Social Fund. Some 69 million ECUs were allocated for the period 1989–93 (Molle 2007). Major budgetary allocations to promote cohesion have followed since then. For the period 1 January 2007–31 December 2013, a budget of €348 billion (35 per cent of the Community budget) was allocated to regional policy. For the period 2014–20 a total of €351.8 billion – out of a total €1,082 trillion – was allocated (European Commission, April 2014). This represents the EU's largest budget allocation.

Despite major progressive budgetary allocations since its inception, cohesion policy has been met by a constant stream of criticism (Manzella and Mendez 2009). Both academia and the European Commission have acknowledged that disparities between regions remain wide (Martin 2003, de Sousa Santinha *et al.* 2009; European Commission, Directorate General for Regional and Urban Policy 2014). Following the economic and financial crises in its sixth report on economic, social and territorial cohesion the Commission noted:

> regional disparities in employment and unemployment rates have widened as have those in GDP per head in many countries while in others they have stopped narrowing. These developments mean that the Europe 2020 employment and poverty targets are now significantly further away than when they were first set and it will require a substantial effort over the next 6 years to achieve them in a context of significant budgetary constraints.
> (European Commission, Directorate General for Regional and Urban Policy 2014)

It has been held that as the EU develops an overarching EU-wide cohesion policy, Member States will become increasingly constrained in their ability to intervene in their eonomies to support the areas that they consider are in need (Colomb and Santinha 2014). If a region is not sufficiently disadvantaged it does not qualify for assistance under the provisions of the EU's regional aid map. This leads to a lacunae for regions that, although not sufficiently disadvantaged to qualify for regional aid, still merit support. Once regions fall outside the EU's regional aid map, support through regional aid instruments is severely constrained (Wishlade 2008). The main argument is that the process of liberalisation clashes (Wishlade 2008) with 'the special arrangements introduced by all countries to protect certain activities in the public interest' (Wishlade 2003) for the pursuit of social and territorial cohesion.

Notwithstanding the fact that the promotion of social and territorial cohesion are now enshrined in the the Treay of Lisbon, there is still a lack of a common definition. Delhey notes that the European Commission interprets cohesion according to how similar Member States are with respect to their equality of living and working conditions (Delhey 2004). This he regards as more a matter that reflects upon convergence. For Delhey, however, a social understanding of cohesion – and hence of integration – is a matter that needs to reflect upon *inter-relations* rather than convergence. As such, he adopts a relational perspective on social integration and places an emphasis on bonds and ties. Delhey (2004: 14) defines social integration as being 'transnational and macro-social', and regards the EU as 'a social space of non-state actors of different nationality, and collectivities involved in the amalgamation process' (Delhey 2004).

People as national collectivities or groups comprise the European social space. 'Social integration of the European social space rests on the intergroup relations of members of these different nationalities, not on the extent of ingroup relations' (Delhey 2004: 14) – hence the reason why European social integration is defined as transnational and macro-social. According to Delhey, transnational relations can also occur within single societies. A case in point is when EU citizens live permanently in another Member State. He therefore argues that it would be a mistake to interpret transnational interactions as solely being cross border transactions.

Delhey (2004: 16) conceptualises social integration by presenting a two-by-two matrix, which for ease of understanding is reproduced below. Such conceptualisation comprises a quantitative and a qualitative component. The quantitative component of social integration is referred to as *mutual relevance*. The notion of mutual relevance seeks to capture not only direct observable transactions, but also cognitive ones. The example provided by Delhey is as follows: '[I]f the Italians were to use other European countries as yardsticks for evaluating their own living conditions as satisfying or dissatisfying, this would be a sign of transnational relevance, and thus of European integration' (Delhey 2004: 15).

Table 2.1 A general concept of social integration

Mutual relevance (share in each actor's transaction flows)	Cohesiveness of actor's behaviour and attitudes	
	cohesive ←——————→ non-cohesive	
High ↑↓ Low	(highest level of integration) tied amity	(highest potential for conflict) tied hostility
	untied amity	untied hostility (lowest level of integration)

Source: Delhey, J. (2004). 'European Social Integration – From convergence of countries to transnational relations between peoples', Wissenschaftszentrum Berlin für Sozialforschung (WZB) Reichpietschufer 50, 10785 Berlin www.wz-berlin.de. ISSN 1612-3468, p. 16.

The qualitative component of social integration is referred to as *cohesion*. Delhey (2004: 15) interprets cohesion as meaning that 'the elements behave in a way that at least prevents negative consequences (negative solidarity) or, at best, causes positive consequences (positive solidarity) either for other actors or for the systems as a whole'.

According to Delhey, the most dangerous level of EU social integration is *tied hostility* because it denotes that although actors are mutually relevant they behave in a non-cohesive manner. Alternatively, when a level of *tied amity* is reached this reflects 'exactly the condition Monnet had in mind when speaking of uniting the peoples of Europe'.

A relational approach to European social integration – as configured by Delhey – makes it possible to reformulate European goals of social integration while also retaining the integrity of national welfare systems. Delhey's definition of European social integration envisages an arena in which a socially just model of integration – as prosposed in this book – is possible through the flexible application of public procurement processes in which the European citizen sits as the key actor in the integration process.

Notes

1 Most contemporary accounts of European integration begin with the aftermath of the Second World War. However, such accounts need also to be considered over a much longer timeframe since calls for European integration were articulated long before the twentieth century – including the call in 1693 by a prominent English Quaker, William Penn, for a European parliament and the end of the state mosaic in Europe (Urwin 1995).
2 It is worth noting that the term 'Economic' was deleted from the treaty's name by the Maastricht Treaty – which was put into force in 1993 and renamed the Treaty Establishing the European Community (TEC). The Treaty of Lisbon, which was brought into force in 2009, brought further amendments and was renamed, the Treaty on the Functioning of the European Union.
3 See Articles 2 and 3 of the Treaty of Rome, 1957.
4 Article 2 of the EEC reads as follows: 'The Community shall have as its task, by establishing a common market and progressively approximating the economic policies of Member States, to promote throughout the Community a harmonious development of economic activities, a continuous and balanced expansion, an increase in stability, an accelerated raising of the standard of living and closer relations between the States belonging to it.'
5 The application of Marshall's classic definition of 'social policy' as the use of 'political power to supesede, supplement or modify operations of the economic system in order to achieve results which the economic system would not achieve on its own', applies here (Marshall 1964: 15).
6 This article is now covered by Article 106 (2) of the Treaty on the Functioning of the European Union.
7 This article is now covered by Article 93 of the Treaty on the Functioning of the European Union.
8 This article is now covered by Article 107 (2) of the Treaty on the Functioning of the European Union.
9 This article is now covered by Article 107 (3) of the Treaty on the Functioning of the European Union.

60 *The status quo*

10 Provisions on social policy in the Treaty of Rome are covered by Articles 117–28. Provisions on social policy are now headed under Title X of the Treaty on the Functioning of the European Union and include Articles 151–61. Title XI of the Treaty on the Functioning of the European Union covers provisions on the European Social Fund (see Articles 162–164). Title XII of the Treaty on the Functioning of the European Union provides for education, vocational training, youth and sport (see Articles 165–166). Title XIII of the Treaty on the Functioning of the European Union provides for Culture (see Article 167). Title XIV of the Treaty on the Functioning of the European Union covers provisions for public health (see Article 168). Title XV of the Treaty on the Functioning of the European Union covers provisions for consumer protection (see Article 169).
11 Charles de Gaulle (1890–1970), first President of France's Fifth Republic.
12 The fundamental social rights of workers, as contained in the Community Charter, were later developed in the Charter of Fundamental Rights of the European Union. The Charter of Fundamental Rights of the European Union is legally binding by way of the Treaty of Lisbon – which entered into force on 1 December 2009.
13 According to Scharpf, the *frustrations of democratic governance* are due to the limited range of available policy options for governments at domestic level, combined with the lack of democratic legitimacy at EU level.
14 The Maastricht Treaty entered into force on 1 November 1993.
15 The Treaty of Amsterdam entered into force on 1 May 1999.
16 The Treaty of Nice came into force on 1 February 2003.
17 The Lisbon Treaty came into force on 1 December 2009.
18 See Article 3 (3) TEU.
19 Article 160 TFEU assigns the following tasks to the Social Protection Committee: '[T]o monitor the social situation and the development of social protection policies in the Member States and the Union; – to promote exchanges of information, experience and good practice between Member States and with the Commission; – without prejudice to Article 240, to prepare reports, formulate opinions or undertake other work within its fields of competence, at the request of either the Council or the Commission or on its own initiative.'
20 To date, the amending treaties do not provide for a general regime on public procurement. Article 132 (4) EC, now repealed, was the only provision which explicitly referred to public procurement. Article 45 (1) (b) TEU is the only instance where procurement is explicitly referred to: it states that the European Defence Agency is tasked to 'promote harmonisation of operational needs and adoption of effective, compatible procurement methods' (Fernández Martin 1996).
21 During the period 1950–73 the annual average economic growth was more than twice that for the period 1973–87.
22 See also the Commission (1973), wherein public procurement began to be considered within the framework of a common industrial policy in the 1970s.
23 It is worth noting that the term 'Economic' was deleted from the treaty's name by the Maastricht Treaty (which came into force in 1993), and instead renamed the Treaty Establishing the European Community (TEC). The Treaty of Lisbon, which was brought into force in 2009, brought further amendments and was renamed the Treaty on the Functioning of the European Union.
24 See Council Directive 71/305/EEC of 26 July 1971.
25 See Council Directive 77/62/EEC of 21 December 1976.
26 Both the utilities and defence sectors are regarded as key industrial sectors and thus highly sensitive areas when it comes to open competition.
27 It is worth noting that the adoption of a new legislative package for the modernisation of EU public procurement was agreed upon by the Council in June 2013, and by the European Parliament in January 2014. For this purpose:

- Directive 2004/18/EC of the European Parliament and of the Council of 31 March 2004 – coordinating procedures for the award of public works contracts, public supply contracts and public service contracts (30 April 2004) – will be repealed with effect from 18 April 2016, and replaced by Directive 2014/24/EU of the European Parliament and of the Council of 26 February 2014 on public procurement.
- Directive 2004/17/EC of the European Parliament and of the Council of 31 March 2004 – coordinating the procurement procedures of entities operating in the water, energy, transport and postal services sectors (30 April 2004) – will be repealed with effect from 18 April 2016, and replaced by Directive 2014/25/EU of the European Parliament and of the Council of 26 February 2014 on procurement by entities operating in the water, energy, transport and postal services sectors.
- A new Directive 2014/23/EU of the European Parliament and of the Council of 26 February 2014 was drafted concerning the award of concession contracts. Member States are to take the necessary measures to transpose this Directive and comply with its provisions by 18 April 2016.

References

Atkins, W.S. Management Consultants, 1988. *The Costs of Non-Europe in Public Sector Procurement. Basic Findings Vol. 5, Part A and B*. Luxembourg: Office for Official Publications of the EC.

Bovis, C., 1998. *The Regulation of Public Procurement as a Key Element of European Economic Law*. London: Wiley-Blackwell.

Cecchini, P., 1988. *The European Challenge, 1992: The benefits of a Single Market*. Aldershot, Hants: Wildwood House Limited.

Colomb, C. and Santinha, G., 2014. 'European Union competition policy and the European territorial cohesion agenda: An impossible reconciliation? State aid rules and public service liberalization through the European spatial planning lens' in *European Planning Studies*, vol. 22, no. 3, pp. 459–80.

Cox, A., 1993. *The Single Market Rules and the Enforcement Regime After 1992*. United Kingdom: Earlsgate Press.

Craig, P. and De Búrca, G., 2011. *EU Law – Text, cases and materials*. Oxford: Oxford University Press.

Crouch, C. and Le Galès, P., 2012. 'Cities as national champions?' in *Journal of European Public Policy*, vol. 19, no. 3, pp. 405–19.

De Sousa Santinha, G., Rodrigues, C. and Almeida, A., 2009. *Rumo a um novo ciclo de apoio comunitário: o caso do município de Arouca*. Master's thesis, Universidade de Aveiro.

Delhey, J., 2004. *European social integration: from convergence of countries to transnational relations between people*. Wissenschaftszentrum Berlin für Sozialforschung (WZB) Reichpietschufer 50, 10785 Berlin, www.wz-berlin.de. ISSN 1612–3468, pp. 1–25.

Europa Glossary., 'Structural Funds and Cohesion Fund', available at: http://europa.eu/scadplus/glossary/structural_cohesion_fund_eno.htm [accessed December 2010].

Fernández Martin, J.M., 1996. *The EC Public Procurement Rules: A Critical Analysis*. Oxford: Clarendon Press.

Geyer, R., 2000. 'The State of European Social Policy' in *Policy Studies*, vol. 21, no. 3, pp. 245–61.

Gillingham, J., 2003. *European Integration 1950–2003 – Superstate or New Market Economy?* Cambridge: Cambridge University Press.

Keohane, R.O. and Hofmann, S., 1991. *The new European Community: decision making and institutional change*. Boulder, CO: Westview Press.
Manzella, G.P. and Mendez, C., 2009. *The turning points of EU cohesion policy*. Brussels: European Commission.
Marshall, T., 1964. *Class, Citizenship and Social Development*. Garden City, NY: Doubleday.
Martin, P., 2003. 'Public policies and economic geography' in Funck, B. and Pizzati, L. (eds), *European Integration, Regional Policy, and Growth*, pp. 19–32. Washington DC: The World Bank.
Mathieu, C. and Sterdyniak, H., 2008. *European social model(s) and social Europe*. Paris: OFCE.
Milward, A.S., 1981. *The Integration of the European Economy since 1815*. London: George Allen & Unwin Ltd.
Molle, W., 2007. *European cohesion policy*. London: Routledge.
Moravcsik, A., 1991. 'Negotiating the Single European Act: national interests and conventional statecraft in the European Community' in *International Organization*, vol. 45, no. 1, pp. 19–56.
Moravcsik, A., 1993. 'Preferences and power in the European Community: a liberal intergovernmentalist approach' in *JCMS: Journal of Common Market Studies*, vol. 31, no. 4, pp. 473–524.
Nelson, B.F. and Stubb, A. (eds), 2014. *The European Union: readings on the theory and practice of European integration*. USA: Lynne Rienner Publishers, Inc.
Sauter, W., 2009. *State and Market in European Union Law: The Public and Private Spheres of the Internal Market before the EU courts*. Cambridge: Cambridge University Press.
Scharpf, F.W., 1997. 'Economic integration, democracy and the welfare state' in *Journal of European Public Policy*, vol. 4, no. 1, pp. 18–36.
Scharpf, F.W., 1999. *Governing in Europe: effective and democratic?* Oxford: Oxford University Press.
Scharpf, F.W., 2009. 'Legitimacy in the multilevel European polity' in *European Political Science Review*, vol. 1, no. 2, pp. 173–204.
Scharpf, F.W., 2012. 'Perpetual momentum: directed and unconstrained?' in *Journal of European Public Policy*, vol. 19, no. 1, pp. 127–39.
Schiek, D., Liebert, U. and Schneider, H., 2011. *European economic and social constitutionalism after the Treaty of Lisbon*. Cambridge: Cambridge University Press.
Schömann, I., 2010. 'The Lisbon Treaty: a more social Europe at last'. *ETUI Policy Brief – European Social Policy*, vol. 1, no. 6.
Urwin, D., 1995. *The Community of Europe: A History of European Integration*. London: Longman.
Van Hamme, A., 1990. 'EC Public Procurement Rules in the Wake of the Single European Market: A Survey of Recent Changes' in *Studia Diplomatica*, vol. 43, no. 3, p. 6.
Wishlade, F.G., 2003. 'Regional State Aid and Competition Policy in the European Union' in Colomb, C. and Santinha, G. (2014) 'European Union Competition Policy and the European Territorial Cohesion Agenda: An Impossible Reconciliation? State Aid Rules and Public Service Liberalization through the European Spatial Planning Lens', *European Planning Studies*, vol. 22, no. 3, p. 471.
Wishlade, F.G., 2008. 'Competition and cohesion – coherence or conflict? European Union regional state aid reform post-2006' in *Regional Studies*, vol. 42, no. 5, pp. 753–65.

Official documents

Directives

Council Directive 71/305/EEC of 26 July 1971, *Concerning the coordination of procedures for the award of public works contracts*, OJ No L 185, 16 August 1971, p. 5.

Council Directive 77/62/EEC of 21 December 1976, *Coordinating procedures for the award of public supply contracts*, OJ No L 13, 15 January 1977, p. 1.

European Council

Presidency Conclusions, 2000. *Lisbon European Council 23 and 24 March 2000, Presidency conclusions*.

European Commission

COM 85 (310) final, 1985. *Completing the Internal Market. White Paper from the Commission to the European Council*. Milan: Commission of the European Communities.

COM (89) 568 final, 29 November 1989. *Communication from the Commission Concerning its Action Programme Relating to the Implementation of the Community Charter of Basic Social Rights for Workers*. Brussels: European Commission.

European Commission, 1973. *Memorandum on Technological and Industrial Policy Programme*. Brussels.

European Commission, April 2014. *The European Union explained: Regional policy Luxembourg*. Luxembourg: Publications Office of the European Union.

European Commission, Directorate General for Regional and Urban Policy, 2014. *Investment for jobs and growth – Promoting development and good governance in EU regions and cities*. Sixth report on economic, social and territorial cohesion. Brussels: European Commission.

3 The effectiveness of EU public procurement

3.1 Introduction

Public procurement is a highly dynamic policy tool through which works, services and supplies are purchased for use by the public sector in delivering public services. When utilised intelligently, public procurement can go beyond the scope of mere purchasing. It can greatly influence and change policy practices and is a major tool for the implemenation of other strategies. Public procurement can further industrial development, promote environmenal and social objectives, encourage innovative solutions and create more affluence.

In the Europe 2020 strategy for smart, sustainable and inclusive growth public procurement plays a key role. The Europe 2020 strategy calls upon public procurement to improve conditions to enable businesses to innovate and to support the shift towards a resource efficient and low carbon economy. It stresses the need for obtaining optimal procurement outcomes through efficient procedures, as well as stressing that procurement markets must be kept open EU-wide. In the Europe 2020 strategy public procurement is recognised as one of the market-based instruments capable of achieving these objectives.

The economic approach to the regulation of public procurement seeks to promulgate the notion of free trade through integration of the Single European Market by institutionalising the principles of transparency, non-discrimination and objectivity when awarding public contracts. As such, companies from across the Single Market are expected to be able to compete better for public contracts (that is, contracts with an estimated value that is equal to or above the defined thresholds)[1] – thereby facilitating cross border procurement with the resultant increase in import penetration in the public sector across the EU.

The total public procurement expenditure on works, goods and services across the EU as a percentage of GDP stood at 17.4 per cent in 2006, 17.6 per cent in 2007, 18.1 per cent in 2008, 19.9 per cent in 2009, and 19.7 per cent in 2010 (European Commission 2011b); and at 19 per cent for the year 2011 (European Commission 2012). However, one needs to exercise caution when referring to total public procurement expenditure. The methodology has been clearly explained by the Commission in various working documents (European Commission 2010a, 2010b, 2011b, 2012).

When it comes to interpreting the total amount of public procurement expenditure as a percentage of GDP such expenditure is based on estimates that includes payments in the form of social transfers in kind.

> For example, this measure includes the costs of health care and medical products reimbursed through statutory health insurance funds or by government (which alone accounts for approximately 4.5% of EU27 GDP) as well as other public transfers not organised through the form of public contracts or which are disbursed by non public entities.
> (European Commission 2010a: 2)

The estimated value of tenders published in the *Official Journal of the European Union* through the Tenders Electronic Daily database (TED) appears to provide a more realistic picture of public procurement spending. More specifically, this indicator attempts to represent the volume of procurement for which there has been a call for competition across the EU. This figure stood at €367.20 billion in 2007, €392.42 billion in 2008, €420.44 billion in 2009, €447.03 billion in 2010, and €425.44 billion in 2011 (European Commission 2012: 3). It is worth noting that this estimate – which is calculated by the services of the Commission – does not represent actual values but is an estimate based on the values contained in Contract Award Notices (available for only 64 per cent of published tenders) together with a correction factor (European Commission 2010a: 3). The Commission notes that in view of the large proportion of contracts for which the awarded contract value is unavailable, the application of a correction factor is regarded as necessary in order to be able to arrive to a global estimate for all published procurement (European Commission 2010a: 3). Therefore, in the methodology applied, the *number of calls* as published in the *Official Journal* and the TED database is

> multiplied by an average based, in general, on all the prices provided in the contract award notices published during the relevant year.
> Contracts above €100 Million have been taken at their own value but not included for the calculation of these averages. An estimate is necessary because the value of the contracts awarded is not always provided in the published contract award notices. It should also be noted that the indicator measures what is competitively advertised, rather than contracts actually awarded: a small proportion of all procedures advertised are either abandoned or for various reasons do not lead to a contract award.
> (European Commission 2011b: 2–3)

A picture of the magnitude of direct EU public procurement spending that falls within the remit of EU legislation is demonstrated in the value, as a percentage of GDP, of calls for tender published in the *Official Journal*. This percentage stood at 3 per cent of Community GDP in 2007, 3.1 per cent in 2008, 3.6 per cent in 2009 and 2010 (European Commission 2012a: 7).

66   The status quo

It is noteworthy that Member States are obliged to forward to the Commission yearly statistical reports in order to enable assessment of the results of applying the Directive.² However, consistent failure to rely on actual data reports when presenting public procurement statistics, illustrates the lack of transparency. The following discussion will assess the impact of EU public procurement legislation by way of its effectiveness in increasing transparency, cross border procurement, participaation by small- and medium-sized enterprises, and procurement in the international public procurement market.³

3.2 EU public procurement and its impact on transparency

Given the objective of creating flawless intra European community trade between the public and private sector, the elimination of preferential and discriminatory purchasing behaviour is crucial. Hence, the legal significance of such economic logic has put an emphasis on the issue of transparency. Transparency, it is claimed, generates competition and this in turn helps bring about anticipated savings. In order to ensure transparency the European Directives on public procurement adopted various measures which include:

- *The publication of notices* on the TED (Tenders Electronic Daily) official website for public contracts in Europe; and the *Official Journal of the European Union (OJEU)*.⁴ Such notices can come in the form of:
    - a Prior Information Notice (PIN) providing information on forthcoming procurement. The publication of such notices is not mandatory by law;
    - a Contract Notice (CN) or invitation to tender. Publication is mandatory except under special circumstances as stipulated by law;
    - a Contract Award Notice (CAN) provides information on the awarded contract. Its publication is mandatory as stipulated by law.
- *The application of selection criteria* – responses need to be evaluated against prequalifying criteria reflecting the minimum level of standards possibly required. These represent tests of good standing (probity), technical competence, and financial strength or capability. Such tests are independent of each other. While the test of probity is an absolute test, the others are relative to the size and complexity of the project.
- *The application of award criteria* – contracts need to be awarded on the basis of objective criteria that are linked to the subject matter of the procurement with a view to compliance with the principles of transparency, non-discrimination and equal treatment, therefore ensuring that tenders are assessed in a transparent and objective manner under conditions of effective competition.
- *The application of technical specifications* – the subject matter of the purchase needs to be defined in accordance with non-discriminatory technical specifications, for example specifications elaborating upon the requirements

of a material, service quality, environmental performance or accessibility for disabled persons.
- *The application of established procurement procedures* – the Directives provide for the conduct of established public procurement procedures.

In 2004, following an assessment of the performance of the public procurement markets over the preceding ten years (European Commission 2004), it was reported that there was 'overwhelming evidence' (p. 24) that the procurement regulations had contributed to increased transparency, and, in consequence, to an increase in cross border competition and price savings for public authorities. An upward trend in the number of Contract Notices published in the *Official Journal of the European Union* between 1995 and 2002 was noted, with the number of publications for 2002 being almost twice that recorded in 1995. This steady growth appears to have been maintained across the EU25 and the EU27 (European Commission 2010a). In the 2004 report (European Commission 2004), despite the upward trend in the publication of Contract Notices it was noted that only 16 per cent of the estimated public procurement was being published. The transparency rate – defined as 'the value of procurement published in the Official Journal as a percentage of estimated total public procurement' (European Commission 2004) – was found to vary between Member States and between different government levels and sectors. However, as was noted by the Commission itself, an increase in transparency rates does not necessarily mean an increase in transparency because large value public procurement projects can easily skew this measure. As highlighted by the Commission in their 2010 working document report, 'This ratio will, inter alia, be influenced by the extent to which indicator 1 includes expenditure which should not be construed as procurement' (European Commission 2010a: 3). As it transpires, indicator 1 refers to the *total EU public procurement spend* – now referred to by the Commission as *Total Public Expenditure on Works, Goods and Services*. This captures other components of public expenditure not necessarily relating to EU public procurement contracts and which, for some Member States, 'may be significant and result in particularly inflated figures for this indicator' (European Commission 2010a: 3).

Drawing on a comprehensive body of evidence and new independent research, the Commission claimed in 2011 that

> EU public procurement Directives have helped to establish a culture of transparency and outcome-driven procurement in the EU. This has triggered competition for public contracts, and generated savings and improvements in the quality of procurement outcomes. Open and competitive public procurement has driven down costs by around 4%, generating savings of approximately €20 billion. This far exceeds the costs generated by the regulatory framework, which are estimated to be €5 billion.
>
> (IP/11/785, 2011)

One of the reports that appears to have contributed to such claims is based on econometric analysis conducted by Europe Economics for DG internal market (Europe Economics 2011). Their analysis has been based on a sample which contains information on 175,167 awards covering the years 2006–09 and is derived from the MAPPS database which includes all notices published in the online European public procurement journal, Tenders Electronic Daily (TED) since 1993. Although the MAPPS database covers the publication of notices for all Member States the researchers note that the distribution of specific awards across Member States is uneven. Moreover, it is also noted that the sample is not a representative one. Nevertheless, the researchers attempt to justify extrapolation, 'because exclusion of observations seems to be at random (or at least not correlated with the dependent variables of our models) so that there are no obvious sample selection problems' (Europe Economics 2011: v).

The analysis is based on two models, the *outcome model* and the *number of bidders model*. The outcome model postulates a relationship between final award value and procurement-related indicators (Europe Economics 2011: iv). The number of bidders model postulates a relationship between the number of bidders and the procurement-related indicators (non-weighted) (Europe Economics 2011: iv). The researchers claim that the procurement-related indicators identify with the European public procurement Directives as measures aimed at opening the procurement market. Such procurement-related indicators include those that relate to:

- *transparency* – as reflected through the publication of notices (PIN, CN and CAN);
- *openness* – as reflected through the use of standard procedures; that is, the open or the restricted procurement procedure or the use of non-standard procedures which are used in exceptional circumstances;
- *aggregation* – as reflected through procurement that is conducted through central purchasing authorities.

In terms of transparency (transparency being equated with the publication of notices), it was found that when a contract notice is published[5] this leads to a reduction of roughly 1 per cent of contract award value when compared to the initial estimated total value. In terms of procedure, it was found that when the open procedure is adopted this increases the estimated savings by 3 per cent.

The Commission appears to build further on such findings and argues that the findings are consistent with previous reports that also attribute savings to the procurement Directives (European Commission 2011a: 20). In this respect the Commission claims that previous estimates of savings as a result of EU-advertised procedures are in the region of 2.5–10 per cent lower than the initial estimated contract value (European Commission 2011a: 20). Hence, and on the basis of hypothetical savings of 5 per cent realised on €420 billion[6] of public contracts, the Commission further argues that this would translate into estimated savings of over €20 billion. It is therefore postulated that such savings 'could generate increases in employment and GDP of between 0.08 and 0.12% after one decade (160,000–240,000 jobs)' (European Commission 2011a: 20); and that were such savings to be 'realised for all public procurement, the gains would be correspondingly greater (0.5% GDP and employment)' (European Commission 2011a: 20).

And here is where we come in sync with the Cecchini Report – in which efficiency gains amounting to 0.5 per cent ($c.17.5$ billion ECUs or 21.5 billion ECUs if defence procurement is included) of 1986 Community GDP were projected (Cecchini 1988: 17). However, it is worth noting that such projections need to be interpreted with great caution since they do not appear to take into account other highly relevant factors. Indeed, in the report presented by Europe Economics, the researchers noted that they had not been able to identify the source of the changes in the procurement disciplines. Nonetheless, they noted that this 'will become important in interpreting the results because, although we can see the effects of different procurement tools, we cannot disentangle the effects strictly derived from the compliance with the Directives, as some of the measures envisaged are voluntary' (Europe Economics 2011: 10). But the researchers were able to make the following claim: '[B]ased on our modelling exercises, we find that good procurement practice in general has a beneficial effect on procurement outcomes' (Europe Economics 2011: v). However, such a sweeping claim that is made on the basis of the study in question is highly dubious, and although it opens the floor for potential debate it is within this light that the following issues also need to be factored in.

First, the study in question examines relationships between so-called procurement practices and procurement outcomes. However, correlations between the two can in no way be interpreted as causation. All that can be established is that there *appears* to be some sort of relationship between procurement practices and their proclaimed beneficial outcomes.

Second, the study in question appears to define the general notion of good procurement practice on the basis of procurement indicators comprising transparency, openness and aggregation.

- transparency as reflected by the publication of notices (PIN, CN and CAN);
- openness as reflected through the conduct of standard procedures; that is, the open or the restricted procurement procedure or the use of non-standard procedures which are used in exceptional circumstances;
- aggregation as reflected through procurement that is made through central purchasing authorities.

Such indicators touch only in a very superficial manner on 'good procurement practices'. Various other unobservable factors that potentially affect the procurement process are not taken into consideration. Such unobservable factors may not necessarily take into account good procurement practices and yet may have had an impact on the proclaimed beneficial effects of the procurement outcomes.

A case in point concerns the declaration of assurance by Director General (DG) Regional Policy in connection with the regularity and legality of the applicable EU budget. In 2011 DG Regional Policy made various reservations, one of which was in respect of 'serious deficiencies in the management and control systems with regard to the compliance of the operations with the public procurement rules' (European Commission 2012b: 6). Indeed, the Commission is well aware of the recurring problems with Member States' lack of respect for public procurement rules – as highlighted on various occasions by the Court of Auditors of the European Union (hereafter referred to as the Court of Auditors) in their audits concerning projects co-financed by European Regional Development Fund (ERDF) and the Cohesion Fund under cohesion policy. Irregularities relating to public procurement have accounted for 41 per cent of the cumulative quantifiable errors (Court of Auditors 2010)[7] identified by the Court of Auditors in the years 2006–09 concerning projects co-financed by the ERDF and Cohesion Fund (European Commission SEC (2011) 1179 final). For the financial year 2009 the Court of Auditors noted as follows: 'The non-respect of public procurement rules alone accounts for 43% of all quantifiable errors and makes up for approximately three quarters of the estimated error rate' (Court of Auditors 2010: para. 4.21). In its report for the financial year 2010 the Court of Auditors noted:

> Public procurement is one area where the Court often finds errors. EU public procurement law consists essentially of a series of procedural requirements. To ensure the basic principle of competition foreseen in the Treaty the contracts have to be advertised; bids must be evaluated according to specified criteria; contracts may not be artificially split to get below thresholds, etc.
> (Court of Auditors 2010: para. 4.21)

A repeat of the above statement can also be found in the auditor's financial report for the year 2011(Court of Auditors 2012: para. 10) in which serious failures to respect public procurement rules were also noted. The errors observed affected a quarter of the transactions audited, and the combined estimated contract value for the 298 audited public procurements amounted to €6.7 billion (Court of Auditors 2012: para. 5.31, C344). Such errors accounted for 44 per cent of all quantifiable errors. The following presents some of the examples reflecting serious failures to respect public procurement rules as identified by the Court of Auditors in their 2011 financial report:

> *Use of direct award without justification*: In the case of an EEPR project concerning the construction of a gas pipeline, the contracts related to the works in the second and third stage of the project were awarded without tendering to the consortium that had been awarded a contract for the first stage of the pipeline five years earlier. This is not in line with the applicable EU and national public procurement laws.

Direct award of additional works in the absence of unforeseeable circumstances: In the case of a CF project related to road construction, additional works relating to amendments made subsequent to the approval of the original plan were awarded directly to the same contractor. These additional works were not due to unforeseeable circumstances, therefore a breach of public procurement rules occurred.

Significant changes in scope of the contracted works: In the case of a CF project related to the construction of a new metro line, the scope and budget of a related service contract was changed significantly through the involvement of experts who initially had not been foreseen. The additional tasks to be carried out were not due to unforeseeable circumstances, but rather to the way the contracting authority had planned the project.
(Court of Auditors 2012: para. 5.31, C344)

The Court of Auditors have consistently noted that the errors relating to public procurement are not specific to cohesion policy but refer to non-compliance with internal market rules (SEC (2011) 1179 final; Court of Auditors 2012: para. 5.31). Notwithstanding the fact that contracting authorities are well aware that eligibility for EU funds is dependent on compliance with the EU public procurement rules, one would have thought that this gives contracting authorities more good reason to abide by public procurement legislation. However, given the scenario as is, such lack of compliance can only be interpreted as reflecting the tip of an iceberg when it comes to EU public procurement in general.

Third, the study conducted by Europe Economics (2011: p. iii) claims to investigate 'the relationships between procurement practices and procurement outcomes'; that is, the relationships between the selected procurement indicators and their relationship with 'final' award values. The author claims that the cut-off line delineating where procurement outcomes are measured is myopic. Reliance on the so called 'final' award values – which capture nothing other than the award price as published in the Contract Award Notices – is not sufficient and can be highly misleading. What counts is the actual final price that the public purchaser pays. There can be major discrepancies between the initial award price (i.e. the price that the researchers capture in their analysis by way of the published Contract Award Notices) and the actual final price – especially for works and service contracts where cost overruns can occur during the contractual period. In the case of large construction projects cost overruns are a common feature due to various unforeseens such as inflation in construction industry costs (wages and materials) and unforeseen additional works.[8] The Directives are silent when it comes to the post-contractual phase. But, as the Commission notes, '[T]he ultimate test of the effectiveness of public procurement legislation is the impact on prices actually paid for goods and services by public procurement authorities' (European Commission 2004: 14) However, measuring actual prices that incorporate variations arising during the contractual period appears to be a mammoth task.

3.3 EU public procurement and its impact on cross border procurement

According to the Commission's 2004 report (European Commission 2004: 14) on the performance of the public procurement markets, it was claimed on the basis of the new evidence[9] that the level of cross border procurement had increased. However, this increase – which the Commission claims comes as a result of the increasing level of transparency – is mostly attributed to indirect cross border procurement as foreign firms make use of local subsidiaries (30 per cent of the bids in the sample). Only 3 per cent of the total number of bids in the sample engaged in direct cross border public procurement.

In the meantime, Alan Wood presented to the UK Chancellor of the Exchequer and Secretary of State for Trade and Industry a report in which he was requested to investigate the difficulties UK suppliers were confronted by when competing for public contracts in other EU countries (Wood 2004). The report notes that competing for public contracts in other EU countries is not an easy task, is time consuming, and is resource intensive. However, although it was argued that EU public procurement rules were not a hindrance for UK suppliers, grey areas remain – including a strong belief that local firms were being favoured. Nevertheless, UK firms were not apparently interested in challenging procurement decisions even when direct discrimination was believed to have occurred: maintaining good relations was their preferred option. Most interestingly, cultural preferences – where buying locally constituted an integral part of the culture – was identified as one of the main hindrances affecting the openness of public procurement markets. Other highlighted trade barriers to intra EU trade included political factors as well as industrial policy. In addition, each industry appeared to possess its own specific concerns. Local integration – for example, through locally based subsidiary companies – was found to be one of the main success factors for winning public procurement contracts in other EU countries. This finding is also in line with the Commission's 2004 report and a more recent report presented by Ramboll Management Consulting together with the University of Applied Sciences HTW Chur (hereafter referred to as the Ramboll Report) to DG Internal Market and Services in 2011 (Ramboll and University of Applied Sciences HTW Chur 2011).

The Ramboll Report aims to provide an update on the measurement of cross border procurement in Europe. Data for 1995, 2000 and 2005 reveal an increasing trend towards import penetration. Such a trend could be observed in both the public and private sectors. Nevertheless, public sector import penetration remains significantly lower (7.5 per cent in 2005) than in the private sector (19.1 per cent in 2005). The study makes a distinction between direct and indirect cross border procurement. When it comes to the public sector, direct cross border procurement accounts for 1.6 per cent of awards (or approximately 3.5 per cent of the total value of contract awards) published in TED for the period covering 2007–09. In the case of indirect cross border procurement for the same time period, 11.4 per cent occurs through affiliates when measured by the number of awards, or 13.4 per cent when contract values are used. Indirect cross border procurement through wholesalers/distributors also appears to be a common channel for procurement. For the period 2007–09 this type of procurement accounted for 11.9 per cent when both the number of awards and volume procured were taken into consideration.

The Ramboll Report also compares the impact of cross border procurement between Category 'A' services and Category 'B' services – as differentiated by the public procurement Directives and laid down in Annex II of Directive 2004/18/EC and Annex XVII of Directive 2004/17/EC. In essence, Category 'B' services are not subject to the detailed procedural rules of the Directives – especially those pertaining to selection and award.[10] The reason for this is because these services were acknowledged as being less suited for cross border procurement in comparison to category 'A' services.

According to the Ramboll Report, Category 'A' service contracts have a share of 1.4 per cent of direct and 11.0 per cent of indirect cross border procurement – when examined on the basis of number of awards (the total number amounting to 218,644) (Ramboll and University of Applied Sciences HTW Chur 2011). When compared to Category 'B' services – 0.7 per cent and 3.3 per cent for direct and indirect cross border procurement respectively (the total number amounting to 91,078 awards) (Ramboll and University of Applied Sciences HTW Chur 2011) – Category 'A' services appear to have a higher share of cross border procurement. On examining the value of procurement it was found that the share of 'A' services amounted to 2.8 per cent of direct and 16.2 per cent of indirect cross border procurement (total value amounting to €117,186 million (Ramboll and University of Applied Sciences HTW Chur, 2011). In the case of Category 'B' services the volume of cross border procurement amounted to 1.2 per cent and 12.1 per cent (total value amounting to €40,157 million (Ramboll and University of Applied Sciences HTW Chur 2011). In their report the researchers noted:

> In line with the distinction between A and B services, it might be expected that the share of cross-border procurements (direct and indirect through affiliates) would be significantly higher for A services than for B services. This can be confirmed, at least to a certain extent.
> (Ramboll and University of Applied Sciences HTW Chur 2011)

They further argue that

> For some of the B service subjects, direct cross-border procurement plays only a very small role, with a share of less than 0.5%. However, in other categories of B service the extent of cross-border procurement is even higher than the average for A services. However, this study only covers contract awards that were published in the OJ/TED, i.e. the cross-border performance of B services contracts which were not published in the OJ/TED could not be analysed. Thus, the proportion of B services contracts awarded cross-border could be different in reality.
> (Ramboll and University of Applied Sciences HTW Chur 2011)

It is worth noting that the same argument in respect of 'B' services contracts not being published in the *Official Journal* and TED database also holds true for Category 'A' services. Furthermore, despite the fact that in both categories the publication of a Contract Award Notice is mandated by the Directives, 'on average contract award notices are published for 80% of procedures which are publicly tendered through TED' (European Commission Working Document Public procurement Indicators 2008: 3). Therefore the real picture could be quite different.

It is interesting to note that according to the Ramboll Report certain Category 'B' services were identified as having higher than average cross border procurement than 'A' services. For example, 1.9 per cent of the total number of contracts for legal services were awarded cross border, compared to the average of 1.4 per cent for Category 'A' services (Ramboll and University of Applied Sciences HTW Chur 2011). However, in terms of their *value*, this worked out at 21.2 per cent of the total value of contracts for legal services awarded directly cross border, compared to the average of 2.8 per cent of Category 'A' services (Ramboll and University of Applied Sciences HTW Chur 2011). In the case of hotel and restaurant services – which comprised 10.9 per cent of the total number of contracts awarded indirectly cross border (compared to an average of 11 per cent of Category 'A' services) – their total value accounted for 39.1 per cent of indirect cross border procurement in this category compared to the average of 16.2 per cent for Category 'A' services.

The Commission notes that 'as far as some sectors are concerned, the distinction between tradable and non-tradable sectors is somewhat arbitrary' (European Commission 2011: 16). Indeed it could be argued that for some sectors the adoption of a lighter public procurement regime resulted in apparently more effective cross border trade than in those sectors that are exposed to a fuller regime. Such conclusions need to be interpreted in the light of previous empirical research such as that conducted by Geroski (1991), Head and Mayor (2000) and Nevan and Rollers (1991) – in which serious doubts are expressed about the claimed impact of non-tariff barriers as identified by the Commission on Europe's Single Market programme. Other factors, such as consumer bias, are also identified as being a determinant of market fragmentation. Such empirical reports appear to support the reality that Europe faces today – a reality in which overall cross border procurement in the public sector over the past 20 years has remained relatively low. Notwithstanding such facts, the Commission – in its proposal for a Directive of the European Parliament and of the Council on public procurement – noted the following:

> The traditional distinction between so-called prioritary and non-prioritary services ('A' and 'B' services) will be abolished. The results of the evaluation have shown that it is no longer justified to restrict the full application of procurement law to a limited group of services. However, it became also clear that the regular procurement regime is not adapted to social services which need a specific set of rules.
>
> (COM (2011) 896 final: 8)

Previous attempts – albeit failed ones – demonstrating the Commission's desire to expose category 'B' services to the full public procurement regime are clearly reflected in the Irish An Post case (Case C-507/03, 2007). In proceedings under Article 226 EC,[11] the European Commission alleged failure to fulfil obligations on grounds of infringements of Articles 43 EC and 49 EC.[12] In this case the European Commission sought to extend the obligations of Member States with respect to services coming within the ambit of Annex 1B of Directive 92/50 relating to the coordination of procedures for the award of public service contracts. In its judgment the Court held that '[a] mere statement by it that a complaint was made to it in relation to the contract in question is not sufficient to establish that the contract was of certain cross-border interest and that there was therefore a failure to fulfil obligations' (Case C-507/03, 2007).

In essence, it could be argued that on the basis of the Ramboll Report cross border public procurement was, and remains, significantly and persistently low. In the case of certain 'B' services – such as legal, and hotel and restaurant services – a lighter public procurement regime has resulted in apparently more effective cross border trade than has been the case in other sectors exposed to the fuller public procurement regime.[13] Indeed, such findings expose the fact that there remains much scope for better utilisation of the EU public procurement regime.

3.4 EU public procurement and its impact on small- and medium-sized enterprises

Small- and medium-sized enterprises[14] (hereafter referred to as SMEs) have been described as the true backbone of the European economy, being primarily responsible for wealth and economic growth while playing a key role in innovation and R&D (DG Enterprise 2011). Notwithstanding this, it becomes difficult to comprehend how SMEs remain under-represented in above-EU threshold public procurement, a fact long acknowledged by the Commission.[15] It is worth noting that one of the acclaimed beneficial effects that the 1992 Single Market programme was expected to reap was for SMEs; and that this would provide greater opportunities for their participation in public procurement contracts.

In a study conducted on behalf of the Commission in 2007 (GHK 2007) it was estimated that in 2005, 64 per cent of the number of contracts above EU thresholds were awarded to SMEs (this corresponds to 42 per cent of the procurement value above EU threshold). This figure does not take into account subcontracts secured by SMEs. In addition, major discrepancies across Member States were also found. For example, in Slovenia and Slovakia, SMEs captured 78 per cent and 77 per cent of the public procurement market, while France and the UK captured 35 per cent and 31 per cent respectively.

According to a follow-up report (GHK 2010) the share of public contracts awarded to SMEs for the period 2005–08 captured lower values. In the period 2006–08 an estimated 60 per cent of above-EU threshold contracts were awarded to SMEs. This accounted for 34 per cent of the market share in terms of value.

76 *The status quo*

In another empirical study, the analysis covered the 27 EU Member States and the three European Economic Area (EEA) countries (Iceland, Liechtenstein and Norway) for the period between 2008–11 (PwC *et al.* 2014). An estimated 56 per cent of all public procurement contracts above the EU thresholds were awarded to SMEs. In terms of contract value this corresponds to 29 per cent of market share. However, it was also noted that SMEs benefit from public procurement awards through other routes: for instance through joint bid arrangements or as subcontractors. Therefore, when such routes are also taken into consideration, it was estimated that 46 per cent of aggregate public procurement value above EU threshold were awarded to SMEs. SMEs' participation in below-threshold procurement was found to be between 58 and 59 per cent of contracting value.

With a view to facilitating access by SMEs to public procurement contracts the Commission issued a European Code of Best Practice in 2008 in order to ensure a level playing field for all economic operators (SEC (2008) 2193). A Commission communication entitled 'Think small first, a "Small Business Act" for Europe'[16] was published in 2008, and in 2010 a European small business portal was established.[17] In 2010 the European Parliament called upon the Commission to take stock of the situation and encourage wider dissemination across Member States of the Small Business Act's European Code of Best Practices because SMEs were struggling to gain access to public procurement markets (European Parliament, Committee on the Internal Market and Consumer Protection 2010).

3.5 EU public procurement and its impact on the international public procurement market

When it comes to the international scenario, EU suppliers in the utilities public procurement market are facing discriminatory practices that in effect close off their exporting opportunities (COM (2009) 592 final): 'Most of the EU's major trading partners operate restrictive public procurement practices which discriminate against EU suppliers. The current economic crisis increased the use of such practices' (COM (2009) 592 final: 18). To date, the Agreement on Government Procurement (GPA) is the only legally binding instrument for opening up multilateral obligations within the World Trade Organisation (WTO). Although the EU is strongly committed to the multilateral trading system, and keen on focusing on areas not covered by the multilateral WTO rules – including public procurement – the plurilateral WTO Government Procurement Agreement remains the main instrument for opening up international procurement markets. This, as the Commission points out, is mainly due to the highly sensitive political nature of government procurement (COM (2009) 592 final: 18). GPA parties are reluctant to further open public procurement to international competition. Thus, for example, the US, Japan and Korea maintain set asides (when a proportion of public procurement contracts are reserved in order to favour particular firms) for their national SMEs; and the Japanese preclude other international economic operators from accessing their railway procurement market (COM

(2009) 592 final: 18). Meanwhile, and as noted by the Commission, when procurement opportunities are not offered in finalised negotiations, the other party nevertheless is fully aware that EU procurement is not 'sheltered with a wall, which would be impossible to penetrate' (COM (2009) 592 final: 18). With a view to addressing imbalances, the Council requested the Commission to *rebalance the agreement* – and so the revised offer in February 2008 took into account the possibility for other GPA parties to reciprocate the opening of the procurement markets (Council meeting, n. 6039, 2007: 6). When reciprocity is not met, this notion is interpreted more strictly by the EU. Furthermore, in cases where external parties are profiting from the EU's general openness, the EU now appears to be contemplating the imposition of carefully targeted restrictions in order to encourage reciprocity.[18] On 6 April 2014 the revised GPA, concluded in December 2011, entered into force. According to Internal Market and Services Commissioner Michael Barnier, for those countries that are party to the agreement the revised GPA will enable significant opportunities in each other's public procurement markets since public procurement rules in GPA jurisdictions become more transparent and predictable (IP/14/381, 4 April 2014). This remains to be seen.

3.6 Concluding remarks

European challenges need not rely solely upon European economic efficiency logic of the sort that today manifests itself as an overriding and unconditional attitude. Public procurement as a highly dynamic policy tool can be used in various ways. Thus, in order to to ensure its optimisation one needs also to take into consideration all of its potential uses. Restricting the use of public procurement solely for the achievement of an economic efficiency logic means closing the door on other valid opportunities. Therefore, in order to ensure optimisation of the public procurement regime, a reordering of how we conceive public procurement is essential. This, in effect, calls for a paradigm shift wherein a departure from dogmatism becomes a must.

It is argued that the intertwined social threads constitute the very fabric of Europe's economic dimension; and that Europe's building capacity is located therein – potentially weaving the way towards European integration. The alternative is for the EU public procurement regime to have a social dimension standing at its core – one that extends into a social model of European integration in which the European citizen becomes the key actor in the integration process.

Notes

1 By Council Decision 94/800/EC (22 December 1994), 'Concerning the conclusion on behalf of the European Community, as regards matters within its competence of the agreements reached in the Uruguay Round multilateral negotiations', the public procurement Directives are to comply with the obligations as laid down in the agreement. See Commission Regulation (EU) No. 1251/2011 of 30 November 2011 amending Directives 2004/17/EC, 2004/18/EC and 2009/81/EC of the European Parliament and of the

Council in respect of their application thresholds for the procedures for the awards of contracts. For revised threshold values see Commission Regulation (EU) No 1336/2013 of 13 December 2013 amending Directives 2004/17/EC, 2004/18/EC and 2004/81/EC of the European Parliament and of the Council in respect of the application thresholds for the procedures for the awards of contracts, OJEU, L 335/17.

2 Member States are obliged to present to the Commission statistical reports of the preceding year by the end of 31 October of each year. The following Articles apply: Article 67 of Directive 2004/17/EC of the European Parliament and of the Council of 31 March 2004 coordinating the procurement procedures of entities operating in the water, energy, transport and postal services sectors (30 April 2004); Article 75 of Directive 2004/18/EC of the European Parliament and of the Council of 31 March 2004 on the coordination of procedures for the award of public works contracts, public supply contracts and public service contracts (30 April 2004); Article 42 of Directive 98/4/EC of the European Parliament and of the Council of 16 February 1998 amending Directive 93/38/EEC coordinating the procurement procedures of entities operating in the water, energy, transport and telecommunications sectors; Article 39 of the European Parliament and Council Directive 97/52/EC of 13 October 1997 amending Directives 92/50/EEC, 93/36/EEC and 93/37/EEC concerning the coordination of procedures for the award of public service contracts, public supply contracts and public works contracts respectively; Article 31 of Council Directive 93/36/EEC of 14 June 1993 coordinating procedures for the award of public supply contracts; Article 34 of Council Directive 93/37/EEC of 14 June 1993 concerning the coordination of procedures for the award of public works contracts; Article 42 of Council Directive 93/38/EEC of 14 June 1993 coordinating the procurement procedures of entities operating in the water, energy, transport and telecommunications sectors; Article 39 of Council Directive 92/50/EEC of 18 June 1992 relating to the coordination of procedures for the award of public service contracts.

3 It is worth noting that a new legislative package for the modernisation of public procurement – that seeks to attain greater simplification and flexibility in public procurement procedures across the EU – was adopted by Member States and needs to be complied with by 18 April 2016. The legislative reforms will be put into context in Chapter 9.

4 To this effect see Articles 35–7, 69, 70, Annexes VII, VII A, VII B, VII C, VII D, VIII of Directive 2004/18/EC; Articles 41–4, Annexes XIII, XIV, XV A, XV B, XVI of Directive 2004/17EC; and Articles 30–2, 64, Annexes IX, V, VI of Directive 2009/81/EC.

5 According to the researchers over a quarter of contracts do not publish a CN or a PIN. See Europe Economics 2011: v.

6 It appears that the €420 billion of public contracts reflects the estimated value of tenders published in the online European public procurement journal, Tenders Electronic Daily (TED), for year 2009. See European Commission 2011b.

7 The calculation of error rates is based on representative statistical samples with a 95 per cent confidence level.

8 See examples above, as reported upon by the Court of Auditors.

9 See European Commission 2004: 9, fn 9). This new evidence is based on a sample study of 1,500 firms actively involved in procurement ('COWI. Monitoring Public Procurement in the European Union using Firm Panel Data', Lot 1, final report July 2003). This study is based on questionnaires addressed to a sample of firms from Austria (60), Belgium (60), Denmark (60), France (360), Germany (450), Ireland (40), Spain (120) and the UK (360). The targeted sample of firms was drawn from nine economic areas corresponding to Common Procurement Vocabulary sectors 24 (chemicals), 29 (machinery), 30 (office equipment), 33 (medical products), 34 (motor vehicles), 50 (motor repair), 45 (construction), 74 (business services) and 90 (sewage). These sectors account for 66 per cent of all published tenders.

10 Pursuant to Article 21 of Directive 2004/18/EC, contracts referring to services listed in Annex II B shall be subject solely to Articles 23 relating to technical specifications and Article 35 (4) which refers to the publication of the Contract Award Notice. Pursuant to Article 32 of Directive 2004/17/EC, contracts referring to services listed in Annex XVII B shall be subject solely to Article 34 relating to technical specifications and Article 43 which refers to the publication of the Contract Award Notice.
11 Article 226 EC has now been replaced by Article 258 TFEU.
12 Articles 43EC and 49EC have been replaced by Articles 49 TFEU and 56 TFEU respectively.
13 With the coming into force of the new public procurement Directives (Directive 2014/24/EU replacing Directive 2004/18/EC and Directive 2014/25/EU replacing Directive 2004/17/EU) the distinction between Category 'A' and 'B' services have been abolished. In their stead, a list of services belonging to the so-called *light regime* are identified and different rules for such services apply. The simplified regime applies to contracts above €750,000. Contracting authorities are obliged to publish in advance their intention to award contracts and to publish the contract award decision. No procedural rules apply but contracting authorities are obliged to treat bidders equally. Services covered – social services, health services, cultural services, educational services, certain legal services and hotel and restaurant services. See Article 74 of Directive 2014/24/EU and Article 91 of Directive 2014/25/EU.
14 Pursuant to Commission Recommendation 2003/361/EC of 6 May 2003 concerning the definition of micro, small- and medium-sized enterprises (SMEs), these are considered to be any entity engaged in an economic activity, irrespective of its legal form. SMEs employ fewer than 250 persons and have an annual turnover not exceeding €50 million, and/or an annual balance sheet total not exceeding €43 million.
15 To this effect see, for instance, COM (1989) 400 final: para. 41, and European Commission 2010: 25.
16 See COM (2008) 394 final.
17 See European Commission, Small Business Portal, available at: http://ec.europa.eu/small-business/index_en.htm.
18 According to the Commission this approach is not targeted at the poorer, developing countries. See COM (2009) 592 final: 19, footnote 42).

References

Cecchini, P., 1988. *The European Challenge, 1992: The benefits of a Single Market*. Aldershot, Hants: Wildwood House Limited.

Europe Economics, 2011. *Estimating the Benefits from the Procurement Directives – A report for DG Internal Market*. London: Europe Economics, Chancery House

Geroski, P., 1991. '1992 and European Industrial Structure' in: Mackenzie, G. and Venables, A.J. (eds), *The Economics of the Single European Act*. London: Macmillan.

GHK, 2007. *Evaluation of SME Access to Public Procurment Markets in the EU, Final Report*. Brussels: European Commission.

GHK, 2010. *Evaluation of SMES' Access To Public Procurement Markets In The EU*. Brussels: DG Enterprise and Industry.

Head, K. and Mayer, T., 2000. 'Non-Europe: The Magnitude and Causes of Market Fragmentation in the EU' in *Review of World Economics*, vol. 136, no. 2, pp. 284–314.

McCrudden, C., 2007. *Buying social justice: Equality, government procurement, & legal change*. Oxford: Oxford University Press.

Neven, D.J. and Rollers, L.H., 1991. 'European Integration and Trade Flows' in *European Economic Review*, vol. 35, no. 6, pp. 1295–1309.

80 *The status quo*

PwC, ICF, GHK and ECORYS, 2014. *SMEs' access to public procurement markets and aggregation of demand in the EU.* Brussels: DG Internal Market and Services.

Ramboll, M.C. and University of Applied Sciences HTW CHUR, 2011. *Final Report – Cross-border procurement above EU thresholds.* Denmark: Ramboll.

Wood, A., 2004. *A report to The Chancellor of the Exchequer & Secretary of State for Trade & Industry.* UK: Office of Government Commerce.

Official documents

Cases before the Court of Justice of the European Union

Case C-507/03, *Commission of the European Communities* v. *Ireland, 2007.* ECR I-09777.

Court of Auditors

Court of Auditors, 2010. 'Annual report concerning the financial year 2009 (2010/C 303/01)', *Official Journal of the European Union.*

Court of Auditors, 2012. 'Audit report concerning financial year 2011 (2012/C 344/01)', *Official Journal of the European Union.*

European Council

Council Meeting, 2780th External Relations, C.M., 2007. Nr 6039/07, p. 6. Brussels.

European Parliament

European Parliament – Committee on the Internal Market and Consumer Protection, 2010. 'New Developments in Public Procurement, INI/2009/2175, Report Adopted 18 May 2010'. Brussels.

European Commission

COM (1989) 400 final, 1989. *Public Procurement Regional and Social Aspects (Communication from the Commission).* Brussels: European Commission.

COM (2008) 394 final, 25 June 2008. *Communication from the Commission to the Council, the European Parliament, the European Economic and Social Committee and the Committee of Regions, 'Think small first, a "Small Business Act" for Europe'.* Brussels: European Commission.

COM (2009) 592 final, 2009. *Report from the Commission concerning negotiations regarding access of Community undertakings to the markets of third countries in fields covered by the Directive 2004/17/EC.* Brussels: European Commission.

COM (2011) 896 final, 2011. *Proposal for a Directive of the European Parliament and of the Council on public procurement.* Brussels: European Commission.

DG Enterprise, A.I., *European Small Business Portal – Facts and Figures.* European Commission.

European Commission, 2004. *A report on the Functioning of Public Procurement Markets in the EU: Benefits from Application of EU Directives and challenges for the future.* Brussels.

European Commission, 2010a. *Working Document – Public Procurement Indicators 2008*. Brussels.
European Commission, 2010b. *Public Procurement Indicators, 2009*. Brussels.
European Commission, 2011a. *EU Public Procurement Legislation: Delivering Results Summary of Evaluation Report*. Brussels.
European Commission, 2011b. *Public Procurement Indicators 2010*. Brussels.
European Commission, 2012a. *Public Procurement Indicators 2011*. Brussels.
European Commission, 2012b. *2011 Annual Activity Report – Directorate General Regional Policy*. Brussels.
SEC (2008) 2193, 2008. *European Code of Best Practices Facilitating Access By SMEs To Public Procurement Contracts*. Brussels: Commission of the European Communities.
SEC (2011) 1179 final, 2011. *Commission Staff Working Paper – Analysis of errors in cohesion policy for years 2006–2009. Actions taken by the Commission and the way forward*. Brussels: European Commission.

European Commission – press releases

European Commission, IP/11/785, Press Release, 24 June 2011. 'Single Market Act: EU public procurement framework has saved around 20 billions euros'. Brussels.
European Commission, IP/14/381, Press Release, 4 April 2014. 'Commission welcomes the revised World Trade Organisation's Agreement on Government Procurement'. Brussels.

4 Free trade
What about it – myths or realities?

4.1 Introduction

The intellectual rationale behind the opening up of public procurement forms part and parcel of Europe's drive to create an integrated political and economic union. It has been held that 'political and economic integration are inextricably inter-related' (Cox 1993: 11). It has been assumed as long as Member States maintain preferential national public procurement patterns in order to protect their domestic industries from competition – there will always be vested interests for resisting an integrated political and economic union, thus eradicating any hope that Europe can ever become properly integrated both politically and economically. Furthermore, in such a situation, and in the light of global competition, the consequence of such market fragmentation is that European firms would not be able to compete successfully in world markets since they lack the necessary economies of scale given that they operate in relatively small domestic markets (Cox 1993).

The liberalisation of public procurement was said to play a key role in European integration via the Single Market Initiative (Cecchini 1988). Once public procurement was removed from the clutches of the Member States it was assumed that one could get away with local parochialism and trigger into motion industry's competitive market forces. This would be made possible through a reformulation of the public procurement rules: in other words, through a reformulation of the public procurement rules a domino effect on the Single Market Initiative was to be expected. Thus it was assumed that uncompetitive suppliers would be forced to restructure themselves if they were to survive in a competitive environment, mergers and acquisitions would be encouraged, and greater opportunities would open up for small- and medium-sized enterprises to participate in public contracts. As a consequence, efficiency gains amounting to 0.5 per cent (approximately 17.5 billion ECUs or 21.5 billion ECUs if defence procurement is included) of 1986 Community GDP was expected to result (Cecchini 1988: 17). Such efficiency gains were to emanate from three major supply-side effects (Cecchini 1988). First, the *static trade effect* brought about by liberalised procurement would make it possible for the public purchaser to buy from the cheapest suppliers. Second, the *competition effect* would cause prices to fall in the face of real competition. And third, the *restructuring effect* would lead to long-term savings through economies of scale and international competition.

The economic rationale behind EU public procurement regulation is based on neoliberal economics. Various community documents, as well as famous studies such as the Cecchini and the Atkins Reports, reflect this (Cecchini 1988; Atkins 1988; European Commission 1988, 1989; Bovis 1998). In essence, it is assumed that once rules to eradicate market barriers are put into place the efficient operation of the market – when left to its own devices – would ensure that the public sector is served by the most efficient suppliers. This in turn would lead to significant savings in public expenditure. It has also been assumed that most of the gains would flow into higher levels of employment and increases in economic growth.

But there are various criticisms to this line of thought since it assumes that market inefficiencies are located on the demand side of the economic equation – that is, through inefficient public purchasing – and it is the correction of public purchasing behaviour (such as the eradication of protectionism and the defence of national champion firms) that would naturally generate positive supply-side ripple effects on the economy (Siebert 1989; Cutler 1989). However, such arguments fail to take into account purchasing behaviour on the supply-side – which has been held to be of equal importance – and regulation in this respect is not included in public procurement legislation (Bovis 1988).

Other researchers appear not at all convinced that the trade barriers – as identified in the Cecchini Report – are the main reason for market fragmentation across the EU. Geroski (1991) attributed market fragmentation to the diversity in national and regional tastes, and claimed that the 1992 Programme would do little to reduce this type of fragmentation. Head and Mayer (2000) appear to lend further support to Geroski's conjecture in their empirical research – which was mainly concerned with the examination of the border effect vis-à-vis non-tariff barriers and the consumption of foreign goods relative to the consumption of domestic ones. Head and Mayer make use of a trade model derived from monopolistic competition. The researchers found no relation between market fragmentation and the barriers that were identified and removed by Europe's Single Market programme prior to the implementation of the Single European Act – i.e the period 1984–86. In effect, industries related to the personal consumption of goods (and not those identified by the Commission) appeared as the ones on which the border effects were higher. Border effects were defined by Head and Mayer (2000: 26) as the 'extent that domestic subunits trade more with each other than with foreign units of identical size and distance'. The researchers went on to argue that border effects appear to be linked more closely with variety in tastes than to formal barriers to trade. Other research (Neven and Rollers 1991) also examining the impact of non-tariff barriers on the share of EU imports in four major EC countries for the years 1975–85 found no relationship to their impediment on trade. What is more, the results suggested that the Single Market programme may actually generate more benefits to firms *outside* the EU.[1] Head and Mayer also conducted empirical research on the impact of non-tariff barriers and the border effect post-implementation of the Single Market programme. They noted a declining trend with respect to the impact of borders. However, this downward trend could be traced back at least a decade before the Single Market programme was implemented.[2] Moreover, the researchers noted that none of the different measures for the removal of non-tariff barriers covering the industries earmarked by the Commission could explain the changes in the border effect. Thus, their removal did not provide the greatest benefits to the targeted industries. In other words, the expected rise in the ratio of trade over the consumption of domestic products – for those industries labelled by the Commission as high barriers to trade – did not materialise. Head and Mayer say their results suggest that whereas differences in taste could be invoked prior to the implementation of the Single Market programme, following 1986 the fall in border effects did not seem to be larger in industries comprising mainly final goods. Instead, consumer bias is given as their explanation for the border effects.

Another study (Ilzkovitz et al. 2007) – funded by the Commission and prepared by the Directorate General for Economic and Financial Affairs (although the Commission inserted a disclaimer noting that the views expressed represented those of the authors) – aimed to analyse the effects of the implementation of the internal market programme. The study put together a comprehensive body of empirical evidence in order to take stock of what has been achieved in terms of European economic integration. It is claimed that the internal market has been the source of large macroeconomic benefits. However, it also contended that 'the initial expectations that the Internal Market would serve as a catalyst for creating a more dynamic, innovative and competitive economy at the world level have not been met' (Ilzkovitz et al. 2007: 1, 18). The researchers identify various reasons for this, all of which point towards various inefficiencies – slow, and at times incomplete, implementation of Directives; inadequacy of some instruments; persistence of barriers to cross border trade and investment; and a slow development of an internal market for knowledge. It is argued that if the removal of most of the remaining cross border barriers could be achieved, Europe would have attained substantially larger gains.

As noted earlier, the reasoning that grounds the liberalisation of the European public procurement market draws on neoliberal economics – which is itself based on a strong support for the market economy. At the heart of this rests the theory of comparative advantage. Nothwithstanding the fact that the theory of comparative advantage is one of the oldest and most successful economic theories – and enjoys widespread support – various economists have exposed certain difficulties with its underlying assumptions, particularly in light of today's market realities. Therefore, when taking into consideration the fact that essential components underpinning the rationale remain debatable, it is all the more natural to expect robust justifications that hold tightly to the European Union's overriding stance when utilising public purchasing[3] as a tool that directly promotes the market economy – particularly when this comes at the expense of its potential use by Member States to promote domestic social policies.

Free trade: what about it? 85

This chapter will continue its discussion in section 4.2 – 'On framing economic theories' – by exposing the difficulties that economists face when it comes to theorising in economic terms. Such facts need to be factored into our understanding, given the overriding importance that Europe assigns to neoliberal economics. We then move on to section 4.3, 'The theory of comparative advantage – a general idea', in which we introduce very briefly a general idea of the theories that relate to free trade, and some of the ongoing critiques, with a view to allowing the reader who may not be as well versed with such theories understand slightly better the arguments that emanate in this respect. Section 4.4, 'Moving beyond theory: free trade and the Europe 2020 strategy' puts into perspective free trade as captured within the Single Market Act and its assumed role in the Europe 2020 strategy. The discussion in section 4.5 attempts to put into context 'The liberalisation of the network industries as an illustration of the EU's overriding and unconditional attitude towards the Single Market project'; section 4.6 presents our concluding remarks.

4.2 On framing economic theories

Differences in economic analysis should not come as a surprise (Unger 2007).[4] One needs only to look at the history of economics – which is replete with examples of economic theories that were later drastically revised. Burtt (1972) explains that when economists differ in their analysis this is not because their methods have been employed incorrectly or in an unscientific manner. For Burtt these differences stem from other phenomena that are more deeply ingrained within the nature of economics itself. Burtt lists three factors that contribute to such differences. First, there is the difficulty of *verifying economic hypotheses*. The conduct of controlled experiments in economics is generally not possible. History cannot be rerun to see, for example, whether a different monetary policy could have produced greater economic stability. Thus, the ability of economic hypotheses to explain the real world is seriously questioned. The procedures economists employ are almost always indirect and their judgements almost always conditional. Second, there is the difficulty of *open-endedness of economic behaviour*. According to Burtt, economic action is usually concerned with the choice of scarce economic resources in order to achieve specified goals and which, in turn, produce income. However, he argues that the dividing line between economic and non-economic goals and motives is drawn differently by different economists. The achievement of non-economic goals such as prestige, status, security, or, alternatively, the achievement of economic goals, falls largely within the discretion of the economist. Different decisions on such preliminary questions and motives lead to different predictions. The third factor – and for Burtt the most fundamental in explaining economic controversy among economists – revolves around the *need for an element of valuation in all economic judgements*. In view of the fact that economic valuations are not conducive to measurement or ranking, what may appear for one economist as a significant bit of analysis, can be dismissed and hence regarded by another as insignificant. Burtt argues (1972: 3) that 'each age writes its own history books and stamps upon the contents the value judgments of that age'. He presents a multitude of examples. For instance, he explains how Malthus' theory of effective demand was demolished by Ricardo. But a century later John Maynard Keynes revived Malthus' theory and claimed that he was right after all, and that Ricardo was wrong. François Quesnay – the first to develop an input-output analysis, a tool that is today recognised as being of great importance – was dismissed for generations, only to be valued 150 years later. Anti-mainstream writers such as Sismondi and Karl Marx were rejected outright at the time. However, some of their insights – such as techniques of dynamic analysis – were acknowledged in the twentieth century.

Burtt notes three approaches in the attitudes of economists. In the first approach – during the seventeenth century – economists assumed that their value judgements were based on scientific conclusions, that they were desirable for society, and that they were therefore necessary to support certain government policies. But these attitudes had reversed by the end of the nineteenth century. The separation of positive analysis from normative judgements was recognised as essential for the growth of pure scientific economics. John Stuart Mill and John E. Cairnes advanced the idea that the economist should not and cannot draw political conclusions. By the middle of the twentieth century it was recognised that no matter how positivist the economist is, the valuation process is implied in all forms of analysis. Myrdal (1969: vii) is quoted as stating: 'This implicit belief in the existence of a body of scientific knowledge acquired independently of all valuations is, as I now see it, naive empiricism.'[5] For Myrdal, economic theories require *a priori* social judgements because otherwise 'there are no scientific facts but only chaos'. For Burtt (1972: 8) '[t]he social relevance of the valuation systems of the men who frame theories and draw inferences becomes, then, a fundamental issue in economic theory'. Indeed, we cannot rely and be guided solely by studies that adopt too narrow a perspective on social life because they fail to take sufficient consideration of the intertwined social threads that ultimately weave out the EU's economic fabric.

4.3 The theory of comparative advantage – a general idea

The early logic that free trade could be beneficial to countries was postulated by Adam Smith in 1776. He argued that

> If a foreign country can supply us with a commodity cheaper than we ourselves can make it, better buy it of them with some part of the produce of our own industry, employed in a way in which we have some advantage.
>
> (Smith 1776: 12)

Thus was the concept of *absolute advantage* in production conceived. In *The Wealth of Nations* (Smith 1776b) Adam Smith postulated that the progress of human well-being is primarily attributed to free exchange, which in turn makes possible the division of labour. The work of philosophers, scientists and engineers are examples that reflect such a division of labour. Progress, it is argued, is not the result of advances brought about by technology; but rather by a division of labour which makes possible the development of technology. Thus, specialisation sits at the very heart of human well-being. Furthermore, it is argued that all this evolves through a natural process. Governments cannot hasten such a process and as such their main function is to protect freedom of exchange by upholding justice, i.e. property rights.

Some 39 years later the basic idea of *absolute advantage* – as described by Adam Smith – was claimed to be erroneous (Torrens 1815). It was demonstrated that the chosen specialisation good of any country should be that which enjoyed a *comparative advantage* in its production. The idea of *comparative advantage* was formalised by David Ricardo and thereafter referred to as the 'Ricardian model'. In the 1817 book, *On the Principles of Political Economy and Taxation*, David Ricardo presented his theory by way of a numerical model using his famous example of two imagined countries – England and Portugal, producing two commodities: wine and cloth. To identify a country's *comparative advantage* one must compare the *opportunity* costs.[6] Ricardo's argument was that there are gains from trade if each country specialises completely in the production of the good in which it enjoys a *comparative advantage* in producing – then trades with the other country for the other good.

Ricardo's theory emerged during turbulent times when the Industrial Revolution gave rise to heated political debates over the extent of control of industrial capitalism. Sympathetic towards capitalist enterprise's desire for greater freedom from government restriction, his theory was capable of withstanding various criticisms (Unger 2007). The idea of comparative advantage has since got to the nub of justification for universal free trade – on the basis of productive specialisation. The notion for free trade derives its main support from claims that it can raise aggregate economic efficiency both within national borders, and across them.

The Ricardian model is based on various assumptions. First and foremost it assumes that perfect competition prevails in all markets. It is based on the assumption of two countries, producing two goods, with labour as the only factor of production. Goods are assumed to be homogenous across firms and countries, while labour is homogenous within a country but heterogeneous across countries. Transportation costs do not feature in the equation (Suranovic 2010). The exchange is assumed to be costless and it is further assumed that there are similar tastes across trading countries (Leamer 1994). Other key assumptions underlying the theory of comparative advantage are that costs and benefits arising during the process of consumption are internalised since they are taken into full account and borne by economic operators. As such, no externalities are seen to exist because total private costs and total social costs are considered equivalent (Prasch 1996). The theory of comparative advantage assumes full employment of all capital and labour, and further assumes that labour is capable of relative mobility at no cost. Trade between countries is always assumed to be balanced in that the value of imports is equal to the value of exports for each country (Robinson 1980). Furthermore, the theory of comparative advantage assumes that capital does not cross international borders.

With the passage of time, alterations were made to the Ricardian model – notably the Heckscher–Ohlin model originally developed in the 1920s. Other elaborations to this model were also provided in the 1930s, 1950s and 1960s (Suranovic 2010). The following explanation attempts to capture the most salient points.

Whereas under the Ricardian model production technologies are assumed to differ across countries, this is not the case with the Heckscher–Ohlin model, in which they are assumed to be the same – that is, the Heckscher–Ohlin model assumes that economies have a static set of technologies, including labour skills (Prasch 1996: 42). The Heckscher–Ohlin model, as with the Ricardian model, assumes that perfect competition prevails in all markets. The model takes into account two factors for production, namely labour and capital. It is through the use of capital that income for the capital owner is generated (referred to as 'rents'). A distinctive characteristic within this model is that it assumes that countries differ in their endowments of labour and capital as inputs in the production process. Consequently, the differing capital:labour ratios in production processes across countries and industries make it possible for trade to occur whilst influencing prices, wages and rents.

In an attempt to further explain international trade flows vis-à-vis comparative advantage, other theories were developed over the years – such as those based on variety and scale economies (Krugman 1980; Ethier 1982; Helpman and Krugman 1985), or in-firm heterogeneity (Melitz 2003; Helpman *et al.* 2003; Bernard *et al.* 2007). In 1980 Deardorff's theorem of the law of comparative advantage made it possible to establish the theory's general validity (Deardorff 1980). Empirical support for the prediction of Deardorff's theorem was later presented by Bernhofen and Brown (2004) using Japan's historical product-specific data on autarky prices for the period 1851–53 (i.e. before Japan opened to foreign trade) and trade data for the period 1868–75 (i.e. after Japan opened to foreign trade). The authors claimed that their findings presented robust support for the law of comparative advantage. Kiyota (2011) revisits the findings presented by Bernhofen and Brown (2004) and presents empirical support for the law of comparative advantage, even after trade imbalances are taken into account. In testing trade theory one of the key assumptions underlying Deardorff's theorem is balanced trade. However, Kiyota demonstrates empirical validity of the law of comparative advantage even after unbalanced trade is taken into account. Kiyota asserts that while Deardorff's propostion holds true under unbalanced trade conditions, an additional assumption needs to be factored in; that is, the representative consumer has homothetic preferences. According to Kiyota this assumption presents empirical restrictions.

From an economic standpoint Deardorff (2005) asserts that the two-good model of Ricardo provides strong results that support the theory of comparative advantage, but that 'under more general assumptions such strong results no longer are assured. Instead one can derive much weaker results, usually in the form of correlations between comparative advantage and trade, and these hold in a much wider variety of circumstances' (Deardorff 2005: 1). He contends:

> A single concept can hardly be expected to explain every aspect of something as widespread and complicated as trade. But the theory gives good reason to believe that comparative advantage works, on average, to provide the potential for gain from trade and to explain what the nature of beneficial trade is likely to be.
>
> (Deardorff 2005: 23)

The case for free trade appears to be particularly strong when arguments in its favour emerge from the political side. Academic arguments concerning free trade take a more sophisticated course. And while free trade can cause harm as well as good, the same could be said of protectionist policies (Suranovic 2010). The following are some of the main issues concerning free trade that academia appears to have settled on (Suranovic 2010):

- the main support for free trade arises because it can raise aggregate economic efficiency;
- trade theory shows that some people will suffer losses in free trade;
- a country may benefit from free trade even if it is less efficient than all other countries in every industry;
- a domestic firm may lose out in international competition even if it is the lowest-cost producer in the world;
- protection may be beneficial for a country;
- although protection can be beneficial, the case for free trade remains strong.

Roberto Mangabeira Unger (2007) delves into the very heart of the theory of comparative advantage – on which the doctrine of free trade is based. Although in no way denying the power of the concept, Unger claims that the problem lies more in what the doctrine on comparative advantage leaves unsaid. As such, it remains beyond the reach of economic theorising. He argues that the theory is incomplete in three major ways.

First: 'Incompleteness: Indeterminacy resulting from failure to justify unique assignments of comparative advantage' (Unger 2007: 28). As soon as more than two countries with more than two commodities are analysed one realises that there can be multiple, infinite or no solutions. In the case of multiple or infinite solutions the doctrine of comparative advantage becomes inadequate. Further, Unger argues that the doctrine of comparative advantage deals with *static efficiency*. That is, it does not tell us anything on the possibilities deriving from innovation.

Second: 'Incompleteness: Confusion Resulting from Uncertainty about the limits of our power collectively to shape comparative advantage' (Unger 2007: 36). Comparative advantage can be acquired or shaped. But when it comes to shaping comparative advantage institutions tend to be biased, to a greater or lesser extent, towards their own reputations and arrangements of productive specialisations, and hence such bias restrains the way they are organised. Because the doctrine of comparative advantage deals with *static efficiency* it traps us into believing that there is a single natural expression of what constitutes a market economy. Unger claims that the fact that a market economy – although acknowledged in principle – can be realised within various institutional formats, is given little force. Hence, in order to dispel such confusions when producing and reshaping comparative advantage, one needs to cross boundaries. An inclusive market economy requires innovation in all its institutional forms. Experimentation is crucial in this respect – advancing with the benefit of hindsight gathered through experimentation, rather than through blueprint, becomes the key driver. However, neither the market economy nor democratic politics as presently organised can be trusted to promulgate this much needed experimentation. In order to go beyond the world of *static efficiency* and produce comparative advantage through experimentation, Unger finds scope in the creation of alternative regimes that could be assigned to different sectors or scales of production. The power to experiment, for Unger, should not only come during times of crisis but be maintained at a continuous pace in small steps through the appropriate institutional settings.

Third: 'Incompleteness: Embarrassment resulting from the assumption that the world is divided into sovereign states' (Unger 2007: 44). Herein lies the paradox. Consistent with the claim to increased efficiency through freedom to trade and by combining factors of production, the right of labour to cross boundaries features as a vital aspect congruent to the doctrine of comparative advantage. And yet, various States across the globe exert restrictions on the mobility of labour – thus withholding the possibility of a universal right to live and work abroad. As soon as we acknowledge this, one realises that such political divisions, in effect, support substantive differences across States as to how they organise their work and arrange their economies. Indeed, the existence of separate States induces an everlasting diversity to the range of economic and institutional set-ups. Most importantly, diversity increases the opportunity to develop new and original institutional arrangements, including the regimes of property and contract between government and private enterprise. Diversity enables varying ways of organising work, combining ideas and machines while moulding a market economy into its distinctive shape. According to Unger, the political separation of States grounds the theory of international trade, for without it trade would collapse (Unger 2007: 48).[7] But in standard economic trade theory terms, division is considered a costly burden. The relation between diversity and efficiency gains does not feature within the classical conceptions of comparative advantage. To this end the theory is blind. Indeed, various complexities drive world trade, and the relevance of economic theories vis-à-vis free trade does not always appear to impart practical value.

4.4 Moving beyond theory: free trade and the Europe 2020 strategy

Politics play a vital role in driving world trade. For the EU the relaunch of the Single Market Act, adopted in April 2011, has been considered an essential element of the Europe 2020 strategy which sets ambitious goals for the attainment of smart, sustainable and inclusive growth. According to President Barroso, 'Europe 2020 is about what we need to do today and tomorrow to get the EU economy back on track. The crisis has exposed fundamental issues and unsustainable trends that we cannot ignore any longer' (IP/10/225 2010). The Europe 2020 strategy sets out Europe's vision for Europe's social market economy over the next decade. In this respect it proposes seven flagship initiatives:

- an innovation Union;
- youth on the move;
- a digital agenda for Europe;
- a resource-efficient Europe;
- an industrial policy for the globalisation era;
- an agenda for new skills and jobs;
- a European platform to tackle poverty.

According to the European Commission, '[A]n up-to-date single market is the common foundation of all these structures' (COM (2010) 608 final: 4). It is considered as the 'real growth engine within the European economy' (COM (2011) 206 final: 3). Twelve priority actions were identified in the Single Market Act adopted in April 2011, and the reform of public procurement legislation constitutes one of these actions. Budgetary constraints have directed attention towards the need for more efficient use of public money, and have thus moved public purchasing up the policy agenda for all Member States. The public procurement legislation reform attempts to incorporate greater simplification and flexibility to reduce costs, the duration of contracting procedures, and better access to public procurement markets – in particular for SMEs (IP/11/785 2011).

In effect, the relaunch of the Single Market seeks to address the shortcomings of the internal market. Such shortcomings were highlighted by Professor Mario Monti (2010) in his report, and by the European Parliament in Louis Grech's (2010) report. Accordingly, the remedial actions incorporated in the relaunch of the Single Market seek to address such shortcomings by

> putting an end to market fragmentation and eliminating barriers and obstacles to the movement of services, innovation and creativity. It means strengthening citizens' confidence in their internal market and ensuring that its benefits are passed on to consumers. A better integrated market which fully plays its role as a platform on which to build European

competitiveness for its peoples, businesses and regions, including the remotest and least developed.

(COM (2011) 206 final: 3)

It is worth recalling that the pursuit of freer trade, and the economic integration of Europe has, and remains, the central source for the construction of the European Union since the signing of the Treaty of Rome that established the European Economic Community in 1957. In 1986, by way of the White Paper (COM 85 (310) final), market failures were acknowledged. The White Paper set out a whole list of barriers that had to be removed by the end of 1992 in order to address market fragmentation. The elimination of all remaining barriers was the object of the 1992 Single Market programme, and hence Europe's challenge at the time. In this respect the Single European Act – which was signed on the 17 February 1986 – revised the Treaties of Rome in order to add momentum to European integration and the completion of the internal market. Some 20 years after the 1992 Single Market programme, Europe remains engrossed in *'putting an end to market fragmentation and elimination of barriers'* (COM (2011) 206 final: 3, emphasis in original).

The challenges that Europe faces today are no greater than those faced after the Second World War, or during the time when the technical revolution coincided with the recession of the 1970s. As the facts now clearly reveal, addressing European challenges exclusively through the economic dimension is insufficient. Europe need not constrain itself and adopt such an overriding and unconditional attitude towards the Single Market project even though it now attempts to camouflage this by inserting the term 'social market economy' in the Europe 2020 strategy. But what is actually meant by a 'social market economy' is highly obscure. We sink into further obscurity when the Single Market route is said to lay the common foundation for the seven flagship initiatives that set out Europe's vision for the Europe 2020 strategy. Despite these efforts we remain more or less trapped in the belief that there is a single natural expression of what, exactly, constitutes a market economy. Our institutions are biased towards this end. There are other various market routes for the taking, and failure to acknowledge this is to deprive Europe of alternative opportunities.

As we further configure our rational understandings in order to be able to assess the arguments in favour, or otherwise, of free trade vis-à-vis the EU public procurement regime, it is best to have a clear and concise standard that frames our personal expectations when deriving comparative judgements that define what we expect from an optimal market economy. As such a distinction needs to be made between expectations that explicate an *ideal* (Parasuraman *et al.* 1988)[8] or a *wished-for* level of performance from expectations that explicate the *anticipated* level of performance. Herein we make use of an *ideal* reference standard and thus define the *wished-for* or *ideal* market as that being the one that exploits the potential and provides the greatest opportunities for all those wanting to engage in it in a sustained manner. Attaining this *ideal* standard or *ideal* market exposes the presence of a gap between what the market economy embraces today, and what we *wish for*. The closing of this gap calls for a reordering of Europe's economic and social dimensions, a matter that will be further elaborated as we work our way through. In Chapter 8 we will revert to such *wished-for* or *ideal* market in the hope that at that point we may have acquired better understandings that empower our personal judgements on how we can operationalise this *ideal* market.

4.5 The liberalisation of the network industries as an illustration of the EU's overriding and unconditional attitude towards the Single Market project

During the past two decades growth in Europe – according to the European Commission – is attributed to the creation of the Single Market and the opening of borders (COM (2010) 608 final). Accordingly, the combined effect of these two forces – that is, 'internal market integration, in particular through the liberalisation of network industries, and enlargement has been to create 2.75 million additional jobs and growth of 1.85% in the period 1992–2009' (COM (2010) 608 final: 2). The 70 per cent drop in mobile phone call charges and the 40 per cent reduction in airfares have been described as 'concrete examples' of the Single Market creating advantages for both businesses and European citizens (COM (2010) 608 final: 2).

However, it is argued that one cannot attribute the drop in mobile phone call charges or the reduction in air fares solely to the creation of the Single Market, in view of the fact that additional factors have also contributed significantly to such outcomes. For instance, technological advancements and organisational restructuring have had a crucial impact on falling prices. In the case of air transport, the major hurdles limiting competition do not relate to trade barriers but rather to shortages of available slots in major airports and airspace congestion. Indeed, the 'concrete examples' as set out by the Commission (COM (2010) 608 final) fail to take into consideration other equally important factors which may have nothing to do with the Single Market. One would expect that over a period of more than two decades since the gradual opening of the network industries, more tangible indicators reaffirming the effectiveness of the liberalisation programme would present themselves. In 2007 the European Commission published a staff working document on the evaluation of the performance of network industries that provide services of general economic interest, and noted as follows:

> Network industries are generally still characterised by high levels of market concentration and a slowly developing state of competition. While competition has picked up most in the telecommunications sector, the electricity and gas sectors are still largely dominated by incumbents, who often benefit from an insufficient level of separation of their supply activities on the one hand and their transmission activities on the other. This simultaneous

control tends to discourage new entrants and consequently hampers the development of competitive markets.

(SEC (2007) 1024 final: 6)

What follows is a very brief overview of the performance of the network industries since the implementation of the EU's gradual liberalisation programme, given that (according to the Commission) 'there can be no denying the contribution made by the single market' (COM (2010) 608 final: 2) and that 'internal market integration, *in particular through the liberalization of network industries*' (COM (2010) 608 final: 2, my emphasis) is one of the major forces behind growth in Europe.

In the telecommunications sector reforms were introduced in the 1990s. On the basis of a market opening index developed by Copenhagen Economics for work commissioned by the European Commission, it was revealed that market opening in the telecommunications sector remained below 50 per cent up to the year 2000. This has been explained as being partly due to the time lag between legislation and implementation (Mehmet 2009: 8). Prices in this sector have fallen significantly over time. As a result of market opening price convergence between EU countries were claimed to have been attained (Mehmet 2009: 10–11). Productivity levels (per employee and per hour) have also been on the increase. By 1996 the reported productivity levels exceeded those of the total industry level. Yet it has been argued that it would be difficult to attribute such productivity gains to the liberalisation process (Mehmet 2009) given that market opening in the telecommunications sector remained below 50 per cent until the year 2000. On the other hand, the increase in productivity gains as a result of technological developments that started a long time before the liberalisation process, and the gradual fall in employment levels, have been considered as possible influences (Mehmet 2009: 13).[9] Despite the reforms – according to a European Central Bank report (Martin *et al.* 2005) – effective competition remains limited in the telecommunications sector as incumbent operators remain dominant, especially for local calls. This position has also been reaffirmed by the Commission – however, they appeared optimistic at the time since it was argued that market players continued to increase between 2004 and 2005 with competition being stronger in the mobile markets than in fixed telecommunications (SEC (2007) 1024 final). In September 2013 the Commission acknowledged that the European Single Market for telecoms is far from realised as it operates largely on the basis of 28 national markets (IP/13/828, 2013). The telecoms sector was described as fragmented along national borders, lacking regulatory consistency and predictability, with unfair high prices and a lack of investment (COM (2013) 634 final). According to the Commission the need for 'substantial progress towards a European single market for telecoms is essential for Europe's strategic interests and economic progress' (IP/13/828, 2013). With a view to developing this, the matter was accordingly taken a step further with the Commission proposing a legislative package for a 'Connected Continent: Building a Telecoms Single Market'. This builds on the 2009 Telecoms Framework Directive and envisions a single EU regulator responsible for interpreting and implementing a harmonised legal framework (COM (2013) 634, final).

EU reforms in the postal sector started in 1992 (COM (2008) 884 final) with the Postal Directive setting out the Community framework.[10] Germany, the Netherlands and Sweden have been described as the frontrunners in the postal liberalisation process and do not appear to have experienced problems (Martin *et al.* 2005). The organisational and ownership restructuring initiatives by Member States – from state-owned to limited or joint stock company – has been described as almost complete by 2010 (Okholm *et al.* 2010). Nevertheless, Member States appear to maintain a controlling stake in such firms, with the exception of Germany, Malta and the Netherlands (Okholm *et al.* 2010). Where restructuring has not brought about a separation of network and operation, access for new entrants, distortion of competition and protectionism remain problematic. Driven by fierce competition from the electronics sector, new entrants operating in the postal sector have adopted low-cost business strategies relying on a younger, less well educated workforce, and short-term contracts (Okholm *et al.* 2010: 151).[11] As a consequence, fears of declining working conditions and wage dumping in the postal sector have been expressed (Okholm *et al.* 2010). When it comes to consumer prices these have been found to differ greatly across Member States.[12] But on the whole prices have been found to be on the increase in most postal markets (Okholm *et al.* 2010), while competition in this sector appears to be progressing more slowly than expected (COM (2008) 884 final: 7). Notwithstanding the heterogeneous demand for postal services, the market is rapidly declining across Member States – although demand for parcel delivery services has been growing (WIK-Consult 2013). In 2011 the volume of letter items that were delivered in the EU28 decreased by approximately 15 billion when compared with year 2007 (82 billion letter items were delivered in 2011; 97 billion letter items were delivered in 2007) (WIK-Consult 2013). Despite full market opening competition in the postal market has been described as stagnant because very little competition has emerged (WIK-Consult 2013).

Prior to 1987, European air transport services could be described as a fragmented market enjoying a high degree of government protection. Between 1987–97 gradual liberalisation took place in three successive packages of liberalisation measures.[13] Since 1997 the EU regulatory framework provided unrestricted market access to Community air carriers holding a Community licence – including the freedom to set fares. Nevertheless, and despite the adoption of a cautious regulatory reform process, the European Commission found that in 1997 more than 90 per cent of EU air routes were still monopolistic or duopolistic (Martin *et al.* 2005: 24). This finding was further confirmed by an OECD 2000 report (Martin *et al.* 2005). The shortage of available slots in major airports and airspace congestion have been identified as the major bottlenecks limiting competition (Martin *et al.* 2005). In 2014 the Chief Executive Officer of the International Air Transport Association (IATA) commented as follows: 'The single aviation market created enormous demand for air connectivity. But this was not matched with a Single European Sky. The result is an inefficient and fragmented air traffic management system that is a burden on European competitiveness' (IATA 2014). He contends that 'airspace is finite. So capacity can only grow with efficiency' (IATA 2014) – and thus advised the Gulf region, during the April 2014 global aerospace summit in Abu Dhabi, to base their aviation growth strategy on the basis of regional cooperation and global standards and to 'learn from the mistakes of Europe' (IATA 2014).

In the meantime, as low-cost carriers slash air fares and offer alternative routes, and with the introduction of electronic air tickets, the competitive structure of the air transport industry appears to be changing substantially. While the overall market size for all air carriers remained broadly the same in the period 2007–12, in 2011 low-cost airlines exceeded the market share of incumbent air carriers for the first time (market share for low-cost airlines stood at 42.4 per cent, while that of incumbent air carriers stood at 42.2 per cent). The trend for low-cost airlines to increase their market share continued in 2012 (44.8 per cent share, as against a market share of 42.4 per cent for incumbent carriers) (SWD (2013) 208 final). EU airlines face numerous challenges and threats both from within the internal EU market, and from the external non-EU market.

In July 1996 the Commission issued a White Paper laying out 'A strategy for revitalising the Community's railways' (COM (96) 421 final). At the time the railway sector was described as being in decline, and with a falling market share – hence the need to respond to market changes and customer needs. Further reforms were proposed by way of the so called *rail infrastructure package*. The first package[14] that aimed at making legislation more effective was adopted in 2001. In 2002 the Commission issued the *second railway package*[15] aiming at improving safety and interoperability – including the establishment of a European Railway Agency in order to support such. In 2004 the *third railway package*[16] was adopted with a view to completing the European regulatory framework. In 2006, the Commission – and more specifically, DG Energy and Transport – commissioned a report in 'response to perceived failings of railways such as falling market shares in both passenger and freight markets and especially poor performance in international freight traffic where rail should naturally have a competitive advantage over road' (European Commission 2006: 1). From the findings it was observed that 'both the path and speed of the reforms differ from country to country and that there may be several ways to undertake reforms' (European Commission 2006: 1).

In 2011 the Commission issued a White Paper – 'Roadmap to a Single European Transport Area – Towards a competitive and resource efficient transport system' – in which it endeavoured 'to create a genuine Single European Transport Area' (COM (2011) 144 final). Accordingly, 40 initiatives for the next decade are set out for the building of a competitive transport system. The White Paper envisions that by year 2030, 30 per cent of road freight travelling 300 km or more will shift to other modes such as rail or waterborne transport; by 2050 rail is to substantially expand its modal share over medium and long distances for both passenger and freight; a European high speed rail network is to be completed by 2050; and the length of the existing high speed network is to be tripled by 2030. By 2020 a European multimodal transport system is to be established, with moves being made towards full application of the 'user pays' and 'polluter pays' principles. The proposals are expected to dramatically reduce Europe's dependence on imported oil and cut carbon emissions in transport by 60 per cent by 2050, with research and innovation playing a crucial role for the development of cutting-edge technology.

Reforms calling for liberalisation in the electricity market began progressively through the adoption of the 1996 Electricity Market Directive (Directive 96/92/EC) that called for the initial liberalisation of at least 25 per cent of the national electricity markets by 1999, subsequently increasing to a third by 2003. In the gas market sector partial liberalisation of 20 per cent was envisaged by 2000, and subsequently to a third by 2008 (Directive 98/30/EC: 1). However, in 2003 an agreement to speed up the liberalisation process in the energy market was reached, with the adoption of new Directives that repealed the former.[17] The new target deadlines were 1 July 2004 for non-household users, and 1 July 2007 for household users.

Despite the reforms, 'the electricity and gas sectors are still largely dominated by incumbents' (SEC (2007) 1024 final: 6) with three major companies tending to control between 100 per cent and 75 per cent of the market – except in Germany and the UK where the share ranges between 39 per cent and 68 per cent (Mehmet 2009: 18). The relationship between productivity gains and market opening in the electricity and gas sectors is not clear-cut as an upward trend in productivity levels was already in existence before the EU reforms took effect (Mehmet 2009: 12). In addition, the gradual fall in employment levels could be regarded as another contributory factor responsible for the productivity gains (Mehmet 2009: 13). As to the evolution of prices in the electricity and gas sectors, it is worth noting that a downward trend was already in existence across the EU15 before the Community reforms commenced (Fiorio and Florio 2010). According to reported empirical research across the EU15, the overall effect of the reforms in the electricity and gas sector on prices was never found to be statistically significant for electricity; while negative correlations were found with gas prices (Fiorio and Florio 2010). In addition, prices were found to show strong and different dynamics across countries. Furthermore, the researchers found strong evidence of higher consumer satisfaction with prices when services were under public ownership (Fiorio and Florio 2010). In another study based on findings across the EU15 it was noted that 'Irrespective of what the cause is, it is clear that the relationship between price convergence and competition is not as straightforward as the proponents of liberalisation would expect' (Mehmet 2009: 11). It is argued that in line with the *theory of second best*,[18] partial removal of market distortions will not necessarily lead to Pareto-optimality or welfare improvement (Mehmet 2009).

On the one hand the Commission appears to acknowledge that substantial barriers continue to hamper market integration in the network industries – including the protectionist behaviour of governments vis-à-vis their domestic incumbents (SEC (2007) 1024 final: 8) – while on the other hand it remains adamant that the creation of the Single Market constitutes one of the main driving forces behind Europe's growth in the period 1992–2009 (COM (2010) 608 final). It is worth recalling that the aim of progressively establishing the internal market expired on 31 December 1992.[19] Nevertheless, two decades later 'the aim of *establishing* or ensuring the functioning of the internal market in accordance with the relevant provisions of the Treaties'[20] remains topical.

4.6 Concluding remarks

The 1992 Single Market programme made fervent calls for greater European economic integration. A total of 282 measures – of which public procurement played but a small part – sought to abolish the physical, technical and fiscal restraints. The ultimate goal in this purposeful and forceful drive centred on the achievement of prosperity for the people of Europe.

We now come full circle and revert back to the expected benefits that were expected to emanate from the opening up of public procurement,[21] and put into context the findings of Geroski (1991) and Head and Mayer (2000) – who claimed that market fragmentation was attributable to the diversity in national and regional tastes and that the 1992 programme would do little to reduce this type of market fragmentation. We combine their findings with the Wood (2004) Report, in which cultural preferences appeared deeply ingrained and featured as one of the main trade barriers. It is also worth bearing in mind that we are holding on to an early nineteenth century doctrine of free trade that leaves various facets wide open for debate.

As a consequence, evaluations become too discretionary. This is highly relevant when it comes to institutions that are not directly accountable to their elected representatives. Accountability by results is said to be an important standard of substantive legitimacy – a powerful tool to control the discretion of administrative bodies (Majone 1998). Can all this be attributed to an accountability problem, or perhaps a democratic deficit (Majone, 1998)?

The main argument here, and one which in no way attempts to lessen the significance of the issue concerning the accountability problem/democratic deficit, is that Europe is utilising the EU public procurement regime as a tool to directly promote the market economy. Far too much attention, energy and resources have been given, and continues to be given, in this respect. By adopting such an overriding and unconditional attitude, Europe is overlooking alternative opportunities for achieving its desired objectives.

Notes

1 It has been noted by the Commission that within the WTO – even when procurement opportunities are not offered in the final negotiated deal – other trading parties are well aware that procurement opportunities across the EU are not 'sheltered with a wall, which would be impossible to penetrate' (COM(2009) 592 final: 19).

2 This finding is consistent with other empirical reports from the power supply industry that have also presented evidence that long-term restructuring in the market commenced well before the implementation of the Single Market programme (McGowan and Stephen 1989; Ninni 1990).
3 The terms 'public purchasing' and 'public procurement' are used interchangeably.
4 'There are any number of models that make contradictory stipulations in the hope of justifying, by different routes, the program of free trade conducted on the basis of comparative advantage' (Unger 2007: 32).
5 The work cited was written by Myrdal in 1953, and his book was translated from German by Paul Streeten. Myrdal did not always hold such a belief because in 1929 he was of the opinion that through determined effort one could eliminate the metaphysical elements from positive economics.
6 Choices often involve trade-offs that deny the possibility of other alternatives. The opportunity cost in Ricardo's example is the amount of wine that England must give up in order to produce another unit of cloth. England is said to enjoy comparative advantage if it must give up relatively less wine to produce another unit of cloth than Portugal. So let England produce only cloth while Portugal produce only wine.
7 'That such a collapse would occur is made explicit in the idea of "integrated world equilibrium", or IWE, associated with Paul Samuelson and then with Avinash Dixit and Victor Norman' (Unger 2007: 48).
8 Expectations are viewed as the desires or wants of consumers; that is, what they feel a service provider *should* offer rather than what they *would* offer. This standard is similar to the *ideal standard* referred to as the *wished-for* level of performance (Miller 1977).
9 According to Copenhagen Economics, 2005 market opening reforms have led to 500,000 jobs (Copenhagen Economics in Mehmet, U., 2009, *Liberalisation in a World of second best: evidence on European network industries*, MPRA Paper No. 17873, Munich).
10 See Postal Directive 2008/06/EC of the European Parliament and of the Council of 20 February 2008 amending Directive 97/67/EC with regard to the full accomplishment of the internal market of Community postal services. This is the third Postal Directive amending the first Postal Directive (97/67/EC) as amended by Directive 2002/39/EC indicating 2010 (and in the case of some other Member States, the year 2012) as the final step in the process of gradual market opening. ('European Commission. The EU Single Market – EU Postal legislation', available at: http://ec.europa.eu/internal_market/post/legislation_en.htm#proposal [accessed 9 May 2011]). As of 1 May 2013, all 28 Member States (except Cyprus and Romania) have adopted legislation to transpose the Third Postal Directive into national law.
11 According to the research findings by Copenhagen Economics this scenario has been observed in Sweden, Germany, Austria and Belgium (Okholm *et al.* 2010).
12 Prices for 20g letters ranged between €0.23 and €0.81, and for 1kg parcels between €0.90 and €15.10 (prices are for 2009 after purchasing power standard adjustment) (Okholm *et al.* 2010: 36).
13 Regulatory measures in connection with the first package of 1987, laying down the procedure for the application of competition rules, included the following regulatory instruments: Regulation 3975/87, OJ L374/1 1987; Regulation 3976/87, OJ L374/9 1987; 87/601, OJ L374/12 1987; Decision 87/602, OJ L374/19 1987. The second package of 1990 – adopting measures for further relaxation – included the following regulatory instruments: Regulation 2342/90, OJ L217/1 1990; Regulation 2343/90, OJ L217/8 1990. The 1992 third package on the liberalisation of the internal aviation market included the following regulatory instruments: Regulation 2407/92, OJ L; Regulation 2408/92, OJ L Regulation 2409/92, OJ L.
14 The first *rail infrastructure package* included the following regulatory instruments: Directive 2001/12/EC of the European Parliament and of the Council of 26

100 *The status quo*

February 2001 amending Council Directive 91/440/EEC on the development of the Community's railways, Official Journal L 75 of 15 March 2001; Directive 2001/13/EC of the European Parliament and of the Council of 26 February 2001 amending Council Directive 95/18/CE on the licensing of railway undertakings, Official Journal L 75 of 15 March 2001; Directive 2001/14/EC of the European Parliament and of the Council of 26 February 2001 on the allocation of railway infrastructure capacity and the levying of charges for the use of railway infrastructure and safety certification, Official Journal L 75 of 15 March 2001. See Europa, 'Summaries of EU legislation – White paper: A strategy for revitalising the Community's railways', available at: http://europa.eu/legislation_summaries/environment/tackling_climate_change/l24014_en.htm [accessed 11 May,2011].

15 The proposals presented in the second railway package were based on the White Paper presented by the Commission on 12 September 2001: 'European transport policy for 2010: time to decide' (COM (2001) 370 final – not published in the Official Journal). The package comprised the following regulatory instruments: Directive 2004/49/EC of the European Parliament and of the Council on 29 April 2004 on safety on the Community's railways and amending Council Directive 95/18/CE on the licensing of railway undertakings and Directive 2001/14/CE on the allocation of railway infrastructure capacity and the levying of charges for the use of railway infrastructure and safety certification, Official Journal L 164 of 30 April 2004; Directive 2004/50/EC of the European Parliament and of the Council of 29 April 2004 amending Council Directive 96/48/EC on the interoperability of the trans-European high-speed rail system and Directive 2001/16/EC of the European Parliament and of the Council on the interoperability of the trans-European conventional rail system, Official Journal L 164 of 30 April 2004; Directive 2004/51/EC of the European Parliament and of the Council of 29 April 2004 amending Council Directive 91/440/EEC on the development of the Community's railways, Official Journal L 164 of 30 April 2004. Regulation (EC) No 881/2004 of the European Parliament and of the Council of 29 April 2004 establishing a European Railway Agency, Official Journal L 164 of 30 April 2004. See Europa, 'Summaries of EU legislation – White paper: A strategy for revitalising the Community's railways', available at: http://europa.eu/legislation_summaries/environment/tackling_climate_change/l24014_en.htm [accessed 11 May 2011].

16 See COM (2004) 140 final, Directive 2004/51/EC, Directive 2004/50/EC, Directive of the European Parliament and of the Council of 29 April 2004 amending Council Directive 96/48/EC on the interoperability of the trans-European high-speed rail system and Directive 2001/16/EC of the European Parliament and of the Council on the interoperability of the trans-European conventional rail system, Official Journal L 164 of 30 April 2004. See Europa, 'Summaries of EU legislation – White paper: A strategy for revitalising the Community's railways', available at: http://europa.eu/legislation_summaries/environment/tackling_climate_change/l24014_en.htm [accessed 11 May 2011].

17 See Directive 96/92/EC, which was repealed and replaced by Directive 2003/54/EC of the European Parliament and of the Council of 26 June 2003 concerning common rules for the internal market in electricity, OJ L 176, 15 July 2003: 37. Directive 98/30/EC concerning common rules for the internal market in natural gas was repealed and replaced by Directive 2003/55/EC.

18 The OECD defines the *theory of second best* as follows: 'The theory of the second best suggests that when two or more markets are not perfectly competitive, then efforts to correct only one of the distortions may in fact drive the economy further away from Pareto efficiency.' See OECD, 'Glossary of statistical terms. Theory of Second Best', available at: http://stats.oecd.org/glossary/detail.asp?ID=3306 [accessed 18 March 2015].

19 Article 14 (1) EEC held that 'The Community shall adopt measures with the aim of progressively establishing the internal market over a period expiring on 31 December 1992.'
20 See Article 26 (1) TFEU, emphasis added.
21 See discussion in Chapter 3.

References

Atkins, W.S. Management Consultants, 1988. *The Costs of Non-Europe in Public Sector Procurement. Basic Findings Vol. 5, Part A and B*. Luxembourg: Office for Official Publications of the EC.

Bernard, A.B., Redding, S.J. and Schott, P.K., 2007. 'Comparative advantage and heterogeneous firms' in *The Review of Economic Studies*, vol. 74, no. 1, pp. 31–66.

Bernhofen, D.M. and Brown, J.C., 2004. 'A direct test of the theory of comparative advantage: the case of Japan' in *Journal of Political Economy*, vol. 112, no. 1, pp. 48–67.

Bovis, C., 1998. 'The regulation of public procurement as a key element of European economic law' in European Law Journal, vol. 4, no. 2, p. 220.

Burtt, E.J.J., 1972. *Social Perspectives in the History of Economic Theory*. New York: St Martin's Press.

Cecchini, P., 1988. *The European Challenge, 1992: The benefits of a Single Market*. Aldershot, Hants: Wildwood House Limited.

Copenhagen Economics, *Market Opening in Network Industries: Parts I and II. (Report no. 6201 for DG Internal Market)*. Copenhagen Economics for the Commission.

Cox, A., 1993. *The Single Market Rules and the Enforcement Regime After 1992*. United Kingdom: Earlsgate Press.

Cutler, T., 1989. *1992-The Struggle for Europe*. Oxford: Berg Publishers.

Deardorff, A.V., 1994. 'Exploring the limits of comparative advantage' in *Weltwirtschaftliches Archiv*, vol. 130, no. 1, pp. 1–19.

Deardorff, A.V., 1980. 'The general validity of the law of comparative advantage' in *The Journal of Political Economy*, vol. 88, no. 5, pp. 941–57.

Deardorff, A.V., 2005. 'How robust is comparative advantage?' in *Review of International Economics*, vol. 13, no. 5, pp. 1004–16.

Ethier, W.J., 1982. 'National and international returns to scale in the modern theory of international trade' in *The American Economic Review*, vol. 72, pp. 389–405.

Fiorio, C.V. and Florio, M., 2010. 'A Fair Price for Energy? Ownership versus Market Opening in the EU15'. CESifo Working Paper no. 3124, Category 1: Public Finance.

Geroski, P., 1991. '1992 and European Industrial Structure' in: Mackenzie, G. and Venables, A.J. (eds), *The Economics of the Single European Act*. London: Macmillan.

Head, K. and Mayer, T., 2000. 'Non-Europe: The Magnitude and Causes of Market Fragmentation in the EU' in *Review of World Economics*, vol. 136, no. 2, pp. 284–314.

Helpman, E. and Krugman, P.R., 1985. *Market structure and foreign trade: Increasing returns, imperfect competition, and the international economy*. Cambridge, MA: MIT Press.

Helpman, E., Melitz, M.J. and Yeaple, S.R., 2003. 'Export versus FDI with heterogeneous firms' in *American Economic Review*, vol. 94, pp. 300–16.

IATA, Remarks of Tony Tyler at the Global Aerospace Summit, Abu Dhabi, 7 April 2014. Available at: www.iata.org/pressroom/speeches/Pages/2014-04-07-01.aspx [accessed 13 June 2014].

Ilzkovitz, F., Dierx, A., Kovacs, V. and Sousa, N., 2007. *Steps towards a deeper economic integration: the Internal Market in the 21st century – A contribution to the Single Market Review*. Brussels: Directorate-General for Economic and Financial Affairs.

Kiyota, K., 2011. 'A test of the law of comparative advantage, revisited' in *Review of World Economics*, vol. 147, no. 4, pp. 771–8.

Krugman, P., 1980. 'Scale economies, product differentiation, and the pattern of trade' in *The American Economic Review*, vol. 70, pp. 950–9.

Leamer, E., 1994. 'Testing trade theory' in: Greenaway, D. and Winters, L.A. (eds), *Surveys in International Trade*. Cambridge, MA: Blackwell.

Majone, G., 1998. 'Europe's "Democratic Deficit": The Question of Standards' in *European Law Journal*, vol. 4, no. 1, pp. 5–28.

Martin, R., Roma, M. and Vansteenkiste, I., 2005. *Regulatory Reforms in Selected EU Network Industries, Occasional Paper Series, no. 28*. Germany: European Central Bank.

McGowan, F. and Stephen, T., 1989. 'Restructuring in the Power-Plant Equipment Industry and 1992' in *World Economy*, vol. 12, no. 4, pp. 539–56.

Mehmet, U., 2009. *Liberalisation in a World of second best: evidence on European network industries*. MPRA Paper No. 17873, Munich.

Melitz, M.J., 2003. 'The impact of trade on intra-industry reallocations and aggregate industry productivity' in *Econometrica*, vol. 71, no. 6, pp. 1695–725.

Miller, J.A., 1977. 'Studying Satisfaction, Modifying Models, Eliciting Expectations, Posing Problems and Making Meaningful Measurements' in H.K. Hunt (ed.), *Conceptualisation and Measurement of Consumer Satisfaction and Dissatisfaction*. Indiana University: Bloomington School of Business, pp. 72–91.

Monti, M., 2010. *A new strategy for the single market: At the service of Europe's economy and society – Report to the President of the European Commission*. Brussels.

Myrdal, G., 1969. *The Political Element in the Development of Economic Theory*. New York: Simon and Schuster.

Neven, D.J. and Rollers, L.H., 1991. 'European Integration and Trade Flows' in *European Economic Review*, vol. 35, no. 6, pp. 1295–309.

Ninni, A., 1990. 'Recent Changes in the Power Equipment Industry and the Opening Up of Public Procurement' in *Energy Policy*, vol. 18, no. 4, pp. 320–30.

OECD. 3 January 2002. 'Glossary of statistical terms. Theory of Second Best', available at: http://stats.oecd.org/glossary/detail.asp?ID=3306 [accessed 18 March 2015].

Okholm, H.B., Winiarczyk, M., Möller, A. and Nielsen, K.C., 2010. *Main developments in the postal sector (2008–2010)*. Copenhagen: Copenhagen Economics.

Parasuraman, A., Zeithaml, V. and Berry, L., 1988. 'SERVQUAL: A Multiple-Item Scale for Measuring Consumer Perceptions of Service Quality' in *Journal of Retailing*, vol. 64, pp. 12–40.

Prasch, R.E., 1996. 'Reassessing the theory of comparative advantage' in *Review of Political Economy*, vol. 8, no. 1, pp. 37–56.

Ricardo, D., 1817. *On the Principles of Political Economy and Taxation*. London: John Murray.

Robinson, J., 1980. *Reflections on the theory of international trade, Collected Economic Papers, Volume V*. Cambridge, MA: MIT Press.

Siebert, H., 1989. *The Completion of the Internal Market*. Tubingen, JCB Mohr: Institut fur Weltwirtschaft an Der U Kiel, Symposium.

Smith, A., 1776a. *Book Four, Of Systems of Political Economy*. Introduction, p. 12.

Smith, A., 1776b. *The Wealth of Nations, Books I-III*. London: Penguin Books.
Suranovic, S.M. Last updated 15 February 2007. 'International Trade Theory and Policy', available at: http://internationalecon.com/Trade/Tch40/T40-2.php [accessed 28 June 2010].
Torrens, R., 1815. 'Essay on the External Corn Trade' in Suranovic, S.M., *International Trade Theory and Policy*. Available at: http://internationalecon.com/Trade/Tch40/T40-0A.php [accessed 4 April 2015].
Unger, M.R., 2007. *Free trade reimagined: the world division of labor and the method of economics*. Princeton, NJ: Princeton University Press.
WIK-Consult, August 2013. *Study for the European Commission, Directorate General for Internal Market and Services – Main Developments in the Postal Sector (2010–2013)*. Germany: Bad Honnef.
Wood, A., 2004. *A report to The Chancellor of the Exchequer & Secretary of State for Trade & Industry*. UK: Office of Government Commerce.

Official documents

Directives

Directive 96/92/EC, *Directive of the European Parliament and of the Council of 19 December 1996 concerning common rules for the internal market in electricity*, OJ L 27, 30 January 1997, p. 20.
Directive 98/30/EC, *Directive of the European Parliament and of the Council of 22 June 1998 concerning common rules for the internal market in natural gas*, OJ L 204, 21 July 1998, p. 1.
Directive 2004/51/EC, *Directive of the European Parliament and of the Council of 29 April 2004 amending Council Directive 91/440/EEC on the development of the Community's railways*, Official Journal L 164 of 30 April 2004.

European Parliament

Grech, L., 2010. *Delivering a single market to consumers and citizens*. European Parliament.

European Commission

COM 85 (310) final, 1985. *Completing the Internal Market. White Paper from the Commission to the European Council*. Milan: Commission of the European Communities.
COM (96), 421 final, 1996. *A strategy for revitalising the Community's railways*. Brussels: European Commission (not published in the Official Journal). Available at: http://europa.eu/legislation_summaries/environment/tackling_climate_change/l24014_en.htm [accessed 11 March 2015].
COM (2004) 140 final, 3 March 2004. *Communication from the Commission – Further integration of the European rail system: third railway package*. Brussels: European Commission.
COM (2008) 884 final, 22 December 2008. *Report from the Commission to the Council and the European Parliament on the application of the Postal Directive (Directive 97/67/EC as amended by Directive 2002/39/EC)*. Brussels: European Commission.

COM (2009) 592 final, 28 October 2009. *Report from the Commission concerning negotiations regarding access of Community undertakings to the markets of third countries in fields covered by the Directive 2004/17/EC.* Brussels: European Commission.

COM (2010) 608 final, 27 October 2010. *Towards a Single Market Act for a highly competitive social market economy.* Brussels: European Commission.

COM (2011) 144 final, 28 March 2011. *White Paper: Roadmap to a Single European Transport Area – Towards a competitive and resource efficient transport system.* Brussels: European Commission.

COM (2011) 206 final, 13 April 2011. *Communication from the Commission to the European Parliament, the Council, the Economic and Social Committee and the Committee of the Regions – Single Market Act – Twelve levers to boost growth and strengthen confidence – 'Working together to create new growth'.* Brussels: European Commission.

COM (2013) 634 final, 11 September 2013. *Communication from the Commission to the European Parliament, the Council, the European Economic and Social Committee and the Committee of the Regions on the Telecommunications Single Market.* Brussels: European Commission.

Europa, last updated 22 January 2007. *Summaries of EU legislation – White paper: A strategy for revitalising the Community's railways.* Available at: http://europa.eu/legislation_summaries/environment/tackling_climate_change/l24014_en.htm [accessed 11 May 2011].

European Commission, 1988. *Public Procurement and Construction: Towards an Integrated Market.* Luxembourg: Office for Official Publications of the EC.

European Commission, 1989. *Opening Up Public Procurement in the European Community.* Luxembourg: Office of Official Publications for the EC.

European Commission, 2006. *Policy effectiveness of rail – EU policy and its impact on the rail system.* Belgium.

European Commission, n.d. *The EU Single Market – EU Postal legislation.* Available at: http://ec.europa.eu/internal_market/post/legislation_en.htm#proposal, [accessed 9 May 2011].

SEC (2007) 1024 final, 12 July 2007. *Commission Staff Working Document – Evaluation of the Performance of Network Industries Providing Services of General Economic Interest 2006 Report.* Brussels: European Commission.

SWD (2013) 208 final, 6 June 2013. *Commission Staff Working Document: Fitness check-Internal Aviation Market – Report on the suitability of economic regulation of the European air transport market and of selected ancillary services.* Brussels: European Commission.

European Commission – press releases

IP/10/225, 2010. 'Europe 2020: Commission proposes new economic strategy in Europe'. Brussels: European Commission.

IP/11/785, 2011. 'Single Market Act: EU public procurement framework has saved around 20 billions euros'. Brussels: European Commission.

IP/13/828, 11 September 2013. 'Press Release, Commission proposes major step forward for telecoms single market'. Brussels: European Commission.

5 Poverty and natural law theory in context

5.1 Introduction

According to the Vice-President of the European Commission, Joaquín Almunia, public services play a key role in Europe's model of society, and certain services such as healthcare, education, social housing, communications, energy and transport cannot be subjected to the whims of market forces (Joaquín Almunia 2010). The Lisbon Treaty has brought about significant changes that clearly support the provision of public services.[1] Thus, all this essentially highlights the pivotal role that the State has in its system of *welfare*. In essence, systems of welfare seek to secure a basic level of well-being and a minimum acceptable level of quality of life for all citizens. Among the various virtues identified with welfare – although these have attracted their fair share of criticism – are that it promotes national efficiency, fosters social cohesion, promotes the potential of individuals, and narrows social inequalities (Heywood 2004: 315). This clearly signifies that the merits of welfare feed back into the economy. The economic and social dimensions are 'mutually reinforcing' and 'offer a vision of Europe's social market economy for the 21st century' (COM (2010) 2020 final: 10). To this end, five measurable EU targets for 2020 have been earmarked. One of these targets relates to the promotion of social inclusion, in particular through the reduction of poverty.[2] It aims at lifting 20 million people out of poverty or exclusion by 2020.

Notwithstanding the various ideological debates pertaining to welfare, there appears to be serious concern over the ability of governments to adequately fund and provide public services (Needham and Murray 2005). But one has to bear in mind that such concerns need to be balanced with the fact that all welfare systems are related to the question of poverty. The concept of poverty raises important political questions because it is fundamentally linked with how society distributes and redistributes its resources and opportunities, and therefore exposes the inadequacy of our current systems.

This chapter will explore the link between poverty and natural law theory. In doing so it will attempt to understand how the EU public procurement regime fits in. By way of introduction, it is hoped that this section will enable the reader to put into perspective the pivotal role of public services on a State's system of welfare. Section 5.2 – 'Poverty across the EU – a snapshot' – attempts to provide the reader with an idea of the extent of poverty.

We then narrow our focus by presenting understandings of poverty as derived from the academic literature. Section 5.3 – 'The nature of poverty: definitions abound' – attempts to reveal the difficulties faced by researchers when conceptualising the notion of poverty. Failure by academia to arrive at a universally accepted definition poses a problem when it comes to measuring the extent of poverty, and identifying its causes and the best way to deal with it. The concept of poverty appears to change over time, and from one society to another. Influential attempts to define the notion of poverty have been presented by Sen, who looks at it from the perspective of *capabilities* – or more specifically, *capabilities to function*. However, Sen found difficulty in identifying a set of *capabilities* and *functionings* that could reflect fundamental values and meanings of life. It is argued that the grey areas encountered by Sen find further illumination and support if we refer to the theory of natural law. There is no discontinuity between Sen's conception of *capabilities* and *functionings*, and natural law theory. In effect, *capabilities to function* seek to bring about the full realisation of one's humanity wherein the dignity of the human person is accorded full respect. According to natural law theory the full realisation of one's humanity – as a free and equal being – forms the basis of the moral good. Natural law theory, as a subject matter, is discussed in section 5.4 – 'Freedom for human flourishing as conceived through natural law theory'. At the heart of natural law theory the respect for human dignity stands as the basic moral premise. The elevated status that dignity acquires in natural law theory can also be found in the Charter of Fundamental Rights. 'Respect for Human Dignity – A Legally Enforceable Fundamental Right' is discussed in section 5.5.

An understanding of poverty requires us also to understand the policies that are drafted in response to it. Such reasoning leads the way to the discussion in section 5.6 – 'The quest for justice in poverty reduction: putting EU public procurement into perspective'. This section reveals how the EU public procurement regime turns the hallowed principles of Europe's social market model on its head as it superimposes potentially dynamic social welfare effects. The vacuum that encroaches upon the attainment of treaty principles and fundamental rights is revealed as the EU public procurement regime helps dislocate Europe's founding values. Section 5.7 – 'Concluding remarks' – focuses on the notion of culture, since European social models are deeply ingrained into European cultures. Culture, in effect, can be used as a device to set up boundaries when the integrity of the self, or of the nation, is felt to be under threat or insecure. It is worth highlighting the fact that culture exerts a powerful determining role when it comes to cross border trade – and yet it does not appear to have been factored in as part of the European Community's list of non-tariff barriers.

5.2 Poverty across the EU – a snapshot

Poverty in the EU is a real problem and its reduction is one of the key targets of the Europe 2020 strategy (COM (2010) 2020 final). The strategy highlights a social inclusion target that is based on a combination of three indicators of poverty and exclusion. Indirect and direct measures of poverty and social exclusion are taken into consideration. This set of indicators – which were agreed to in 2009 – are said to provide a better picture of the diversity of living conditions in the EU (Atkinson and Marlier 2010). They include indicators for measuring the *persons at-risk-of poverty*,[3] *severely materially deprived persons*[4] and *people living in households with very low work intensity*.[5] According to the Europe 2020 strategy – which replaces the 2000–10 Lisbon Strategy (European Council 2000) – the aim is to lower by 20 million the number of people who are at risk of poverty, the severly materially deprived, and the number of people with very low work intensity.

In 2012, 24.8 per cent of the EU population – compared with 24.3 per cent in 2011 and 23.8 per cent in 2008 – were at risk of poverty or social exclusion (Eurostat 2013). This corresponds to a total of 124.2 million people across the EU. Poverty and social exclusion increased in more than a third of the Member States in 2011 and 2012, and the poverty and social exclusion of children has increased in 18 Member States since 2008. The overall trends, however, mask the growing divergence between Member States.

It is worth noting that the total number of people at risk of poverty or social exclusion is lower than the sum of those falling under each of the three categories of poverty or social exclusion. This is because some people experience, simultaneously, more than one of the three indicated situations (Eurostat 2013). In 2012, Bulgaria (49 per cent), Romania (42 per cent) Latvia (37 per cent) and Greece (35 per cent) had the highest share of persons at risk of poverty or social exclusion (Eurostat 2013). The lowest share was recorded in the Netherlands and the Czech Republic (both 15 per cent), Finland (17 per cent), and Sweden and Luxembourg (both 18 per cent).

According to 2013 Eurostat data, 122.6 million people –or 24.5 per cent of the population of the EU – were at risk of poverty or social exclusion. This means that these people were in at least one of the following three conditions: at risk of poverty after social transfers (income poverty); severely materially deprived; or living in households with very low work intensity. The proportion of persons at risk of poverty or social exclusion in the EU28 in 2013 (24.5 per cent) has decreased slightly compared to the previous year (24.8 per cent, 2012), but is higher than in 2008 (23.8 per cent).

The 'at risk of poverty' measure, which has been well established in the EU since 2001, is considered an indirect approach to measuring poverty and social exclusion since its focus is on the lack of financial resources for meeting minimum living standards relevant to the society in which its sufferers live. Nearly one in seven people in the EU are at risk of poverty. During 2011 and 2012 (Eurostat 2012), 17 per cent of the population across the EU were identified as being at risk of poverty. The figure is not so different for the past decade and beyond – 17 per cent (1995); 16 per cent (1997); 15 per cent (2001); 17 per cent (2008) (Frazer 2009). The at risk of poverty rates vary across the EU. In 2012 they ranged from 23 per cent in Greece and Romania, 22 per cent in Spain,

Table 5.1 At risk of poverty or social exclusion, 2012

	Persons at risk of poverty after social transfers	Persons severely materially deprived	Persons aged 0–59 living in households with very low work intensity	Persons falling under at least one of the three criteria (at risk of poverty or social exclusion)			
	% of total population			% of total population			In millions, 2012
				2008	2011	2012	
EU28*	17	9.9	10.4	23.7	24.3	24.8	124.5
Belgium**	14.8	6.5	14.0	20.8	21.0	21.6	2.4
Bulgaria	21.2	44.1	12.4	44.8	49.1	49.3	3.6
Czech Republic	9.6	6.6	6.8	15.3	15.3	15.4	1.6
Denmark	13.1	2.8	10.9	16.3	18.9	19.0	1.1
Germany	16.1	4.9	9.8	20.1	19.9	19.6	15.9
Estonia	17.5	9.4	9.0	21.8	23.1	23.4	0.3
Ireland	–	–	–	23.7	29.4	–	–
Greece	23.1	19.5	14.1	28.1	31.0	34.6	3.8
Spain	22.2	5.8	14.2	24.5	27.7	28.2	13.1
France	14.1	5.3	8.4	18.6	19.3	19.1	11.8
Croatia	20.5	15.4	16.1	–	32.3	32.3	1.4
Italy	19.4	14.5	10.3	25.3	28.2	29.9	18.2
Cyprus	14.7	15.0	6.4	23.3	24.6	27.1	0.2
Latvia	19.4	26.0	11.5	33.8	40.4	36.6	0.7
Lithuania	18.6	19.8	11.3	27.6	33.1	32.5	1.0
Luxembourg	15.1	1.3	6.1	15.5	16.8	18.4	0.1
Hungary	14	25.7	12.7	28.2	31.0	32.4	3.2
Malta	15	8.0	7.9	19.6	21.4	22.2	0.1

Netherlands	10.1	2.3	8.7	14.9	15.7	15.0	2.5
Austria**	–	4.0	7.6	18.6	16.9	–	–
Poland	17.1	13.5	6.8	30.5	27.2	26.7	10.1
Portugal	17.9	8.6	10.1	26.0	24.4	25.3	2.7
Romania	22.6	29.9	7.4	44.2	40.3	41.7	8.9
Slovenia	13.5	6.6	7.5	18.5	19.3	19.6	0.4
Slovakia	13.2	10.5	7.2	20.6	20.6	20.5	1.1
Finland	13.2	2.9	9.1	17.4	17.9	17.2	0.9
Sweden**	14.2	1.3	10.0	14.9	16.1	18.2	1.8
United Kingdom***	16.2	7.8	13.0	23.2	22.7	24.1	15.1
Iceland	7.9	2.4	6.0	11.8	13.7	12.7	0.0
Norway	10.1	1.7	7.0	15.0	14.5	13.8	0.7
Switzerland	15.9	0.8	3.4	18.6	17.2	17.5	1.3

Source: Eurostat; EU SILC Data.

Notes:
* EU27 data for persons at risk of poverty or social exclusion in 2008; EU28 estimates for 2012.
** Belgium and Austria: 2012 data provisional; Sweden: 2012 data provisional for households with low work intensity and persons at risk of poverty or social exclusion.
*** Change of provider of cross-sectional EU SILC data: until 2012 data were collected by the ONS, from 2012 onwards they are collected by the Department for Work and Pensions.
– Data not available.
0.0 = Less than 0.5 million.

Table 5.2 Relative median at risk of poverty gap, evolution in percentage points, 2012–13 and 2008–13

	EU28	EU27	EA18	BE	BG	CZ	DK	DE	EE	IE	EL	ES	FR	HR	IT
2013	23.8	23.8	24.0	19.2	30.9	16.6	23.7	20.4	21.5	n/a	32.7	30.9	16.6	28.1	28.0
2012–13 change in % points	~	~	~	~	~	−2.5	~	~	−2.3	n/a	2.8	~	~	−2.9	2.6
2008–13 change in % points	n/a	2.0	2.8	2.0	3.9	−1.9	5.7	−1.8	1.2	n/a	8.0	2.1	3.1	5.0	

	CY	LV	LT	LU	HU	MT	NL	AT	PL	PT	RO	SI	SK	FI	SE	UK
2013	17.7	27.5	24.8	17.5	21.7	19.1	16.5	21.3	22.6	27.3	32.6	20.4	24.1	15.0	19.8	19.6
2012–13 change in % points	−1.3	−1.1	2.2	2.5	~	3.0	~	1.2	~	3.2	1.7	1.3	3.6	~	~	−1.3
2008–13 change in % points	2.4	−1.1	~	~	4.4	−1.2	1.6	1.4	2.0	4.1	~	1.1	6.0	~	1.8	−1.4

Source: Eurostat (EU-SILC).

Note
i Data not available for IE for 2013; (ii) Major break in series in 2013 in ES for income variables in EU-SILC; (iii) For UK, changes in the survey vehicle and institution in 2012 might have affected the results on trends since 2008, and we must therefore be careful about interpreting data on the longer term trend; (iv) Only statistically significant changes have been marked in (positive/negative changes); (v) For the change 2012–13, Eurostat computations of significance of net change are used; (vi) For the change 2008–13, a 1 percentage point threshold has been used; (vii) "~" refers to stable performance (i.e. statistically insignificant change). (viii) For the at risk of poverty rate, the income reference year is the calendar year prior to the survey year (i.e. 2012) except for the United Kingdom (survey year) and Ireland (12 months preceding the survey).

21 per cent in both Bulgaria and Croatia, 10 per cent in the Czech Republic and the Netherlands, and 13 per cent in Denmark, Slovakia and Finland.

The extent to which the income of those at risk of poverty falls below the average poverty threshold – in other words, the depth of poverty – can be glimpsed via the poverty gap. In 2013 the relative median at risk of poverty gap[6] in the EU27 was 23.8 per cent lower than the at risk of poverty threshold. This reflects an increase of 2 percentage points since 2008. In 2013 the poverty gap in the EU27 countries varied between 15 per cent in Finland to more than 30 per cent in Belgium, Greece, Spain and Romania. It is worth noting that the poverty gap has increased in two-thirds of all Member States since 2008, and in some countries quite substantially (by around 4 percentage points or more in Belgium, Portugal, Hungary, Italy, Denmark, Slovakia and Greece.

Some 10 per cent of Europeans (EU28) experienced severe material deprivation in 2012, compared to 9 per cent in 2011 and 8 per cent in 2010 (Eurostat 2012). This indicator, recognised as a direct approach for measuring poverty and social exclusion, is based on non-monetary indicators of material deprivation and is said to improve further the picture for capturing the multi-dimensional nature of poverty and social exclusion (Atkinson and Marlier 2010). Unlike the at risk of poverty indicator, this measure is not a relative one since the set of items[7] identified are assigned equal weight and therefore a common standard is applied across Member States. The share of severely materially deprived persons across the EU varies significantly. In 2012 this indicator ranged from 1 per cent in Luxembourg and Sweden, to 44 per cent in Bulgaria, 30 per cent in Romania, and 26 per cent in Latvia and Hungary.

In 2012 (in the EU28) – as in 2011 and 2010 (in the EU27) – 10 per cent of people were identified as living in households with very low work intensity (Eurostat 2012, 2013). That is to say, 10 per cent of the population aged 0–59 lived in households where the adults (students excluded) worked at less than 20 per cent of their total work potential for the year. As with the other poverty indicators, discrepancies can be noted across Member States. The highest proportion of those experiencing very low work intensity were reported in Croatia (16 per cent), and Spain, Greece and Belgium (all 14 per cent). The lowest proportions were recorded in Luxembourg and Cyprus (both 6 per cent).

5.3 The nature of poverty – definitions abound

Poverty is a multi-dimensional concept and therefore the challenges posed by it are multi-dimensional also. At the heart of the poverty debate lies the difficulty of arriving at a universally accepted definition. In essence, all this ties up with issues of measurement, causes and solutions – which are all strongly interrelated.

One concept – referred to as *absolute* or *extreme* poverty – prioritises the economic aspect and is based on the notion of subsistence; that is, the minimum needed to sustain life. *Absolute* (or *extreme*) poverty is very often contrasted with *relative* poverty.

an absolute poverty line is one which is constructed as an estimate of families' minimum consumption needs; this is done without reference to the income or consumption levels of the general population. In the same context, a relative poverty line is one which is set as a fraction of the median or mean income or consumption of the population as a whole (generally with appropriate adjustments for family size).

(Fisher 1995)

In other words, absolute poverty perceives poverty as existing when people lack the basic necessities to survive. During the World Summit for Social Development, held in March 1995 in Copenhagen, absolute or extreme poverty was defined as 'a condition characterized by severe deprivation of basic human needs, including food, safe drinking water, sanitation facilities, health, shelter, education and information. It depends not only on income but also on access to social services' (United Nations 1995: 41). The 1995 UN summit left it to individual governments to define poverty and to work towards its reduction according to their own national standards. The UN General Assembly's Millennium Declaration of September 2000 set a target of halving by 2015 the proportion of people worldwide whose income is less than one dollar a day (in purchasing power parity dollars, not nominal exchange rate dollars).

Absolute definitions based on the notion of subsistence and the minimum need for sustaining life, begs the question of what, exactly, constitutes 'life' (Alcock 2006)? Ways of life differ depending upon place and time: it therefore follows that necessities also differ. A donkey may be considered a necessity for a family living in a remote village in Africa, but not for someone living in the city. In other studies it has been noted that with absolute definitions of poverty there is a tendency to raise minimum levels since general living standards tend to improve with the passage of time (Fiegehen et al. 1977). Others (Stitt and Grant 1993) noted that when it came to identifying needs, these were found to reflect cultural norms and consequently incorporated relative judgements (that is, relative to the society in which poverty was being measured). It therefore transpired that absolute definitions of poverty were not solely based on objective logic, as was sometimes claimed.

Relative poverty involves determining a poverty level and comparing it across members of society. This measure is linked to income distribution and takes account of market income and social transfers. Relative poverty includes an element of subjectivity because the determination of the poverty level[8] necessitates that value judgements be made. Poverty levels for people considered at risk of poverty commonly fall below the 40–70 per cent range of equivalised disposable household income. The question as to whose judgement this should be appears to be controversial (Alcock 2006).

The relative definition of poverty was developed by Townsend in his important work on poverty in the UK.

> Individuals, families and groups in the population can be said to be in poverty when they lack the resources to obtain the types of diet, participate

Poverty and natural law theory   113

in the activities and have the living conditions and amenities which are customary ... in the societies to which they belong. Their resources are so seriously below those commanded by the average individual or family that they are, in effect, excluded from ordinary living patterns and activities.

(Townsend 1979: 31)

Therefore, Townsend, in his definition, broadened the concept of poverty and took into account the fact that human beings are not only physical but also social beings. Relative poverty prevents people from participating in activities that are customary in the society in which they live. However, the relative definitions of poverty – as with the absolute ones – are not without their problems. For example, it is argued that when poverty levels change – as may occur during a period of recession – the actual change need not necessarily be reflected when a relative picture of poverty is being captured (Sen 1983).

In essence, according to the debate, absolute definitions of poverty incorporate relative judgements; while relative definitions of poverty need to incorporate an absolute core in order to distinguish them from the broader forms of inequality (Sen 1983). Poverty cannot be depicted through the light of inequality, as seems to be the case when viewed through relative terms. Relatively lower standards of living confirm inequalities – but not necessarily poverty. Nevertheless, while the absolutist approach cannot simply be dismissed as wrong, a workable definition of poverty needs to combine both absolute and relative elements (Alcock 2006).

Sen (1983) contends that the 'relative' view appears to be the generally accepted measure for poverty in advanced countries. This he considers as positive when compared to the simplistic absolute definitions. Nonetheless, Sen argues that poverty contains an 'irreducible absolutist core' (Sen 1983) because when there is poverty there is no denying it, irrespective of the relative situation. Sen moves the definition of poverty by incorporating a different specification. To explain this he draws on the explanation put forth by Adam Smith when discussing the concept of *necessaries*.

By necessaries I understand not only the commodities which are indispensably necessary for the support of life, but whatever the custom of the country renders it indecent for creditable people, even the lowest order, to be without....Custom ... has rendered leather shoes a necessary of life in England. The poorest creditable person of either sex would be ashamed to appear in public without them.

(Smith 1776: 351–2)

Thus, for the typical English citizen of the eighteenth century, being in possession of leather shoes was not simply a question of being *less ashamed* (that is, relatively speaking) – rather was perceived as a basic necessity. This, according to Sen, clearly captured the notion of poverty in absolute terms rather than in relative ones. Not being in possession of leather shoes is a shameful affair and bears a direct effect on one's dignity. Hence, it is this very basic requirement – that is, the *capability* of avoiding shame – that Sen conceives as constituting the absolute notion of poverty. It is within the space of *capabilities* (*capability to function*) that one can derive an *irreducible absolutist core* when it comes to conceptualising poverty. On the other hand, the *commodity* needed to put into effect the *capability* for avoiding shame (in the case exemplified by Adam Smith), was the possession of a pair of leather shoes. Indeed, and as Sen contends, the *commodity* requirement for avoiding shame would be a different *commodity* altogether in richer communities. It is within the *commodity* space that the notion of relative poverty comes to play a part when conceptualising it.

As noted by Sen himself, John Rawls' (1971) analysis of social justice greatly influenced the philosophical underpinnings that helped him conceptualise poverty (Sen 1983). According to Sen, one needs to take account of the *capability to function* when assessing whether or not State support should be offered – rather than going about measuring resources or levels of welfare (Sen 1992). Functioning is what a person can do or can be, and freedom provides the capability to achieve this functioning. Thus, a *capability set* comprises the alternative sets of functionings made possible through the available resources and opportunities. The functionings that feature within the *capability* space, as it is referred to by Sen, differ from both utilitarian and Rawlsian concerns.[9] However, Sen refrained from presenting a definitive list of capabilities and functionings – which has been a cause for criticism. It was claimed that this oversight rendered his theory unworkable in practice, except in a rudimentary form. The possibility of deriving a set of capabilities and functionings that could reflect upon fundamental values and meanings to life were conceived as being either too abstract – and therefore impractical to be put to any use – or insufficiently neutral. Such were the challenges that arose that it left wide open the question of how government and civil society might implement the capabilities approach.[10] Despite such criticisms, however, Sen's contribution has often been regarded as more realistic when it comes to defining poverty (Wolff 2008). It has greatly influenced policy within the United Nations Development Programme (United Nations 2010), and in doing so it has promoted a focus on *lack of basic functioning* whilst moving away from income-based measures.[11] Indeed, the richness of the concept cannot be captured through a single measure in view of its multi-dimensionality. This therefore calls for further methodological development.[12] In its Human Development Report of 1997 (United Nations 1997) the United Nations Development Programme introduced a Human Poverty Index (HPI) which recognises that poverty goes beyond material well-being. It is claimed that the poverty of choice and opportunities is more relevant for policy-makers than the poverty of income. The HPI uses the following indicators to signify the most basic dimensions of deprivation: a short life, lack of a basic education, and lack of access to public and private resources.

5.4 Freedom for human flourishing as conceived through natural law theory

When conceptualising poverty it seems that the grey areas encountered by Sen can find further illumination and support if we refer to the theory of natural law. There does not appear to be any discontinuity between Sen's conception of *capabilities* and natural law theory. For in effect, *capabilities to function* seek to bring about the full realisation of one's humanity wherein the dignity of the human person is accorded full respect. The flourishing of the human being turns out to be the common denominator in both Sen's work and in natural law theory. But Sen apparently found difficulty in identifying a set of capabilities and functionings that might reflect fundamental values and meanings to life. Natural law theory, however, presents a logic that encompasses principles that elucidate the fundamental premise for human flourishing. More specifically, the principles of natural law include:

- a set of basic practical principles that indicate the basic forms of human flourishing as goods to be pursued and realised;
- a set of basic methodological requirements of practical reasonableness (one of the goods), distinguishing sound from unsound practical thinking – i.e. between acts that are reasonable, all things considered, and acts that are unreasonable, all things considered. These distinguish ways that are morally right or morally wrong;
- a set of general moral standards (Finnis 2011).

All of this is in sync with Sen's *capability set*. There is therefore much significance and much potential when a deep-seated commitment underlying any public policy is guided by a vision of human flourishing.

5.4.1 Morality in natural law theory

The notion of morality appears to conjure up various meanings. The term 'morality' is derived from the Latin *mos/moris*, which for the Romans referred to *customs*. However, the term appears to have acquired various conceptual meanings. For instance, every religion is based on certain moral beliefs. In the Hindu morality, *dharma* and *karma* are the underlying principles of nearly all conceptions of morality and ethics.[13] If we consider the 'morality' of marriage from the Roman Catholic perspective, the strict monogamy of a lifelong union ('until death do us part') comes to the fore. On the other hand, according to generic Christian morality, the marriage of one man and one woman can be dissolved at any time through divorce (i.e. there is a concept of loose monogamy). Such morality is now also extending marriage to include unions of the same sex. And according to Islamic morality, it is morally correct for a man to marry and have, simultaneously, more than one wife (polygamy). Thus, 'morality' when conceived through the paradigm of a particular religious belief, provides a clear and comprehensive body of rules. However, the existence of such diverse views about the same thing (for example, marriage) leaves unsolved the pertinent question as to which moral principles are valid.

In view of such conflicting views, when it comes to natural law theory, instead of the term 'morality' Finnis advocates the term 'practical reasonableness'. He argues that this term should be used as the standard of reference for any theorist describing features of legal order (Finnis 2011: 15). Hence, the meaning of 'morality' in natural law theory does not derive its force from any particular religious belief(s) but attempts, rather, to present a universal conceptual meaning. By 'practical reasonableness' it is meant that assessments of what should be considered important or significant for those concerned, be put into perspective when selecting and formulating concepts. Max Weber also acknowledged the importance of practical reasonableness. The Weberian concept of *ideal type* recognises recurring social actions. These exemplify mental constructs that direct individual knowledge through an abstract process. Thus, according to Weber, in order to be able to derive to understanding, such actions need to be recognised by the researcher as standing at the core of every social phenomenon (Corbetta 2003: 9–29). According to personal construct theory, Kelly (1955), an American psychologist, proposed that individuals behave like scientists – striving to make sense of their own universe, of themselves, and of particular situations. As experience is gained, people learn to codify their observations (of events, people and things) into a framework of personal constructs by which they learn to anticipate future events. According to the theory, a person continues to employ constructs within a context to which the user finds their application useful.

5.4.2 Practical reasonableness – distinguishing sound from unsound practical thinking

How, it is asked, can one come up with universal conceptual meanings given the heterogeneity by which mental constructs are derived? Indeed, they differ from person to person, from one society to another, across place and time. Finnis explains how Aristotle regularly employed 'the philosophical device' and referred to it as the 'identification of focal meaning' (Finnis 2011: 9). The explanation given is illustrated by an example – that of *friendship*. Standing at the core is the concept of *friendship*. Emanating from this core are 'watered down versions of the central cases' (Finnis 2011: 11) as in the case of business friendship, friendship of convenience, etc. However, there appears to be some difficulty when it comes to getting to the core of concepts. How can one distinguish what constitutes centrality, for instance, when deciding what is to count as law? According to Finnis, moral obligation constitutes the central case. However, he maintains that usage of the term 'practical reasonableness' is preferable. Therefore, in the case of law, what is relevant for the theorist is the practical viewpoint.

But what is practical? What is reasonable? These are the questions that appear to have pervaded over two millennia since Plato and Aristotle. On the basis of what has been learned through the passage of time a number of methodological requirements – based on philosophical reflection – have been presented by Finnis and which therefore set out the basic requirements for practical reasonableness. These requirements, nine in all, 'express the "natural law method" of working out the (moral) "natural law"' (Finnis 2011: 103). Table 5.3 attempts to capture in a summary format that which has been postulated by Finnis.[14]

The nine basic requirements of practical reasonableness are all interrelated and equally basic. All need to be taken into consideration when one attempts rational thinking. They express the language of morality and are thus not to be considered as simply a mechanism for reaching correct judgements. They are also as a mechanism for expressing human flourishing, from which flows human dignity.

5.4.3 Dignity as the basic moral premise

Despite differing views that emanate from the relationship between morality and law, moral principles are generally assumed as principles of justice and which, in effect, underpin the law (Wright 2000).[15] The concept of *justice* covers both *formal equality* (treating like cases alike) and *substantive equality* (giving each person his or her due as a matter of right). The latter appears largely incompatible with utilitarian thought. From times dating back to Aristotle, the issue concerning substantive equality has been the subject of profound thought and its implications for morality, justice and law form the core of natural law theory. Finnis provides a sophisticated elaboration and reformulation of Thomas Aquinas' account of natural law theory.

Natural law theory calls for rational reflection on human beings in their interaction with other human beings (George 2008).[16] Each and every person, as a rational human being, has *dignity*.

> Man regarded as a person [rather than a mere animal], that is, as the subject of a morally practical reason, is exalted above any price; for as a person (*homo noumenon*) he is not to be valued merely as a means to the ends of others or even to his own ends, but as an end in himself, that is, he possesses a dignity (an absolute inner worth) by which he exacts respect for himself with every other being of this kind and values himself on a footing of equality with them.
>
> (Kant 1991)

This *dignity* flows from the very fact that as rational human beings we have the freedom to make choices and conscious decisions which in turn construct one's self and identity. Immanuel Kant, one of the great philosophers of the Enlightenment, has also emphasised this fundamental point – that as free and equal individuals one's humanity is subjected to the universal law of morality in order to distinguish and hence free ourselves from animal inclinations (Wright 2000).

Morality therefore employs judgement. According to Aquinas, when a person reaches a reasoned conclusion about his/her own duty, then the conclusion reached is a practical judgement. This judgement, according to Aristotle, is

Table 5.3 Summary description of the basic requirements of practical reasonableness, as postulated by Finnis

Number	Basic requirements of practical reasonableness	Summary description
First	A coherent plan of life	A deep and harmonious commitment to one's rational plan of life realisable through intelligent actions, opportunities and a high internal locus of control.
Second	No arbitrary preference among values	A fundamental impartiality of recognition of each of the basic forms of good.[*] Notwithstanding this, a rational commitment to one's plan of life may entail preference to certain values on the basis of one's rational assessment of capacities, circumstances and tastes.
Third	No arbitrary preference among persons	A fundamental impartiality of recognition among human subjects. Everyone is entitled to get for themselves what you are trying to get for yourself.
Fourth and fifth	Detachment and commitment	Meaningful commitments to projects during one's lifetime should not entail an overriding and unconditional attitude so as to feel drained of meaning when projects fail. On the other hand, commitments are not to be abandoned lightly. Creative, new and better ways need to be constantly sought.
Sixth	The (limited) relevance of consequences: efficiency, within reason	Conduct through practical reasonableness must seek to bring about the good in one's own life and the life of others and judgement made in accordance to their effectiveness. One must not waste one's opportunities by using inefficient methods.
Seventh	Respect for every basic value in every act	One should not choose to do any act which of itself does nothing but damage or impede the realisation or participation of any one or more of the basic forms of human good. Reason requires that every basic value be at least respected in each and every action.
Eighth	The requirement of the common good	Favour and foster the common good in one's community.
Ninth	Following one's conscience	One must act in accordance with one's conscience.

Source: This summary table is based upon the discussion presented in Finnis, J. (2011). *Natural Law and Natural Rights*, 2nd edition, Oxford: Oxford University Press, Part II, section V, pp. 100–33 (by permission of Oxford University Press).

Note
[*] An explanation of the basic forms of good is provided in Table 5.4.

referred to as 'psyche', while Aquinas refers to it as 'soul' (Wright 2000). From its very existence each and every individual is armed with this 'soul', even though it is at first somewhat undeveloped. It is this freedom as rational beings that bestows an absolute moral worth, a dignity that is equal among all rational beings. Even in cases where for various reasons the mental capacity to reach reasoned conclusions and employ reasoned judgements remains temporarily or permanently undeveloped, by virtue of his or her human nature he or she nevertheless remains in possession of a profound and inherent dignity (George 2008). It therefore follows that simply by virtue of our humanity it is morally right that this dignity be protected by law. It becomes a human right.

As rational beings empowered with freedom we are capable, through the the good of practical reasonableness, of making choices in pursuit of the 'basic goods'. Finnis lists seven *basic goods* which include: life, knowledge, play, aesthetic experience, sociability (friendship), practical reasonableness and religion (Finnis 2011: 81–97). Table 5.4 attempts to capture the gist of each of these basic goods as postulated by Finnis.

According to Finnis, the basic goods are all equally fundamental. Each and every one is to be given due merit as they all bear a particular mark. All are interrelated and can be regarded as aspects of one another. As such, an objective priority of value among the basic goods cannot be assigned – there is no hierarchy of importance amongst them. However, Finnis acknowledges that the order cannot be described as fixed; rather it is partly stable and partly shifting when *basic goods* are being participated in. That is to say, in view of the particular individual circumstances, certain basic goods are afforded priority.

The ultimate goal in the pursuit of such basic goods is the flourishing of the self, a self-fulfilment, a *'beatitude'*, *'felicitas'*. Therefore, the flourishing of the self is something that goes far beyond the achievement of mere pleasure. It is about the capacity of human beings to live in harmony with rational principles in pursuit of a complete, self-fulfilling life, indeed a human flourishing. As such, these basic goods lay the foundations for moral judgements, including judgements pertaining to justice and human rights (Finnis 2011). Thus, according to natural law, rational human behaviour needs also to recognise its obligations towards others while the flourishing of the self is being pursued.

According to the principles of natural law, the sole purpose of the State – and thus of politics and law – is attainment of the common good via the human flourishing or fulfilment of each person in the community (Finnis 2011). Aristotle views the State as a diverse plurality in which citizens are free and equal. This diverse plurality is essential for the complete flourishing of all citizens. The full realisation of one's humanity as a free and equal being forms the basis of the moral good as conceived in natural law theory. It calls upon humanity to uphold a right which others are bound to respect and protect to the best extent possible (George 2008). However, this conception is found to be in conflict with utilitarian theories and its modern variant, economic efficiency theory, which are more concerned with the maximum distribution of wealth rather than how such distribution is affecting the individual.

Table 5.4 Summary description of the seven basic goods, as postulated by Finnis

Basic good	Summary description
Life	Refers to the value of life, including all aspects of its vitality – such as health.
Knowledge	An intrinsic good, desirable for its own sake and not merely instrumental. May also be described as speculative since it is concerned with the uncovering of truths. Knowledge is to be pursued, while ignorance avoided.
Play	Play can enter any human activity but can always be distinguished from its 'serious' context. Some activities, enterprises and institutions are entirely – or primarily – play.
Aesthetic experience	The valued experience that is found in the creation and/or active appreciation of some work of significant and satisfying form.
Sociability (friendship)	In its weakest form this basic good is manifested by the maintenance of peace and harmony through the forms of human community. In its strongest form it is manifested through the flowering of full friendship. It involves acting for the sake of one's friends' well-being.
Practical reasonableness	The capability to bring one's own intelligence to bear effectively. This requires that one has a measure of effective freedom so as to be able to bring an intelligent and reasonable order to one's own actions, habits and practical attitudes. An order that is characterised through an inner integrity and outer authenticity (i.e. genuine realisations).
Religion	A concern for a good that consists of an irreducibly distinct form of order – one that goes beyond humanity. A concern which has been reasonably thought of as important, irrespective of the answer – even if sceptical or pessimistic.

Note
This summary is based upon the discussion presented by Finnis, J. (2011). Natural Law and Natural Rights, 2nd edition, Oxford: Oxford University Press, Part II, section IV, pp. 81–97.(by permission of Oxford University Press).

5.5 Respect for human dignity – a legally enforceable fundamental right

The Treaty of Lisbon,[17] signed on 13 December 2007 in Lisbon and which entered into force on 1 December 2009, recognises the rights, freedoms and principles set out in the Charter of Fundamental Rights (*OJEU* 2007a). More specifically, Article 6 (1) of the treaty confers on the charter the same legal value as the treaties.

The very first Article in the Charter of Fundamental Rights refers to human dignity and reads as follows: 'Human dignity is inviolable. It must be respected and protected.' The courts of the Union and the Member States are to interpret the charter and give due regard to the explanations put forth by the Praesidium (*OJEU* 2007a).[18] In its explanation of human dignity, the Praesdium elucidates that

> The dignity of the human person is not only a fundamental right in itself but constitutes the real basis of fundamental rights.... It results that none of the rights laid down in this Charter may be used to harm the dignity of another person, and that the dignity of the human person is part of the substance of the rights laid down in this Charter. It must therefore be respected, even where a right is restricted.
>
> (*OJEU* 2007b)

Human dignity in the Charter of Fundamental Rights builds upon the 1948 Universal Declaration of Human Rights. The notion of dignity is recognised as inherent in human nature, and ascribes an equal and inalienable right among 'all members of the human family'. It asserts that respect for human dignity provides the 'foundation of freedom, justice and peace in the world'.

What natural law expresses about human dignity is reflected in the Charter of Fundamental Rights. Respect for human dignity has now become a legally enforceable fundamental right in the European Union. Within the Lisbon Treaty's hierarchy of rights, human dignity acquires an elevated status that is 'superior to human rights and fundamental freedoms who owe their origin and existence to the dignity of the human person' (Aquilina 2010).

5.6 The quest for poverty reduction – putting EU public procurement into perspective

The reduction of poverty is back on the EU's agenda. Europe's 2020 strategy for smart and sustainable growth targets 20 million fewer people being at risk of poverty by 2020 (COM (2010) 2020 final). It is worth recalling that in 2000 the number of people living below the poverty line and suffering from social exclusion was described as unacceptable (Presidency Conclusions 2000). Poverty is an unacceptable state of affairs because, simply put, we all deserve to live in dignity and actively participate in society. Human dignity is inviolable and the Union accords dignity with being a fundamental constitutional right. 2010 was designated as the European year for combating poverty and social exclusion, with the aim of reaffirming the EU's political commitment at the start of the Lisbon strategy (March 2000) so as to 'make a decisive impact on the eradication of poverty' (European Council 2000). Despite this, EU poverty rates have not decreased and social exclusion has risen since the 1980s.

The 'fight' against poverty cannot be undertaken exclusively by the use of strategies and targets – which fail to acknowledge a fuller understanding of the moral dimension (Grima 2008). The principles that stand at the very heart of Europe are reflected in institutions that are ultimately bounded by the stark realities of society's concrete experiences. Europe's concern with economic efficiency appeals to a principle that is more concerned with the maximum distribution of wealth rather than how this is affecting the individual. It is grounded in utilitarian logic. The individual is assigned subordinate status in relation to the maximisation of aggregate utility. Consequently, respect for human dignity – at the conceptual level – holds subordinated status relative to European economic efficiency logic. When economic efficiency logic is assigned with a supremacy to which all other practical logics are subservient it denies rationality and practical reasonableness, and is hence immoral.[19]

A case in point is European public procurement legislation. As an instrument, public procurement is indissolubly linked with national policies and, in particular, social policy (Bovis 2006).[20] Historically, there have been consistent attempts to link public procurement with the government policy of the day. EU public procurement did not always have the economic and open market access objectives.[21] For instance, Italian procurement law made it possible to favour bidders from less developed regions of the country. Dutch procurement law and Danish local government law allowed for the creation of jobs for the long-term unemployed. German rules allowed favourable terms for bidders with a refugee background from the former German lands in Poland, the Soviet Union and Czechoslovakia, to mention only a few (Trybus 2008).

The claim that EU public procurement contributes to the Single European Market is highly questionable. But let us assume, for argument's sake, that EU public procurement is making some sort of contribution and make a distinction between its current contribution and a hypothetical contribution were Member States to utilise public procurement as an instrument for advancing directly their country's socio-economic interests without any of the EU procurement restrictions[22] encountered today. It could still be argued that Member States would work just as hard to produce as much welfare as when they were bound by EU procurement restrictions. Indeed, they might even be better off – especially when it comes to competencies in the field of social policy, since they would not have to give up part of their purchasing power to serve wider European integration aims. For it appears that at EU level, in the so called 'fight' against discrimination, poverty and social exclusion, the EU treads very cautiously and recognises the legitimate freedom of Member States to pursue their own social policy goals. And yet, by the same token, Member States are constrained when it comes to the use of vital policy tools that have the power to steer a State's social policy agenda – as is the case with public procurement. Indeed, public procurement has the potential to serve 'aims and objectives stipulated in the European treaties, such as social cohesion, combating of long-term unemployment, and, finally, the achievement of acceptable standards of living' (Bovis 2006: 24–5). But because public purchasing can also serve Europe's internal market aims the latter takes precedence. And so, it is argued, if the contribution of EU public procurement relating to the internal market is highly vague, do not such restrictions represent a straightforward socio-economic burden on Member States? Is it not the case that in dismantling the so-called 'trade barriers' we are simultaneously erecting 'social barriers' by way of restricting Member States' public purchasing autonomy in pursuit of their own social policies? Does this equate with social justice? Is this in line with Europe's fundamental constitutional values? If in this counter-argument public procurement freed from EU procurement restrictions appears, potentially, to offer a better alternative, would it not therefore yield a morally preferable social Europe?

The justifying point of law according to Aquinas (1947) is the common good. However, this should not be interpreted in the utilitarian mode – *the greatest good for the greatest number* – but rather as a shared good where the dignity and rights of each and every member of the community is respected, including the equal right to have one's dignity respected in the exercise of public authority (George 2008). Moral principles are generally assumed as principles of justice and ones which, in effect, underpin the law. According to Raz (2003) the significant connection between morality and the law is what gives it its intrinsic moral excellence. The only way for the law to claim intrinsic excellence is to claim that it has legitimate moral authority. But legitimate authority cannot be established by those who have *de facto* power and legal control. According to Raz, to meet the conditions of legitimacy two criteria need to be fulfilled. The first concerns the 'success condition' (Raz 2003: 9) wherein the authority of the government is derived from its ability (or likely ability) to succeed in discharging its function (its job). The second legitimacy criterion is related to the 'relevance of the needed job' (Raz 2003: 9) in the sense that the job's success is 'confined to its actions aimed at discharging this job' (Raz 2003: 9). In other words, those in authority are not endowed with a general authority to do whatever they deem fit. Legitimate authority is hence grounded in the success of the morally sanctioned task. Now were we to subject EU public procurement legislation to the *success condition* and the *relevance of the needed job* condition, as specified by Raz, we would no doubt find that even from this dimension EU public procurement falls short of moral ideals.[23]

In an endeavour 'to ensure that decisions are taken as closely as possible to the citizens of the Union', Article 5 of the Treaty Establishing the European Union and Protocol no. 2 establish the principles of subsidiarity and proportionality – including a system of monitoring to assess whether action at Community level is justified in the light of possibilities available at the national, local or regional level. Paragraph 3 of Article 5 TEU holds that

> Under the principle of subsidiarity, in areas which do not fall within its exclusive competence, the Union shall act only if and in so far as the objectives of the proposed action cannot be sufficiently achieved by the Member States.

Paragraph 4 of Article 5 TEU establishes that 'under the principle of proportionality, the content and form of Union action shall not exceed what is necessary to achieve the objectives of the Treaties'. While it has been observed that the principle of subsidiarity has the potential to exert an influential impact upon the development of the EU's social dimension, to date subsidiarity has been most often concerned with arguments between the EU institutions and the Member States as to who is responsible for action and decision-making. The idea of decisions being taken closer to the individual has not fully materialised (Burchill 2004).

The debate on poverty has revealed that it is more than a mere state of hunger or nakedness that relies on whatever remnants are thrown out by wealthy others. For respect to human dignity is as important as the satisfaction of hunger. Rawls has emphasised the importance of primary goods and Sen has emphasised the importance of capabilities. In their idea of social justice the notion of opportunities plays a pivotal role. And who can negate the fact that public procurement is also essentially concerned with the provision of access to opportunities? But, as the current state of affairs reveal, EU public procurement doesn't seem to be improving the opportunities for SMEs. According to a European Commission report[24] there was not much change in the share of public contracts awarded to SMEs during the period 2005–08. In the period 2006–08 an estimated 60 per cent of above-EU threshold contracts were awarded to SMEs, which accounted for 34 per cent of the market share in terms of value (for the period 2008-11 SMEs accounted for 29 per cent of market share in terms of value, see discussion in chapter 3). Does not this look like an injustice that is being served to SMEs in the light of Rawls' second principle of justice, which relates to the equality principle and more specifically the *difference principle* postulating that social and economic inequalities between citizens are to be limited as long as they favour the least well-off members of society? Indeed, we now need to realise that the economic benefits that the European Single Market reaps do not appear to trickle down as easily as imagined.

In advancing Europe's theory of social justice we need to reflect and make a distinction between those things that truly constitute permissible European moral ideals, and those that do not. The European Constitution centres on the human person. The value of respect to human dignity identifies with the social conscience of the people of Europe. It also finds its expression through the principle of democracy. The moral debate relating to EU public procurement – though largely confined to above-EU threshold public procurement – requires that it be extended beyond such boundaries. It points towards a reordering of Europe's economic and social dimensions. Because the acceptance of Europe's founding values is not only about embracing a compassionate understanding: it is also about *living* them. Liberation of the poor calls for unbounded ways of thinking.

5.7 Concluding remarks

Poverty features as a real problem across Europe. In effect it reveals the depth to the gap limiting European integration aims. From the foregoing discussion in this chapter it could be argued that the poverty of choices and opportunities is more relevant for policy-makers than the poverty of income. This has direct implications on the potential impact that public procurement can impart when it comes to reducing poverty. Indeed, public procurement as a vital policy tool that is indissolubly linked to national policies, and in particular social policies, offers great potential in fulfilling European treaty objectives such as social cohesion, combatting long-term unemployment, and the achievement of acceptable standards of living. However, as far as EU public procurement is utilised to promote Single Market objectives and seeks to promote the greatest good for the greatest number, the respect towards human dignity at the very conceptual level is assigned subordinate status.

The full realisation of one's humanity – wherein the dignity of the human person is accorded full respect – transpires to be the common denominator and plays a pivotal role in both Sen's work concerning *capabilities to function* when conceptualising poverty, and natural law theory where the attainment of the common good via the flourishing or fulfilment of each person in the community becomes the sole purpose of the State and thus of politics and the law. Nothwithstandng the pivotal role that respect for human dignity plays, it is worth noting that the notion of dignity intricately links to another important issue that cannot be left ignored: culture.

Europe has been described as a State of culture that finds the strengthening of human dignity through its cultural dimension (Andò 2003). European social models are deeply ingrained into European cultures (Joerges and Rödl 2004). Haberle (2001) contends that the Constitution is a book of culture that defines the people's identity at a given point in history. For culture is not a static phenomenon – it is subject to regular evolution in response to the circumstances in which a society finds itself (Bidney 1967). Culture is viewed as a programme or blueprint for survival that involves strategies by which social groups maximise their perceived advantage. This programme includes a set of ideas and beliefs also referred to as ideologies, so that culture not only contains survival instructions but also elaborates their justification, type and purpose (Bullivant 1984). People thus acquire their culture and use it as a device to solve problems. When the integrity of the self or of the nation is thought to be under threat, or becomes insecure, boundaries are set up (Peterson and Lupton 1996).

> The frontier is both an opening and a closing. All frontiers, including the membrane of living beings, including the frontier of nations, are, at the same time as they are barriers, places of communication and exchange. They are the place of dissociation and association, of separation and articulation.
>
> (Morin 1990)

The case of language recognition in the European Union is a classic example and exposes the fact that Member States are not indifferent to cultural identities. We must thus exercise caution before placing all barriers on the same footing. Let us recall[25] at this point the Wood Report (2004) and the findings of Geroski (1991), and Head and Mayer (2000), who attributed market fragmentation in the case of EU public procurement to the diversity in national and regional tastes and who claimed that the 1992 Single Market programme would do little to reduce such fragmentation. Today, with the benefit of hindsight, such findings appear to have been proved correct, implying that public procurement as a dynamic policy tool needs also be viewed from its cultural dimension. For only when an acceptable level of European social justice is achieved through the unconstrained recognition of social rights – and by implication, cultural rights – can we progress any further.

Notes

1 With the entry into force of the Lisbon Treaty, The Charter of Fundamental Rights of the European Union has achieved a legally binding status. Various Articles contained within the Charter recognise the fundamental nature of public service obligations. According to Article 36, access to Services of General Economic Interest is a fundamental right which is protected by the Union. Furthermore, Article 9 TFEU stipulates that the Union shall 'take into account requirements linked to ... the guarantee of adequate social protection' and 'the fight against social exclusion'. Article 14 TFEU and Protocol (No. 26) on Services of General Interest envisage a role for competition policy in shaping Services of General Economic Interest. Non-economic activities are excluded from the scope of application of the treaty (see Article 2 of Protocol no. 26).
2 The five measurable EU targets for 2020, as proposed by the Commission, are: employment, research and innovation, climate change and energy, education and for combating poverty (COM (2010) 2020 final).
3 Eurostat defines 'persons at-risk-of poverty' as 'those living in a household with an equivalised disposable income below the risk-of-poverty threshold, which is set at 60% of the national median equivalised disposable income (after social transfers). The equivalised income is calculated by dividing the total household income by its size, determined after applying the following weights: 1.0 to the first adult, 0.5 to each other household members aged 14 or over and 0.3 to each household member aged less than 14 years old' (Eurostat 2013).
4 Eurostat defines 'severely materially deprived persons' as having

> living conditions constrained by a lack of resources and experienc[ing] at least 4 out of the 9 following deprivation items: cannot afford (1) to pay rent/mortgage or utility bills on time, (2) to keep home adequately warm, (3) to face unexpected expenses, (4) to eat meat, fish or a protein equivalent every second day, (5) a one week holiday away from home, (6) a car, (7) a washing machine, (8) a colour TV, or (9) a telephone (including mobile phone).
>
> (Eurostat 2013)

5 Eurostat defines 'people living in households with very low work intensity' as 'those aged 0–59 who live in households where on average the adults (aged 18–59) worked less than 20% of their total work potential during the past year. Students are excluded' (Eurostat 2013).
6 The relative median at risk of poverty gap is calculated as the difference between the median equivalised disposable income of people below the at risk of poverty threshold and the at-risk-of-poverty threshold, expressed as a percentage of the at risk of poverty threshold (cut-off point: 60 per cent of national median equivalised disposable income).
7 The nine items that attempt to reflect upon severe material deprivation seek to capture the actual experiences that individuals manage to achieve. They are therefore considered as a direct meausure. For a list of the nine indicators refer to the definition provided by Eurostat on 'severe materially deprived persons' (Eurostat 2013).
8 This involves working out the average or median equivalised household incomes, defined as the household's total disposable income divided by its 'equivalent size', in a country. Comparing relative poverty levels between different countries does not sufficiently take into account the differences in standards of living and thus it is argued, in effect it becomes more a question of measuring and comparing inequality levels rather than poverty levels.
9 According to Sen, Rawls' analysis of social justice differs greatly from utility-based theories because his focus is on primary goods – which are resource-based.
10 Martha Nussbaum has proposed a list of ten capabilities and functionings. These include: the capability for physical survival; the capability for bodily health; the

capability for bodily integrity; the capability for the exercise of imagination; the capability for emotional response and exploration; the capability for practical reason; the capability for love and friendship; the capability for connection with nature and other species; the capability for play; the capability for the exercise of control over the environment, including political control (Nussbaum 1999, 2000, 2003). While Nussbaum emphasises universality of the capabilities and functionings, Sen – by contrast – emphasises the importance of adopting a participatory approach that is open to democratic scrutiny and amendment in order to ensure that capabilities and functionings are put into the right context. See Sen (1996).

11 It is worth noting that Sen's work in this respect is among the contributions that won him the Nobel Prize for Economics in 1998.

12 Further to the recommendations of the UK's 2007 Equality Review – which called for the compilation of a measurement framework based on the capability approach, – Tania Burchardt, a member of the steering committee, presented her work in this area (Burchardt 2008).

13 Dharma is said to be one of the most complex and all-encompassing concepts in Hinduism: it can mean religion, law, duty, order, proper conduct, morality, righteousness, justice and norm. Karma is intimately linked to dharma and is understood as a universal law of cause and effect (Kinnard 2013).

14 This summary table is based on the discussion of Finnis (2011), pp. 100–33.

15 That law and morality are separable is a claim commonly attributed to legal positivists including John Austin, Jeremy Bentham, Hans Kelsen, and H.L.A. Hart. However, Joseph Raz (an esteemed legal positivist) argues that such claims should not be the distinguishing factor that marks the division in legal philosophy. For Raz (2003) the necessary connections between law and morality are obvious. Despite such prevailing scepticism among legal positivists, there are others who maintain the view, and argue for, the separability of law and morality. For arguments in this respect see Kramer (2004).

16 R.P. George (2008) notes how the notion of rationality is disputed by some – notably, David Hume, for whom reason is 'the slave of the passions' (Hume 1888); and Thomas Hobbes (Curley 1994). It is argued that the ends people pursue are driven by non-rational motivating factors such as feelings, emotion and desire.

17 The Treaty of Lisbon amends the Treaty on European Union (TEU, also known as the Maastricht Treaty) and the Treaty Establishing the European Community (TEC, also known as the Treaty of Rome) now renamed the Treaty on the Functioning of the European Union.

18 See Preamble to the Charter of Fundamental Rights of the European Union.

19 The argument for its immorality is deduced from the discussion as set out in sections 5.4.1, 'Morality in natural law theory', and section 5.4.2, 'Practical reasonableness – distinguishing sound from unsound practical thinking'.

20 Fernández Martin (1996: 45) contends that there is wide agreement on the use of public procurement as an instrument of economic and social policy. See also Jeanrenaud (1984), Turpin (1972, 1989).

21 See Article 29 (4) and 29 (a) of the EC Public Works Directive 71/305 and Article 26 of EC Public Supplies Directive 77/62.

22 EU procurement Directives – namely Directive 2004/18/EC and Directive 2004/17/EC – are stated to be based on Article 53 (1) TFEU, Article 59 TFEU and Article 114 TFEU. Arrowsmith and Kunzlik (2009) question whether Community social policies that fall within the fields of activity of EU procurement legislation find authorisation in such a treaty basis.

23 Such conclusions are based on the discussions so far. For instance, Majone (1998) concurs that efficiency-oriented policies need to be legitimated by results, on the proviso that there is an adequate system of accountability. The question of accountability was highlighted in Chapter 4.

24 This study is a follow-up to an earlier report by the European Commission published in 2007 and which has been cited and referred to in Chapter 3, section 3.4, 'EU public procurment and its impact on small- and medium-sized enterprises' (GHK 2010).
25 See discussion in Chapters 3 and 4.

References

Alcock, P., 2006. *Understanding Poverty*. Houndmills: Palgrave Macmillan.

Andò, S., 2003. 'Human Rights And The Protection Of Different Cultural Identities' in *Mediterranean Journal of Human Rights*, vol. 7, no. 3, pp. 17–47.

Aquilina, K., 2010. *Respect for Human Dignity and the Law*. State Care. Available at: www.statecareandmore.eu/index.php/blogs/respect-for-human-dignity-and-the-law-by-prof-kevin-aquilina-.html [accessed 23 November 2010].

Arrowsmith, S. and Kunzlik, P., 2009. *Social and Environmental Policies in the EC Procurement Law – New Directives and New Directions*. Cambridge: Cambridge University Press.

Atkinson, A.B. and Marlier, E., 2010. *Income and living conditions in Europe, Eurostat Statistical Books*. Luxembourg: European Commission.

Bidney, D., 1967. *Theoretical Anthropology*. New York: Schocken Press.

Bovis, C., 2006. *EC Public Procurement Case Law and Regulation*. Oxford: Oxford University Press.

Bullivant, B.M., 1984. *Pluralism: Cultural Maintenance and Evolution*. Avon: Multilingual Matters Ltd.

Burchardt, T., 2008. 'Monitoring inequality: putting the capability approach to work' in Craig, G., Burchardt, T. and Gordon, D. (eds), *Social Justice and Public Policy*. Bristol: The Polity Press, pp. 205–29.

Burchill, R., 2004. 'The EU and European Democracy – Social Democracy or Democracy with a Social Dimension?' in *Canadian Journal of Law and Jurisprudence*, vol. XVII, no. 1, pp. 185–207 (p. 198).

Corbetta, P., 2003. *Social Research Theory, Methods and Techniques*. London: Sage Publications.

Edgar Morin, I.N. and Bennington. G., 1990. 'Postal politics and the institution of the nation' in: Bhaba, H.K. (ed.), *Nation and Narration*. London: Routledge.

Fernández Martin, J.M., 1996. *The EC Public Procurement Rules: A Critical Analysis*. Oxford: Clarendon Press.

Fiegehen, G.C., Lansley, P.S. and Smith, A.D., 1977. *Poverty and Progress in Britain 1953–73*. UK: Cambridge University Press.

Finnis, J., 2011. *Natural Law and Natural Rights*, 2nd edition. Oxford: Oxford University Press.

Fisher, G.M., 1995. *Is There Such a Thing as an Absolute Poverty Line Over Time? Evidence from the United States, Britain, Canada, and Australia on the Income Elasticity of the Poverty Line*. US Census Bureau. Available at: www.census.gov/hhes/www/povmeas/papers/elastap4.html.

Frazer, H., 2009. *Poverty and Inequality in the EU*. Brussels: European Anti Poverty Network Social Inclusion.

George, R.P., 2008. 'Natural Law' in *Harvard Journal of Law & Public Policy*, vol. 31, no. 1, pp. 171–96.

Geroski, P., 1991. '1992 and European Industrial Structure' in Mackenzie, G. and Venables, A.J. (eds), *The Economics of the Single European Act*. London: Macmillan.

GHK, 2010. *Evaluation of SMEs' Access To Public Procurement Markets In The EU.* Brussels: DG Enterprise and Industry.
Grima, G., 2008. *Eradication of Poverty As A Moral Commitment – Paper Presented during the Civil Society Project Conference.* University of Malta. Available at: www.um.edu.mt/edrc/books/CD_CSP4/contents.html [accessed February 2015].
Head, K. and Mayer, T., 2000. 'Non-Europe: The Magnitude and Causes of Market Fragmentation in the EU in *Review of World Economics*, vol. 136, no. 2, pp. 284–314.
Heywood, A., 2004. *Political Theory, An Introduction.* 3rd edition, New York: Palgrave Macmillan.
Hobbes, T., 1588–1679. *Leviathan: with selected variants from the Latin edition of 1668.* Edited with introduction and notes by Curley E., 1994, Indianapolis, Cambridge: Hackett Publishing Co.
Hume, D., 1888. *A Treatise of Human Nature.* Oxford: Clarendon Press.
Renauld, J., 1984. 'Marchés publics et politique économique' in *Annales de l'Économie Publique, Sociale et Coopérative*, vol. 72, no. 2, p. 153.
Joaquín Almunia, 2010. 'The role of public services in "Europe 2020"'. Speech 10/276. CEEP Congress.
Joerges, C. and Rödl, F., 2004. *'Social Market Economy' as Europe's Social Model?* Florence: European University Institute.
Kant, I., 1991. *The Metaphysics of Morals, 1797.* Cambridge: Cambridge University Press.
Kelly, G.A., 1955. *The Psychology of Personal Constructs.* New York: Norton.
Kinnard, J.N., 2015. *Hinduism, Principles of Moral Thought and Action.* Available at: www.patheos.com/Library/Hinduism/Ethics-Morality-Community/Principles-of-Moral-Thought-and-Action.html [accessed 4 April 2015].
Kofi, A.A., 2000. *We the Peoples – The Role of the United Nations in the 21st Century.* New York: United Nations. Available at: www.un.org/en/events/pastevents/pdfs/We_The_Peoples.pdf [accessed 29 October 2010].
Kramer, M.H., 2004. 'On the Separability of Law and Morality' in *Canadian Journal of Law and Jurisprudence*, vol. 17, no. 2, pp. 315–35.
Majone, G., 1998. 'Europe's "Democratic Deficit": The Question of Standards' in *European Law Journal*, vol. 4, no. 1, pp. 5–28.
Needham, C. and Murray, A., 2005. *The future of Public Services in Europe.* UNISON and Ver.di. Catalyst and the Centre for European Reform for UNISON and Ver.di.
Nussbaum, M.C., 1999. *Sex and social justice.* Oxford: Oxford University Press.
Nussbaum, M.C., 2000. *Women and human development: The Capabilities approach.* Cambridge: Cambridge University Press.
Nussbaum, M.C., 2003. 'Capabilities as fundamental entitlements: Sen and social justice' in *Feminist Economics*, vol. 9, no. 2–3, pp. 33–59.
Peterson, A. and Lupton, D., 1996. *The new public health: Health and self in the age of risk.* London: Sage.
Rawls, J., 1971. *A theory of Justice.* Oxford: Oxford University Press.
Raz, J., 2003. 'About Morality and the Nature of Law' in *American Journal of Jurisprudence*, vol. 48, pp. 1–17.
Sen, A., 1983. 'Poor, Relatively Speaking' in *Oxford Economic Papers*, vol. 35, pp. 153–69.
Sen, A., 1992. *Inequality re-examined.* Oxford: Clarendon Press.
Sen, A., 1996. 'Freedom, capabilities and public action: a response' in *Notizie di Politeia*, vol. 12, no. 43–4, pp. 107–25.

Smith, A., 1776. *An Inquiry into the Nature and Causes of the Wealth of Nations.* London: Home University Library.
St Thomas Aquinas, 1947. *Summa Theologica Question 96, Article 1.* Available at: www.sacredtexts.com/chr/aquinas/summa/index.htm [accessed November 2010].
Stitt, S. and Grant, D., 1993. *Poverty.* Avebury: Rowntree Revisted.
Townsend, P., 1979. *Poverty in the United Kingdom: a Survey of Household Resources and Standards of Living.* Harmondsworth: Penguin.
Trybus, M., 2008. *Corporate Social Responsibility, Business Responsibilities for Human Rights and International Law.* Copenhagen: Copenhagen University and Copenhagen Business School.
Turpin, C., 1972. *Government Contracts.* Harmondworth: Penguin Books.
Turpin, C., 1989. *Government Procurement and Contracts.* Harlow: Longman.
United Nations, 1995. *World Summit for Social Development.* Copenhagen, Denmark, 6–12 March 1995, A/CONF.166/9, 19 April 1995. Available at: www.un.org/esa/socdev/wssd/index.html [accessed 29 October 2010].
United Nations Development Programme, 1997. *Human development report 1997 – Human development to eradicate poverty.* Available at: http://hdr.undp.org/en/reports/global/hdr1997/ [accessed 12 November 2010].
United Nations Development Programme, 2010. *Human development report 2010, The real wealth of nations: Pathways to human development.* New York: Palgrave Macmillan. Available at: http://hdr.undp.org/en/media/HDR_2010_EN_Complete.pdf [accessed 12 November 2010].
Wood, A., 2004. *A report to The Chancellor of the Exchequer & Secretary of State for Trade & Industry.* UK: Office of Government Commerce.
Wolff, J., 2008. 'Social Justice and public policy: a view from political philosophy' in Craig, G., Burchardt, T. and Gordon, D. (eds), *Social Justice and Public Policy.* Bristol: The Policy Press, pp. 17–31.
Wright, R.W., 2000. 'The Principles of Justice' in *Notre Dame Law Review*, vol. 75, pp. 1859–93.

Official documents

European Council

Presidency Conclusions, 2000. *Lisbon European Council 23 and 24 March 2000, Presidency Conclusions.*

European Commission

COM (2010) 2020 final, 3 March 2010. *Communication from the Commission Europe 2020: A strategy for smart, sustainable and inclusive growth.* Brussels: European Commission.

Official Journal of the European Union

Official Journal of the European Union (OJEU), 2007a. 'Notices from European Union Institutions and Bodies, European Parliament, Council, Commission, Charter of Fundamental Rights of the European Union', 2007/C 303/01.

Official Journal of the European Union (OJEU), 2007b. 'Explanations (*) Relating to the Charter of Fundamental Rights', 207/C 303/2 (Title I – Dignity Explanation on Article 1 – Human dignity).

Eurostat

Eurostat News Release, 2012. 'At risk of poverty or social exclusion in the EU 27'. 171/2012, Brussels.

Eurostat News Release, 2013. At risk of poverty or social exclusion in the EU28. 184/2013, 5 December. Brussels: European Commission.

Part II
Closing the gap

6 The mission of serving the public
Services of general interest and community law

6.1 Introduction

One of the most contentious issues pertaining to Community law concerns the provision and financing of public services, commonly referred to in European Commission terminology as *services of general interest*.[1] Although Community law does not define the term, it was first introduced by the European Commission in 1996 (COM (1996) 443 final). Accordingly, 'this term covers market and non-market services which the public authorities class as being of general interest and subject to specific public service obligations'.[2] The notion of services of general interest was given an elevated status when placed at the heart of the European model of society (COM (1996) 443 final: 3). Services of general interest reflect core European values such as cohesion, solidarity, and equal treatment within an open and dynamic market. But in an era of globalisation, constantly evolving technology, and ever-increasing consumer demands, serious concerns about securing the future of these services has been expressed (COM (1996) 443 final: 1). Thus, the need for modernisation at European level was highlighted, notwithstanding the fact that '[t]he economic integration of Europe based on the single market and the cohesion policy *has had* to take on board the issue of general interest at European level' (COM (1996) 443 final: 6, emphasis added).

Services of general interest cover a wide spectrum of services and include the multitude of activities associated with the delivery of healthcare, education, social services and services within the so-called big network industries such as energy, electricity, gas, postal services, rail transport, air transport, telecommunications and public service broadcasting. Other services include waste management and water supply.

The debate on services of general interest that was initiated through the Green Paper (COM (2003) 270 final) strongly confirmed the importance of such services as pillars of the European model of society. Indeed, the European Commission issued a multitude of communications in this respect – a matter which in itself should not be underestimated. The discussion in the forthcoming section 6.2, 'The European Commission and its plethora of soft law', attempts to highlight this matter. There have been various attempts within the EU to configure and elevate Europe's social dimension. Section 6.3 looks at the matter of 'Services of general economic interest – forging a bond between European economic efficiency and social cohesion?' This section presents a review of early 1990s European Court of Justice cases. Section 6.3.1 delves further into the matter and focuses 'On internal market tensions and concerns'. Section 6.4 is about 'Services of general interest – an endeavour in untangling chaos in the free thinking zone', and adopts a multidisciplinary approach as it directs attention towards two contentious issues linked to the notion of services of general interest. First, section 6.4.1, 'On economic versus non-economic services – gaining marketing insights' reviews the claimed distinction between services of an economic nature and those of a non-economic one. The matter is examined through the marketing literature lens, and the nature and characteristics of services and cross-cultural behaviour and attitudes on service quality are examined. Second, section 6.4.2, 'The public interest: fiction or fact?' reviews the notion of general interest. In an attempt to add vision to the understandings relating to the public interest, this section also reviews the matter through a philosophical viewpoint that is based on natural law theory. Section 6.5, 'Concluding remarks', attempts to consolidate the various issues explored and come up with rational understandings in order to reflect better upon key elements that make up the so-called 'European model of society'.

6.2 The European Commission and its plethora of soft law

The European Commission's first communication on services of general interest was published way back in 1996 (COM (1996) 443 final). Since then, various communications[3] relating to services of general interest have been published.[4] Before delving further into the notion of services of general interest, it is worth noting the significance of *Commission communications* – commonly referred to by academia as 'soft law'.

Article 288 TFEU on the legal acts of the Union clearly states that 'recommendations and opinions shall have no binding force'. However, this is not to be interpreted as them having no legal effects. In the Dansk Rørindustri case that was brought to appeal in front of the European Court of Justice (hereafter referred to as ECJ) requesting that several Court of First Instance[5] decisions be set aside, it was noted that

> The Court has already held in a judgment concerning internal measures adopted by the administration, that although those measures may not be regarded as rules of law which the administration is always *bound* to observe, they nevertheless form rules of practice from which the administration may not depart in an individual case without giving reasons that are compatible with the *principle of equal treatment*. Such measures therefore constitute a general act.
>
> (Joined Cases C-189, 202, 205, 208 and 213: para. 209, C-171/00: para. 35, emphasis added)

The mission of serving the public 137

Furthermore,

> In adopting such rules of conduct and announcing by publishing them that they will henceforth apply to the cases to which they relate, the [Commission] imposes a limit on the exercise of its discretion and cannot depart from those rules under pain of being found, where appropriate, to be in breach of the *general principles of law*, such as *equal treatment or the protection of legitimate expectations*. It cannot therefore be excluded that on certain conditions and depending on their conduct, such rules of conduct, which are of general application, *may produce legal effects*.
> (Joined Cases C-189, 202, 205, 208 and 213: para. 211, emphasis added)

In the Grimaldi case it was held that

> [N]ational courts are *bound* to take recommendations into consideration in order to decide disputes submitted to them, in particular where they cast light on the interpretation of national measures adopted in order to implement them or where they are designed to supplement binding Community provisions.
> (Hofmann 2006: para.18, emphasis added)

Thus, these 'soft'[6] guiding and non-binding instruments produce substantial indirect external effects and derive their validity through the recognition of general EU legal principles: namely, equal treatment, the protection of legitimate expectations (Joined Cases C-189, 202, 205, 208 and 213: para. 209, 211) and the principle of legal certainty (Hofmann 2006: para. 18).[7] During the last two decades it has been noted that these instruments are featuring in European case law at an increasing rate.[8]

6.3 Services of general economic interest – forging a bond between European economic efficiency and social cohesion?

The term 'services of general economic interest' originated with the Treaty of Rome in 1957 – finding its place under Article 90 (2) EEC.[9] Article 90 EEC, now Article 106 TFEU, is a key provision that takes into account the intersection between the public sphere and the economic sphere. In essence, Article 106 TFEU provides a special regime with respect to both the free movement and competition rules for public monopolies and undertakings that have been granted 'special and exclusive rights'.[10] In order to ensure that such rules – and in particular the rules on competition – do not obstruct the performance of particular tasks in the pursuit of public interest goals, Article 106 (2) TFEU provides a derogation. This Article reads as follows:

> Undertakings entrusted with the operation of services of general economic interest or having the character of a revenue-producing monopoly shall be

subject to the rules contained in the Treaties, in particular to the rules on competition, in so far as the application of such rules does not obstruct the performance, in law or in fact, of the particular tasks assigned to them. The development of trade must not be affected to such an extent as would be contrary to the interests of the Union.

It is up to the Commission to 'ensure the application of the provisions of this Article and shall, where necessary, address appropriate directives or decisions to Member States' (Article 106 (3) TFEU).

Before the 1990s no friction emanated between the application of competition rules, and activities conducted by the State (Jones and Sufrin 2009: 563–4). But the scenario has changed since then. The early 1990s were characterised by a process of liberalisation of the network industries,[11] and gave way to crucial European Court of Justice rulings referred under Article 267 TFEU. We now attempt to put into context the most salient issues deriving from these early 1990s cases.

In order for EU competition law to apply, an entity needs to be engaged in an economic activity. Thus, in the Klaus Höfner and Fritz Elser (1991), the Court held at paragraph 21 that 'in the context of competition law ... the concept of an undertaking encompasses every entity engaged in an economic activity, regardless of the legal status of the entity and the way in which it is financed'. In principle, the competition rules as provided for by Articles 101 TFEU and 102 TFEU apply to undertakings. Therefore, as soon as an entity is classified as an undertaking, the competition rules come immediately into force. When it comes to services of general economic interest, Sauter (2008: 167) succinctly notes that 'services of general economic interest (SGEI) are an EU legal category that provides an exception to the competition rules for the proportionate pursuit of legitimate public interest goals by private undertakings'. Such an exception is made possible through the application of Article 106 (2) TFEU.

Nevertheless, measures undertaken by Member States are not to violate the anti-discrimination provisions, the competition rules, and the rules on State aid. In this respect Article 106 (1) TFEU holds that

> In the case of public undertakings and undertakings to which Member States grant special or exclusive rights, Member States shall neither enact nor maintain in force any measure contrary to the rules contained in the Treaties, in particular to those rules provided for in Article 18 and Articles 101 to 109.

The European Court of Justice's interpretation of this Article – as arrived at through the early 1990 cases – suggests that Member States need to tread with caution when granting monopoly rights, since this may result in a violation of the competition rules. In the 1991 Telecommunications Terminal Equipment case (Case C-202/88) France challenged Commission Directive 88/301/EEC of 16 May 1988 on competition in the markets in telecommunications terminal equipment (*OJEU* 1988, L 131: 73). It alleged that the Commission lacked the powers to adopt the Directive on the basis of Article 106 (3) TFEU. Furthermore, as part of its plea the French government requested that Article 2 of Directive 88/301/EEC be annulled. In this respect the Article held that Member States that had granted special or exclusive rights to undertakings for the importation, marketing, connection, and bringing into service of telecommunications terminal equipment (and/or maintenance of such equipment) were to ensure that such rights were withdrawn.

In its analysis the Court interpreted the notion of exclusive rights in the light of Articles 2 and 3 EEC,[12] which 'set out to establish a market characterized by the free movement of goods where the terms of competition are not distorted' (Case C-202/88: para. 41). Accordingly, the holding of exclusive rights in the telecommunications sector was determined by the Court as capable of restricting intra-Community trade – and thus upheld Article 2 of Commission Directive 88/301/EEC of 16 May 1988 on the withdrawal of such exclusive rights (Case C-202/88: para. 31–44). However, the Court declared void the Commission's decision for the withdrawal of special rights. It was ruled that the Commission had failed to produce justification for such an obligation by virtue of it failing to elaborate on the type of special rights involved, or in what respect such special rights infringed upon treaty provisions (Case C-202/88: para. 45–7).

In a similar case Spain, Belgium and Italy challenged Directive 90/388/EEC of 28 June 1990 (OJ 1990L 192: 10) on competition in the markets for telecommunication services, and requested its annulment (Joined Cases C-271/90, C-281/90 and C-289/90). The Court rejected the appellants' claim for the holding of exclusive rights. In the Régie des Télégraphes et des Téléphones (RTT) case (1991) (Case C-18/88) the Court held that an abuse of Article 102 TFEU is committed when an undertaking holding a dominant position extends its monopoly by its own conduct without any objective necessity by way of reserving for itself ancillary activity that could be carried out by other undertakings (Case C-18/88: para. 18, 19). The Court also pointed out that where the extension of the monopoly results from a State measure without any objective justification, this constitutes an infringement of Article 106 TFEU in conjunction with Article 102 TFEU (Case C-18/88: para. 21, 24).

In the Klaus Höfner and Fritz Elser case (1991) the Court acknowledged that the holding of an exclusive right created a dominant position, and although this was compatible with the treaty in this case it led to an *unavoidable abuse* (Case C-41/90: para. 27–29). The mere fact that the entity enjoying the exclusive right was incapable of satisfying the demand pertaining to the exclusivity resulted into an automatic abuse of its dominant position and thus incompatible with Article 102 TFEU. In the ERT (1991) case (Case C-260/89) the Greek government granted ERT, a public undertaking, exclusive rights in the matter of television and radio broadcasting.

Following an assessment of the case, the Court held as follows:

> [I]t should be observed that Article 90 (1)[13] of the Treaty prohibits the granting of an exclusive right to retransmit television broadcasts to an undertaking which has an exclusive right to transmit broadcasts, where those

rights are liable to create a situation in which that undertaking is led to infringe Article 86[14] of the Treaty by virtue of a discriminatory broadcasting policy which favours its own programmes.

The reply to the national court must therefore be that Article 90 (1) of the Treaty prohibits the granting of an exclusive right to transmit and an exclusive right to retransmit television broadcasts to a single undertaking, where those rights are liable to create a situation in which that undertaking is led to infringe Article 86 by virtue of a discriminatory broadcasting policy which favours its own programmes, unless the application of Article 86 obstructs the performance of the particular tasks entrusted to it.

(Case C-260/89: para. 37, 38)

In the 1991 Merci Case (Case C-179/90) the Court elaborated further on this issue when it noted that 'such rights are liable to create a situation in which that undertaking is *induced* to commit such abuses' (Case C-179/90: para. 37, emphasis added). Given this rationale, it could be argued that in effect any dominant position naturally induces an undertaking to be liable to behaviour that is not conducive to competitive markets (Jones and Sufrin 2010: 583).

As it transpires from the jurisprudence of the early 1990s discussed above, it could be observed that there were two major issues at play. On the one hand, one finds in force vigorous EU policies focused on increasing competitiveness and the breaking down of trade barriers. Such policies generally found backing by the Court. On the other hand, one finds tensions arising among Member States as the forceful efforts towards liberalisation led to the partial loss of their own sovereignty when creating legal monopolies.[15] It has been observed that despite the Commission's legitimate right to enact Directives or decisions, such powers have rarely been used since then (Sauter 2008: 168). The European Parliament and Council have strongly objected to the use of such instruments because they basically allow the Commission to legislate single-handedly – i.e. at the cost of democratic legitimacy (Sauter 2008: 168).

6.3.1 On internal market tensions and concerns

It has been argued that the concept of services of general economic interest has come about largely as a result of

negative integration processes. In particular the use of Article [106 (1) TFEU] to attack public monopolies through the national courts and the use of Article [106 (2) TFEU] to defend services of general interest from the full rigour of the competition and free market rules.

(Szyszczak 2007)

Political tensions arise between those who favour a social solidarity-based approach (associated in particular with France, and manifested in the notion of '*service publique*'), and those who favour a market-based approach (regarded as 'Anglo-Saxon', and commonly associated with the United Kingdom). These tensions have played a major influential role when it comes to broadening the internal market dimension.

Some 30 years after the introduction of Article 90 EEC (now Article 106 TFEU), the Treaty of Amsterdam in 1997 introduced a new Article 16 to the EC Treaty (now Article 14 TFEU). This article attempted to instil a sound legal basis for the notion of *service publique* but was characterised by the French senate as a mere 'consolation prize' (Sauter 2008: 171).

Pursuant to Article 14 TFEU,[16] services of general economic interest occupy a place in the shared values of the Union as well as a role in promoting social and territorial cohesion. Protocol (No. 26) elaborates further on the shared values of the Union with respect to services of general economic interest within the meaning of Article 14 TFEU. Furthermore, in line with Article 14 TFEU, the notion of *service publique* is also reflected in Article 36 of the Charter on Fundamental Rights, which is headed under Title IV, Solidarity.[17] This Article does not create a new right but sets out the principle of respect by the Union for the access to services of general economic interest as provided for by national laws and practices.

The ratification of the Lisbon Treaty in 2009 – which has been viewed by some as being pro-solidarity, in contrast to its previous pro-economic focus with regard to European integration (Spiegel Online 2012; Ross 2009) – included a new legal basis for legislation that was added to Article 14 TFEU. This new addition reads as follows:

> The European Parliament and the Council, acting by means of regulations in accordance with the ordinary legislative procedure, shall establish these principles and set these conditions without prejudice to the competence of the Member States, in compliance with the Treaties, to provide, to commission and to fund such services.

Therefore, in addition to Article 106 (3) TFEU, which empowers the Commission to adopt Directives with respect to services of general economic interest, Article 14 TFEU concurrently provides a further legal basis for legislation based upon co-decisions of the European Parliament and of the Council. This situation has been regarded by Sauter (2008) as increasing Article 14 TFEU's ambiguity. Furthermore, dropping the reference to undistorted competition that was previously found in Article 3 (1) (g) EC,[18] and relocating it to Protocol (No. 27) on the Internal Market and Competition, has been interpreted as France's attempt to give the European Treaty a less 'Anglo-Saxon' flavour (Spiegel Online 2012). France's rejection of the Constitution in 2005 was for reasons that included a perceived lack of democratic accountability and the threat they considered it posed to the European social model (Civitas 2007).

6.4 Services of general interest – an endeavour in untangling chaos in the free-thinking zone

This section endeavours to capture a much broader and explanatory map by seeking further understandings through a conceptual lens posited by other disciplines. In doing so it is hoped that by letting go of bounded ways of thinking, and by treading through terrain that perhaps may not always be so familiar, one is in a better position to engage in 'practical reasonableness'[19] and hence better able to distinguish between sound and unsound practical thinking.

6.4.1 On economic versus non-economic services – gaining marketing insights

The term 'services of general interest' attempts to cover both economic and non-economic services (COM (2011) 900 final). While Community law does not define the term it is up to Member States to define and fulfil the missions of services of general interest. Community rules are applicable only in cases where the activities concerned are economic, and where trade between Member States is affected. The notion of services of general interest encompasses two major interrelated difficulties.

The first difficulty revolves around where the competence to define 'services of general economic interest' is actually placed. Because if on the one hand we have public authorities deciding upon their nature and scope, while on the other the Community frames the principles and conditions for their operation, it therefore follows that

> the definition created by Member States has to be in accordance with Community law. Thus, it seems that the two principles are in conflict with one another and it may be questioned where the competence to define actually is situated, at the Community level or at the Member State level – or somewhere in between.
>
> (Neergaard 2009: 37)

And matters become even more complex because of the fact that a distinction needs to be drawn between economic and non-economic services, since these are subject to different provisions of the treaty. This is where the second major difficulty lies, and it is the one which the author contends is the root of the problem. While the quest for legal clarity continues to grow,[20] 'the distinction between economic and non-economic activities has been dynamic and evolving, and in recent decades more and more activities have become of economic relevance' (COM (2003) 270 final: 14). These activities now extend into the remit of social services since 'a growing proportion of social services in the European Union now fall under the Community rules on competition and the internal market, insofar as they can be considered economic activities' (SEC (2008) 2179: 70). However, as the Commission highlights, this is not to be interpreted as a consequence of EU policies. Member States themselves opened up social services to the market in response to evolving needs – or, as the Commission puts it, in response to *national modernisation processes* (COM (2006) 177 final; SEC (2008) 2179).

The demarcation of services of general interest on the basis of economic versus non-economic characteristics is not a straightforward and clear-cut measure. The Commission itself has argued that while in practice 'in most cases of services of general interest this distinction does not create any problems, *however, the abstract definition of "non economic" service has proven to be very difficult*' (COM (2001) 598 final: 11, emphasis added). In effect, when the production of an *a priori* list of non-economic activities was requested, the Commission argued that because the range of services on the market evolved over time – and were subject to technological, economic and societal change – this made the production of a definitive list unfeasible, although a list of examples could be drawn up (COM (2001) 598 final: 11).

In essence, all this exposes the depth – or lack of it – of the 'concept' that we are dealing with when referring to the notion of services of general interest. What we are confronted with appears to be nothing but a blank label, with the attempt to insert meaning taken up at great length by jurisprudence – although the General Court was quite clear on the fact that there is no clear and precise regulatory definition of the concept of 'services of general economic interest' (Case T-289/03). This perhaps explains in part the inconsistencies and lack of clarity that surround the label. But if concepts are to be of any significance they must have clear operational definitions. In the absence of such, we become lost in intense deliberations that attempt to demarcate the lines of what appears to be an illusionary concept, we construe arbitrary doctrinal categories, and we act as if such classifications bear significance. But in the final analysis it is only a *label* that we confront – one that is devoid of true meaning.

In order to derive a better understanding the following discussion draws upon the knowledge gained by others – we need not reinvent the wheel. In this respect the concept of services will be examined from a marketing perspective for this is an area that has been researched deeply by marketing academia. Marketers are also very interested in understanding purchasing behaviour, how services and products are distinguished by consumers, and how they impact upon consumer behaviour. At no point in the marketing literature – despite the extensive research – do we come across such a thing that categorises the concept of 'services' on the basis of a dichotomous distinction, as in economic versus non-economic services.[21]

By way of introduction, the discipline of marketing has been described as a 'pervasive societal activity that goes considerably beyond the selling of toothpaste, soap and steel' (Kotler and Levy 1969: 10). For some, marketing bears negative connotations and is thought of as an immoral activity. Indeed Plato, Aristotle, Thomas Aquinas and other philosophers have variously described merchants as unproductive and acquisitive. But marketing goes far beyond such reasoning – 'it is the concept of sensitively serving and satisfying human needs' (Kotler and Levy 1969: 52). In fact, marketing offers great opportunities to expand our thinking and to apply knowledge that ties economic activity to a higher social purpose.

Marketing has been defined as, 'the effective management by an organisation of its exchange relations with its various markets and publics' (Kotler and Clarke1987: ix). The *exchange* paradigm sits at the very heart of the marketing discipline (Alderson 1957; Eggert and Ulaga 2002; Enis 1974; Houston 1987; Keith *et al.* 2004; Kotler 1972; McCarthy 1975). *Exchange* can be viewed as a process, and when successful all parties involved are better off. In general, three types of exchange have been identified (Bagozzi 1975: 32–9): *restricted exchange*, *generalised exchange* and *complex exchange*. The following is based on the discussion presented by Bagozzi (1975).

Restricted exchange involves the reciprocal exchange between two parties and encompasses two main characteristics. It is first concerned with maintaining equality in that no attempt to gain advantage at the expense of the other is made. Second, it must involve a *quid pro quo* notion; that is, acquiring something of value in exchange for something of value.[22]

Generalized exchange is characterised by univocal reciprocal relationships involving at least three actors, wherein 'the actors do not benefit each other directly but only indirectly' (Ekeh 1974: 48). In such an exchange each actor gives to another but receives from someone other than to whom they gave.

Complex exchange involves at least three parties organised in an interconnecting web of relationships with at least one social actor involved in a direct exchange. Such exchanges involve, for the most part, conscious systems of social and economic relationships.

It has been argued that covert coordination of generalised and complex exchanges may also manifest in relatively unconscious systems of social and economic relationships. This is akin to what Adam Smith referred to as the 'invisible hand' (Nord 1974) wherein such exchanges are driven in the pursuit of self-interest. However, this presents a departure from the exchange tradition developed by Levi-Strauss, who does not encompass an individualistic approach but one that is 'built on social, collectivist assumptions associated with generalised exchange' (Levi-Strauss 1969).

Various media of exchange – such as power, money and persuasion – serve as vehicles that control the link in the exchange process.[23] Products and services are also considered as media of exchange. Given the multivariate nature of the media in the exchange process, an intricate social system of behavioural relationships which go well beyond the visible exchange of products and money are involved. For exchanges hold meanings. 'Human behaviour is a conjunction of meaning with action and reaction' (Bagozzi 1975: 35). Behaviour is not arbitrary but purposeful and intentional. And the explanation for such behaviour lies 'in the social and psychological significance of the experiences, feelings and meanings of the parties in the exchange' (Bagozzi 1975: 36). Bagozzi identifies three main classes of meanings: *utilitarian, symbolic* and *mixed*.

The *utilitarian* meaning of exchange – also referred to as *economic* exchange – assumes that:

- human behaviour is driven by rational motives;
- individuals are driven to achieve maximum satisfaction in the exchange;
- individuals have access to complete information on the alternatives available in the exchange;
- exchanges are relatively free from external influences.

In essence, human behaviour is guided by that action which is perceived to lead to the most beneficial consequences.

The *symbolic* meaning of exchange acknowledges that '[p]eople buy things not only for what they can do, but also for what they mean' (Levy 1959). The *mixed* exchange process incorporates both utilitarian and symbolic meanings of exchanges, and thus may include the following assumptions:

- behaviour is not always rational;
- behaviour is motivated by tangible and intangible rewards, internal and external forces;
- individuals engage in utilitarian and symbolic exchanges involving psychological and social aspects;
- access to information may not always be complete but one proceeds in the best manner possible and at times one makes unconscious calculations of the costs and benefits that are linked to the exchange;
- although striving for maximisation of profits individuals often resort to less than optimum gains in the exchange;
- exchanges are subject to a host of individual and social constraints.

When it comes to social relationships – as in the case with individuals receiving '*free*' services – the question as to whether exchanges of the type mentioned above occur may arise. One may argue that the recipient of the service is not a buyer and that there is no exchange of values with the service provider. However, Bagozzi strongly asserts that exchanges in social relationships do indeed occur,

> but the exchange is not the simple *quid pro quo* notion characteristic of most economic exchanges. Rather, social marketing[24] relationships exhibit what may be called generalised or complex exchanges. They involve the symbolic transfer of both tangible and intangible entities, and they invoke various media to influence such exchanges.
> (Bagozzi 1975: 38)

Hence, as Bagozzi contends, there is 'a mutual exchange between society and the needy separated, in part, by the passage of time' (Bagozzi 1975: 39). Furthermore, it is noted that there are other tangible exchanges and forces that come into play and 'depending on their balance, give it stability or promote change' (Bagozzi 1975: 39).

As noted earlier, various media of exchange – such as products and services – control the link in the exchange process. The distinction between services and goods appear to be clear-cut in everyday parlance. However, the apparent disagreement that is found in the marketing literature on the characteristics that distinguish this core concept leaves it undefined. From the 1980s onwards four distinctive attributes characterising services were widely observable and used by marketers when designing marketing strategies: *intangibility*, *heterogeneity*, *inseparability* and *perishability*.

Services are *intangible* (Bateson 1977; Egdett and Parkinson 1993; McDougall and Snetsinger 1990; Vargo and Lusch 2004; Wright 1995). Although they can be purchased and sold they do not simply fall at one's feet. (Gummesson 1987). In essence, services cannot be seen, tasted, felt, heard or smelled before they are produced. In view of the intangible character of services, consumers are susceptible to relatively higher levels of uncertainty in their buying decisions and hence their overall perception forms an important aspect of the service experience. In effect, services have been viewed as processes – the outcome of which forms a critical part of the consumer experience (Gronroos 1998; Padgett and Allen 1997). When it comes to physical goods, evaluative judgements are generally easier to make given their visible attributes. In the case of services, consumers consume the outcome of the production process, 'the use of a service can be characterised as *process* consumption as opposed to *outcome* consumption' (Gronroos 1998: 322, emphasis added). This explains, in part, why marketers have been highly concerned with the issue of how consumers perceive services and how they evaluate service quality.

Services – in particular those with a high labour content – have been claimed to be *heterogeneous*. The provision of a service can be highly variable depending on who is providing the service, when it is provided, and who is involved in the service experience. Given the difficulty in obtaining a certain level of standardisation – since consistency of behaviour from service personnel is difficult to assure (Booms and Bitner 1981; Lovelock and Gummesson 2004; Palmer and Cole 1995) – what a service organisation may intend to deliver may be entirely different from what in effect the consumer ultimately receives (Parasuraman *et al.* 1985). In an effort to reduce as much as possible the risk associated with the heterogeneous character of services, prospective consumers may actively engage in inquiring on the level of service quality; while on the other hand service organisations may adopt various measures to ensure a consistent service quality offering.

Production and consumption of many services are *inseparable* (Carmen and Langeard 1980; Edgett and Parkinson 1993; Upah 1980). Very often the service provider is physically present when consumption takes place (Berry 1980). Hence, when it comes to service quality – and in contrast to the production of goods – this cannot be engineered at the manufacturing plant but rather takes place during the interaction between the client and the service provider (Lehtinen and Lehtinen 1982). As such, the consumer's input becomes a critical element in the quality of the service performance.

The *perishability* of services is linked to the difficulty associated with the issue of storage (Beaven and Scotti 1990; Edgett and Parkinson 1993; Vargo and Lusch 2004). In effect, the perishable character of services does not present much of a problem when there is a high demand for services. However, when demand fluctuates, a minimum service capacity still needs to be maintained even when during certain periods there is no demand.

Although the intangible, heterogeneous, inseparable and perishable characteristics of services have been widely acknowledged following a review by Moeller (2010), several criticisms have also been raised (Lovelock and Gummesson 2004; Lovelock and Wright 2001; Vargo and Lusch, 2004). Technology appears to have changed the scenario, and hence the generic attributes characterising services may not always be applicable. For instance, it has been argued that the inseparability of production and consumption, and their perishability, can be overcome by technology-based communications as occurs with interactive distance learning. On the intangible character of services it has been argued that many services include a combination of various tangible items, thus watering down the claim attached to their intangible nature. On the issue of heterogeneity it has been argued that various opportunities for standardisation exist – as, for instance, when banks provide an ATM service. However, rather than eliminating altogether the suitability of the widely held service characteristics, Moeller (2010) maintains and discusses their continued applicability –particularly when they are viewed in relation to the various stages of service provision.

Hill (1977) views services from a different angle. He places an emphasis on the aspect of change, which he contends is a crucial element when conceptualising the notion of services. In seeking to identify the characteristics that distinguish services, he begins by establishing the importance of transactions. The very fact that they can be transacted constitutes an important element. Thus, for instance, the midwife who would like to become a musician cannot just barter her knowledge and skills with a musician who fancies practising the profession of a midwife. Such 'services' are not transactable, and therefore cannot qualify as services in the sense discussed here. According to Hill the conceptualisation of services calls for two crucial elements. First, some change needs to be brought about; and second, the change is derived as a result of the activity of another economic unit. On the basis of these two key elements he defines services as 'a change in the condition of a person, or of a good belonging to some economic unit, which is brought about as the result of the activity of some other economic unit, with the prior agreement of the former person or economic unit' (Hill 1977: 318). For Hill there needs to be an impact/change on the consumer brought about by the producer. Otherwise, he argues, 'no service is actually provided. The mere performance of some activity is not enough if the consumer unit is not affected in some way' (Hill 1977: 318).

Levitt (1980) provides another interesting viewpoint on how services might be differentiated by identifying four levels in a product's offering. Rather than elaborating on the distinctive characteristics that demarcate goods and services he discusses how both can stand out in the commercial world, be differentiated, and hence be distinguishable. According to Levitt, '[t]here is no such thing as a commodity. All goods and services are differentiable' (Levitt 1980: 83). This, he claims, also holds true even in the case where commodities are extremely price sensitive, because 'nothing is exempt from other considerations, even when price competition rages' (Levitt 1980: 84).

In essence, standing at the core of any service or good is the generic product (the term 'product' here refers to both services and goods). However, it is the offered product that gets differentiated. The offered product is a complex cluster of value satisfactions which customers perceive as being capable of solving their problems or fulfilling their needs. Products are a combination of tangibles and intangibles. For instance, in a contract the product not only resides in its substantive and carefully packaged physical content but also in the proposer's reputation or image.

Thus, while the *generic* product represents the most basic elements that constitute it, customers never just buy the generic product. The minimal purchase conditions incorporate both the generic product and the *expected* product. The latter, for instance, reflects customers' expectations about price, delivery time, stock, terms and conditions, and so on. Therefore, failure to meet the minimal expectations of customers may reflect negatively on the generic product. It therefore follows that the generic product can only be sold if customers' wider expectations are met.

The product offering can go beyond customers' expectations by offering things they had never thought about. By providing such enhancements the product is augmented. But not all customers prefer an augmented product. Opting, for instance, for lower prices may be preferred. Beyond the augmented product lies the potential product. This reflects all that can be done in order to attract and maintain customer loyalty – budget and imagination being the limit. How products are perceived depends on customers. Thus, for instance, what may be perceived by one customer as an augmented product, may by another customer be perceived as expected. Levitt notes that differentiation does not only reside within the product itself but in the whole process that is involved in its delivery.

Given that customer perceptions play a vital role when it comes to service delivery the notion of service quality in the marketing literature has received considerable attention. Indeed, the ongoing trend towards the globalisation and internationalisation of services has stimulated research to examine the notion of service quality in an international context. A review of the literature exposes the complexities of this construct – in particular the challenges of measuring a consistent service across countries (Caruana *et al.* 1998; Morales and Ladhari 2010; Ueltschy *et al.* 2007; Zhang *et al.* 2008). Culture has been identified as a significant determinant that impacts individual attitudes, behavioural norms and value orientations (Cleveland and Laroche 2007; McCarthy and Hattwick 1992; Trompenaars and Hampden-Turner 1997). Different cultures may lead to significant differences across customers' and exchange partners' expectations of how service quality is perceived (Berthon *et al.* 1999; Caruana *et al.* 1998; Herbig and Genestre 1996; Smith and Reynolds 2001). Moreover, the impact of culture on perceived service quality appears to be an even greater factor when providing services than when providing goods – in view of the intangible nature of services, which require greater personal interaction between service provider and customer (Mattila 1999; Smith and Reynolds 2001).

One of the major issues when conducting cross-cultural research is contained within the 'abstract, ubiquitous, and complex character of the notion of culture' (Morales and Ladhari 2010). Nationality defined in terms of national borders is now claimed to be irrelevant in view of the complex influences operating at the global, regional, cross-national or sub-national (e.g. urban/rural) levels (Craig and Douglas 2006).

Given that service quality is a dynamic and multi-dimensional construct encompassing various factors (Gabbott and Hogg 1996), one of the fundamental concerns when conducting cross-national research is that of establishing equivalence; that is, whether the constructs being measured across nations/cultures are comparable in the sense that one can confirm their equivalence by way of their internal meaning, function and grouping, and in relation to other constructs (Caruana *et al.* 1998; Singh 1995; Smith and Reynolds 2001; Van der Vijver and Leung 1997). It has been argued that even when consumers appear to share similar expectations of a service, quality evaluations may differ (Winsted 1997). Some researchers have indeed questioned the universal applicability of measurement instruments, and in particular when it comes to service quality measures (Douglas and Nijssen 2003; Smith and Reynolds 2001; Ueltschy *et al.* 2004; Wong *et al.* 2003). Various studies have demonstrated how the relative importance of the various dimensions of service quality differs across countries (Kettinger *et al.* 1995; Yavas 1998). Differences in the number of dimensions may also relate to the nature of the service (Smith 2000; Smith and Reynolds 2001). In a study examining the service quality dimensions in the telecommunications industry in the USA and Germany, the five dimensional determinants established by the SERVQUAL instrument, i.e.:

- *reliability* (ability to perform the promised service dependably and accurately);
- *responsiveness* (willingness to help customers and provide a prompt service);
- *empathy* (providing customers with individualised attention);
- *assurance* (ability of employees to inspire trust and confidence);
- *tangibles* (appearance of service personnel, physical facilities, equipment and written material).

were found to be applicable in both the US and the German sample (Leison and Vance 2001). However, the study also revealed significant differences between the two countries when it came to assessing the relative importance of the service quality dimensions. In the US sample reliability was identified as the only important dimension; but for Germans, reliability, responsiveness and empathy constituted important dimensions. The authors contend that the findings have two major implications. First, that there needs to be a clear understanding of the culturally based different definitions of service quality; and second, any design and delivery of a service must focus on those dimensions that are perceived as being important, so as to ensure lower prices and improved quality.

6.4.2 The public interest – fiction or fact?

In 2009 the Lisbon Treaty came into force. For the first time the European Union incorporated and acknowledged into primary law the right to regional and local self-government (see Article 4 (2) TEU). The right to local self-government has, on several occasions, been emphasised in the various judgements of the European Court of Justice. Thus, in its case law concerning the 'in-house' doctrine, it is not appropriate to apply Community law concerning public procurement contracts in cases 'where a public authority performs tasks in the public interest for which it is responsible by its own administrative, technical and other means, without calling upon external entities' (Case C-458/03: para. 61).

When contracting authorities conclude a contract with a third party that is formally but not substantially independent from it, EU public procurement law is not applicable (Case C-107/98: para. 15). However, two conditions need to be met. The first condition is that of 'control', and necessitates that the contracting authority exercises a control that is similar to that which it exercises over its own departments. The second condition relates to 'the essential part of its activities', which necessitates that these be carried out with the controlling contracting authority or authorities. For the European Court of Justice

> the relationship between a public authority which is a contracting authority and its own departments is governed by considerations and requirements proper to the pursuit of objectives in the public interest. Any private capital investment in an undertaking, on the other hand, follows considerations proper to private interests and pursues objectives of a different kind.
> (Case C-26/03: para. 50)

Thus, in the Stadt Halle case, the Court held that a contracting authority could not exercise in-house control over an entity in whose capital it has a holding, (even a minority one), with one or more private undertakings (Case C-26/03: para. 49). Whether there actually exists a private holding in the capital of the company needs to be determined at the time of the award (Case C-26/03: para. 15, 20). The fact that the company's capital may be open to private investors is not enough to support the conclusion that the condition relating to control by the public authority is not satisfied; that is, unless there exists at the time of the award a real prospect that in the short term this will occur (Case C-573/07: para. 50, 51). However, when the in-house exception is applied, and if during the course of the contract private shareholders were to be permitted to hold capital in the company, this in effect would constitute the alteration of a fundamental condition of the contract and would therefore require the contract to be put out for competitive tender (Case C-573/07: para. 53).

In order to determine whether the contracting authority exercises a control similar to that which it exercises over its own departments, there must be a case of a power of decisive influence over both strategic objectives and significant decisions.[25] When a company enjoys a degree of independence it is not possible for the contracting authority to exercise a control similar to that which it exercises over its own departments (Case C-458/03: para. 67–70). Therefore, in order to examine whether or not the control condition satisfies the in-house doctrine, all legislative provisions and relevant circumstances need to be taken into account (Case C-458/03: para. 37, 69). In the Coditel case the Court reaffirmed that the 'possibility for public authorities to use their own resources to perform the public interest tasks conferred on them may be exercised in cooperation with other public authorities' (Case C-324/07: para. 49), and thus found that the decision-making bodies of the concessionaire in question were under the control of the public authorities and therefore strongly pointing in the direction of an in-house control. Both in the Coditel case and in the Sea Srl case, the Court considered that when the controlled company becomes market-oriented and gains a degree of independence this would render tenuous the control exercised by the contracting authority affiliated to it, and hence incompatible with the in-house doctrine (Case C-324/07: para. 36; Case C-573/07: para. 73). Thus, for example, in the Sea Srl case the Court held that when geographical scope does not extend beyond the territory of the shareholding public authorities, and when the activities are limited to the performance of the tasks of the controlling public authorities, these factors signify a lack of market orientation and therefore denote the existence of an in-house control Case (C-573/07: para. 76).

It is worth noting that the second condition – as laid down in the in-house doctrine – necessitates that the contracting company should carry out the essential part of its activities with the contracting authority. However, this does not prevent such companies from engaging with operators other than the contracting authority – as long as such relationships remain incidental to the contracting authority's core services (Case C-573/07: para. 63). This ensures that EU public procurement law remains applicable if the company becomes active in the market and therefore likely to be in competition with other undertakings (Case C-340/04: para. 60). Furthermore, Community law does not require public authorities to use any particular legal form to carry out their public service tasks on a joint basis (Case C-480/06: para. 47). The Court held that

> such cooperation between public authorities does not undermine the principal objective of the Community rules on public procurement, that is, the free movement of services and the opening-up of undistorted competition in all the Member States, where implementation of that cooperation is governed solely by considerations and requirements relating to the pursuit of objectives in the public interest and the principle of

> equal treatment of the persons concerned, referred to in Directive 92/50, is respected, so that no private undertaking is placed in a position of advantage vis-à-vis competitors.
>
> (Case C-480/06: para. 47)[26]

The 1876 *Munn* v. *Illinois* case (Case 94 US 113, 126) in the USA is the first example in that country of the Supreme Court becoming involved in a case in which a private enterprise was deemed to be 'affected with a public interest', and therefore subject to the need for public regulation. In the Munn case, the regulation by the State of Illinois of rates charged by grain storage elevators in Chicago was found by the Supreme Court to be a reasonable regulation of an enterprise 'affected with a public interest' (Keezer 1936: 200). This was because Chicago elevators were considered to occupy a strategic position that threatened a monopoly in an important area of agricultural commerce. Sixty years later (1936) the number of enterprises held to be *affected with a public interest* was noted to be on the increase. The following observations were made:

> It is practically impossible to generalize about characteristics of 'public interest' enterprises. *In determining what constitutes a public use, legislation cannot be depended upon.* Precedents are of little avail for what is today a public use may not be tomorrow, but each case must be decided upon its facts.
>
> (Keezer 1936: 201, emphasis added)

In a study concerning enterprises *affected with a public interest*, no meaning could be identified to the phrase '*affected with a public interest*' – although it was observed that the term was utilised simply as a way of saying 'that, balancing all factors – economic, ethical, practical convenience, etc. – the business ought to be regulated' (Leys and Perry 1959: 49–50).

The notion of 'the public interest' has been extensively employed and invoked in various situations. At times the public interest became the national interest. So, when President Eisenhower in 1954 ordered the Department of Defence not to testify before Congress on internal matters this was in the public interest; when in 1958 President Eisenhower ordered Marines into Lebanon this was in the national interest (Miller 1961).

In 2009, the UK's Information Commissioner published a report to Parliament in connection with the ministerial veto of the recommended disclosure of cabinet meeting minutes concerning military action against Iraq (Information Commissioner's Office 2009). Following the issuance of a Decision Notice on 19 February 2008, the Information Commissioner ordered the Cabinet Office to disclose copies of the minutes of a meeting in which the Attorney General's legal advice concerning military action against Iraq was considered and discussed. However, the government did not agree with this decision and appealed to the Information Tribunal. The tribunal, in a majority decision, upheld the Commissioner's earlier Decision Notice – but on 23 February 2009 the Secretary of State for Justice issued a 'veto' certificate overruling the Information Tribunal's decision and the minutes thus remained undisclosed.

> 7.3. The certificate confirmed that the Justice Secretary took the view that *the public interest* favoured the continued non-disclosure of the Minutes and therefore that there was no failure by the Cabinet Office to comply with its duty to disclose information on request.
> (Information Commissioner's Office 2009: 12, emphasis added)

In 1961, Professor Miller of George Washington University reported during a public law symposium the absence (and failure) to develop an acceptable and workable criteria by which the 'public interest' could be judged and evaluated (Miller 1961). Quoting Dimock (1958), he said: 'In the modern world even more than in the time of Adam Smith and John Stuart Mill our ship is rudderless unless we are able to attach workable meanings to such key concepts as the public interest.' Miller contended that content needed to be given to such concepts, and that an inquiry into the meaning of 'public interest' was urgently needed.

But even today the ship appears still to be rudderless. 'The public interest' is a notion that is much used and much abused. Making a distinction between private interests and collective/public interests has been described as difficult and perhaps impossible (Heywood 2004: 240–51). To some observers public interest theory is so sick as to be beyond resuscitation (Schubert 1962).

Popular usage of terms such as, 'the public interest', 'the general interest', 'the common interest', 'the common good', and 'the national interest', all incorporate the idea of a 'public interest' – and all share the fact that they originate from an abstract notion. Their usage makes it possible to validate, or otherwise, certain actions. The result is a high level of operational ambiguity meaning that 'those who have the power – the administrators, but also the judges and legislators – may act with a high degree of discretion when making decisions' (Schubert 1962). For simplification purposes such terms will be used interchangeably with the 'public interest'.[27]

When a particular decision or action is decided upon on the basis of somebody's interest, what in effect is such interest meant to be and how does one determine that it be regarded as important? The Greek word use for interest, '$συμφέρον$', means the benefit accruing to someone who pursues something, especially at an individual level. Thus, in general terms, the public interest connotes some public benefit or good. But we still remain ignorant of what this good is comprised of and who is in a position to define it? Sociologists have identified two sets of interests (Heywood 2004: 240). There are those who suggest that interests are '*felt*' – in which case they are subjective and can only be revealed by the individual claiming that they are the best judges of what is good for them. On the other hand, there are those who suggest that interests are '*real*', thus incorporating some objective element in which the public is not capable of identifying its own best interests because it is ignorant, deluded or has been manipulated in some way.

The problem of defining interests appears to run through the discussions that attempt to conceptualise the 'public interest'. Three major explications have been identified by Held (1970) – preponderance, common interest and unitary conceptions.

Preponderance accounts of the general interest represent the predominating interest in the community and thus attempts to put into effect policies that aim to satisfy the majority of individuals or increase aggregate individual satisfaction. That interest, however, may not be representative of the interest of all the participants in the community. Preponderance accounts may be the result of a preponderance of force, opinion, utility or preference of members (Kim Yoo Hwan 2006). In essence, this theory is based on Bentham's utilitarian school of thought – which holds that the formula for reaching the 'right' decisions in any given situation is to avoid pain and maximise happiness for the greatest number of people. This is a formula that we find in use today by economists who use arguments based on interpersonal comparison of utilities in order to solve problems of welfare economics (Hill and Bramley 1986; Musgrave 1966; Saks 1995). The *cost-benefit analysis* logic attempts to enumerate all the costs and benefits of a particular situation in order to provide the basis for decision-making. It can also manifest itself in techniques labelled *cost-effectiveness analysis* – which is utilised in cases where it is difficult to measure benefits in order to determine the public welfare. The preponderance approach can also manifest itself when public opinion is sought directly through the ballot box. Others argue that the public interest is equivalent to the preponderance of actual and potential interest groups in society (Dearlove and Saunders 1984).

Such aggregate views of public interest do not stand up to criticism. Preponderance accounts of public interest have the potential to render individual and minority groups extremely vulnerable (Feintuck 2004). This approach is unlikely to engage citizens in a process of dialogue to assist in bringing about a polity (Feintuck 2004). For instance, under the utilitarian logic potentially harmful clinical trials could be conducted without the consent of patients on the grounds that the data obtained might bring about the greatest happiness of the greatest number through the development of more effective medical products (Campbell 1975). Attempts that conceptualise the public interest under the utilitarian logic face ethical problems,

> namely that it is logically impossible to derive a normative judgement from a set of empirical statements. To the extent that the public interest is a normative notion, therefore, it cannot be based on empirical data about the capacity of the interests of some individuals or groups to outnumber, outweigh or overpower those of some other individuals or groups.
>
> (Held 1970, cited in Saks 1995: 42)

The 'public interest' as *common interest* bases judgements of the public interest on non-conflicting interests. This more radical notion of the public interest portrays the public as a collective entity with distinct common interests. Instead of viewing the public as a collection of individuals whose decisions would ultimately need to be taken from among conflicting interests or preference scales on the basis of aggregation accounts, we have the notion of the 'general will' being advanced (Heywood 2004). Jean-Jacques Rousseau is the leading figure who advanced this view in *The Social Contract*, wherein the *general will* was that 'which tends always to the preservation and welfare of the whole' (Heywood 2004: 242). He proposed that government be based on the general will so as to reflect the collective good of the community – benefiting all citizens as opposed to the particular and selfish wills of each cindividual. According to Rousseau, a clear distinction is drawn between general will and the selfish private will of each citizen, thus acknowledging that what is in the interests of an individual or group may not always be in the public interest; and that individual interests may conflict.

The Pareto criterion of optimality could be viewed as fitting in with the common interest approach. Under this criterion, 'the welfare of a group of individuals can only be considered to increase if at least one individual in the group is made better off without anyone being made worse off' (Sugden 1981, cited in Saks 1995: 43). Indeed, under this type of logic it would not be permissible to ameliorate the disadvantaged position of women pursuing careers in the medical sector since this would likely mean a reduction in the number of men occupying more prestigious medical roles (Saks 1995: 45). There are those who argue that even in the case of a truly *common good* the argument that this should override all other claims does not always hold (Benn and Peters 1959).

> For instance, the common good of defence might not be a good enough reason for uprooting a hundred families to make a rocket range. It might be better to compromise for the benefit of the few, and make do with a somewhat less efficient range elsewhere.
> (Benn and Peters 1959: 272)

It appears that one of the main problems with the common interest approach is that the notion of the general will represents the will of the people were they to act selflessly. But because selfishness continues to persist, the common interest can never be revealed (Heywood 2004).

Unitary conceptions of the public interest assert a frank normative position for the public interest. Claims under this scheme are perceived as moral ones that enable moral judgements to be made in terms of a unitary and coherent system of values that guides decision-making in society. Definitions falling within this scheme include those provided by Plato, Aristotle, Augustine, Aquinas and Hegel. Despite the distinctions that can be drawn from their work it has been noted that all share the belief that what is good for the individual/group is compatible with the good of all (Held 1970). According to Saks (1995) it is important to note that arrangements which serve the public interest cannot validly conflict with individual claims of interest; he also contends that the communist system as explicated by Marx brings out clearly this normative unitary view. As such, Saks appears to find the collateral resting on the basis that 'the real interests of both individuals and the public as a whole coalesced, albeit in a communist system in which the free development of each would be the condition for the free development of all' (Saks 1995: 37). He therefore expresses grave doubts about the relevance of such conceptions of the public interest – and in particular the idea that validly conflicting interests are unjustified under this scheme. Such a situation he describes as alien to liberal-democratic countries. Others argue that a unitary model of the public interest can maintain validity only if based on democratic and constitutional claims (Feintuck 2004). It is thus claimed that there is significant scope for such a normative conception – particularly when the public interest is linked to a notion of citizenship ascribing it with the potential of 'imposing limits on the power of society's dominant groups' (Feintuck 2004: 30). And in doing so it acts as a force that reaffirms the overall liberal-democratic settlement (Feintuck 2004).

Both preponderance and common interest accounts of the public interest appear to be more concerned with where the public interest resides, rather than explaining the process that exposes which values are to be protected (Feintuck 2004). It has also been noted that they fail to take into consideration the interests of future generations (Held 1970). On the other hand, and despite the various criticisms, there appears to be a general consensus that *unitary* conceptions of the public interest have the virtue of underlining the normative content (Feintuck 2004; Held 1970; Saks 1995). Thus there is no reason why we should abstain from exploring further the force of the arguments contained in this unitary approach, by appealing to natural law as advocated by John Finnis (2011).

To *favour and foster the common good in one's community* has been identified as one of the basic requirements, according to Finnis.[28] Its reach is complex and manifold. But, as Finnis argues, before we can proceed in our discussion we need first to obtain an understanding of some of the complexities that the community or society entails.[29] For what, in effect, does the *community* involve?

Community is about relationships and interactions; it is an ongoing state of affairs. According to Finnis there are four basic ways or orders that unify such human relationships/interactions. The orders have no hierarchy or value of importance and are only a convenient way of assembling the complexity of human community. They are as follows:

1   First order – appertains to the physical and biological order and comprises the unity of order as studied by the 'natural sciences'. The example given is that of the listener hearing the sounds made by the lecturer.
2   Second order – appertains to the unity of intelligence, a unity of order as studied, for instance, in logic and epistemology. The example given is when the listener's understanding is in line with that of the lecturer, even if this leads to disagreement.
3   Third order – appertains to the unity of culture: shared language, common technology, techniques, etc.

4   Fourth order – appertains to the unity of common action. The example given is that of the lecturer who devotes part of his/her life to trying to communicate knowledge. Likewise, the listener is committed to devoting part of his/her life to acquiring knowledge from another person. Consequently, part of the unity in human community becomes the unity of common action.

The unity of common action in the fourth order is what we are concerned with here since it finds its place with the subject matter relating to our discussion of the public interest. The unity of common action further explains the common good in three senses. In the first sense, 'basic goods'[30] – which Finnis identifies as life, knowledge, play, aesthetic experience, sociability (friendship), practical reasonableness and religion – are goods which are common to each and every person, and therefore are in themselves a 'common good': common insofar as they can be participated in an infinite number of ways, by an infinite number of people, and on an infinite variety of occasions. In another sense, according to Finnis, there is the common good of the political community.[31] And, in a third sense, the common good is defined as

> a set of conditions which enables the members of a community to attain for themselves reasonable objectives, or to realise reasonably for themselves the value(s), for the sake of which they have reason to collaborate with each other (positively and/or negatively) in a community.
>
> (Finnis 2011: 155)

It is in this third sense that Finnis contends that the common good 'is a justified meaning of the phrases, "the general welfare" or "*the public interest*"' (Finnis 2011: 156, emphasis added). And the common good of the political community 'thus explains the availability and relevance of a common good in the third sense' (Finnis 2011: 156). The set of conditions that need to be obtained if each and every member of the community is to attain his/her own objectives relate to justice, authority and law. Justice, authority and law comprise the content of the common good of the political community 'that ought to (but in practice cannot yet) assume some though not all of the present justified functions and aspects of the political communities' (Finnis 2011: 156).

Thus, the common good under discussion should not be misinterpreted as an aggregative concept: such as that conceived by utilitarianism.[32] Utilitarian logic assigns the principles of autonomy, freedom, right and justice with secondary importance. The common good that we are concerned with here refers to the interdependent and harmonious flourishing or fulfilment of each individual in the community – which can only be made possible through cooperation and coordination within communities. Given the nature and condition of human existence, human nature alone cannot be self-sufficient, and it is precisely due to this fact that human flourishing can only be brought about through community coordination and cooperation. It is only in a very limited sense that the State comes before the individual. The pluralist State is, after all, comprised of free and equal citizens (individuals). The primary aim of both the individual and of the State is, in fact, the flourishing of each *individual* in the community.

6.5 Concluding remarks

The message that one draws from the in-house doctrine is loud and clear. It assumes and draws a clear line of demarcation between 'public interest' tasks and 'private interest' tasks. Accordingly, public authorities perform tasks in the public interest unil the point that private interests become involved. As soon as this happens the notion of the public interest becomes deprived of meaning and fades into insignificance; that is, unless it passes the scrutiny test and therefore becomes subject to the conditions set out in Article 106 (2) TFEU in order to ensure that the effective performance of the general interest task prevails.

But on what grounds does this public interest, this *common stock*, once available to all, get cut short. On what grounds does it lose the very core of its nature and become subject to the dictating forces of the market? From what force do these principles derive so as to dictate and circumscribe the range of this common stock? Is it on the basis of the utilitarian logic? Indeed, Europe appears to hold on to aggregative conceptions of the common good and it is this aggregative conception that infuses the public interest function.

Given that 'the authority of rulers derives from their opportunity to foster the common good, and a fair balance of benefits and burdens within a community is an important aspect of that common good' (Finnis 2011: 263), can the argument hold that market forces foster a better common good? And when we speak of values and the sharing of values, what values are we sharing when it comes to services of general economic interest? Are these not the values that are grounded in the economic belief in the efficacy of competitive market forces? It is worth recalling that the theories on which the market economy is based leave much unsaid.[33] What values do we share when Community actions are grounded on illusionary dichotomous beliefs based on economic versus non-economic services of general interest? Indeed, we appear to cherish hollow values that embrace the status quo, values that reinforce existing inequalities in power relationships. We need only look at the figures to see how poverty and other inequalities feature across Europe.[34] These are the signs and symptoms that chink and tear away at Europe's economic fabric, and serve to consolidate the size of the gap that thwarts European integration aims.

Europe's attempts to close the gap – by way of injecting a notion of services of general interest – have been mainly unsuccessful. The provision of services revolves around the conduct of transactions.[35] 'The mere performance of some activity is not enough if the consumer unit is not affected in some way' (Hill 1977: 318), and 'whatever the producer of the service does [,] must impinge directly on the consumer in such a way as to change the condition of the latter. Otherwise, no service is actually provided' (Hill 1977: 318). It is from this point that we can proceed further with the argument.

When it comes to assessing the impact of services of general economic interest across the EU – on the basis of empirical research concerning the network industries and Commission statements[36] – we cannot derive any conclusive evidence that enables us to comfortably ascertain that services of general economic interest are making 'an important contribution to the overall competitiveness of ... European industry and to economic, social and territorial cohesion' (European Commission 2001/C 17/04: para. 8), and that '*[a]s users of these services*, European citizens *have come to expect high quality services* at affordable prices' (European Commission 2001/C 17/04: para. 8, emphasis added). The process of production cannot be mistaken as the *de facto exchange* because the actual impact that services of general economic interest are exerting in the exchange process[37] is not straightforward or clear. When it comes to service quality – and as has been revealed through the marketing literature – perceptions vary across cultures. Moreover, measuring service quality across cultures has proved to be a major difficulty in view of the failure to come up with measures that are capable of establishing cross-cultural equivalence. Furthermore, we need also to bear in mind that as Bagozzi (1975) contends, social relationships do not simply unfold in a *quid pro quo* approach – as occurs in the *restricted* exchange paradigm involving the reciprocal exchange between *two parties*. The process of exchange that occurs in social relationships is much more complex. It involves more than two social actors and invokes various media.

Public procurement can act as one of those media, and therefore when embarking upon public policy, public procurement needs to be perceived within this complex social exchange paradigm. Such logic makes it possible to come up with a definition – one that defines public procurement contracts as '[a] special category of contracts wherein one of the parties represents the public interest and is manifest through complex exchanges that occur in social relationships and which in the process are separated in part by the passage of time'.[38] Thus, in social exchanges a mixture of forces come into play – and depending on their balance can either favour and promote change or embrace the status quo. When it comes to public procurement – insofar as Community action remains primarily guided by values that are grounded upon the economic belief in the efficacy of competitive market forces – the status quo will be maintained. Should we not therefore be directed by a public interest function that infuses values that are rooted in the *community*[39] – such as those that foster the common good of the community wherein the participation of all and the flourishing of all becomes the primary and superseding objective?

Services of general interest reflect values that convey special meanings for each and every Member State. They reflect the evolution of the country's identity construction through the passage of time, thus translating the role and manner by which the country needs to operate. They provide Member States with distinctive features that define Europe.[40] It is a known fact that complete reliance on the market to ensure the delivery of socially desirable objectives is insufficient.[41] When poverty strikes, health problems emerge, unemployment pops up, substance addiction creeps in, and family and housing problems

160 *Closing the gap*

arise – the inherent structural nature of market forces are not directed to deal with such matters. This is why Member States have a vital task in the delivery of high quality services of general interest, and the public sector plays a major role in this respect through regulation and government spending. Services of general interest bear a direct impact upon the life of each and every individual citizen. They

> underpin human dignity and guarantee the universal right to social justice and to full respect of fundamental rights, as set out in the Charter of Fundamental Rights and in international commitments such as the revised European Social Charter and the Universal Declaration of Human Rights. They help to ensure the effective exercise of citizenship.
> (Opinion of the European Economic and Social Committee, 2007/C 161/22 2007: para. 2.1)

Picard (1998: 94) argues that the fundamental right to freedom is losing its meaning, and that its inherent content is being gradually eroded. Services of general economic interest seek first and foremost to meet the ends of Europe's *economic* constitution. This comes at the expense of freedom – and according to *service publique* such freedom was initially utilised to constitute and institute the State with the aim of guaranteeing the very fundamental right to freedom for *its* members. 'Once freedom is on the way to losing its initial (and true) meaning, there is no longer any principle of an intellectual, moral, or political nature left to contain the public sphere' (Picard 1998: 94).

This matter goes far beyond seeking justification for how services of general interest can be demarcated. It is a question that needs to open the floor for discussion of the role of the State in society.

Notes

1 On various occasions in its plethora of communications relating to services of general interest, the Commission has made a distinction between 'services of general interest' and 'public service' – and has noted upon the latter's ambiguity (COM (2011) 900 final: 4). The author contends to the contrary in that the ambiguity is specifically located with the term 'services of general interest' rather than with the term 'public service' – as the discussion in this chapter hopes to reveal. Indeed, it is understood that usage of the term 'public service' can potentially tighten manoeuvring space at the supranational level. However, for the sake of clarity the discussion in this chapter will retain usage of the term 'services of general interest' and the sub-categories related to this term as utilised by the Commission and which will be further elaborated upon as we proceed with the discussion.

2 Over the years the definition attached to the term 'services of general interest' have undergone various modifications. In one of its more recent communications the European Commission defined the term as follows:

> Services of General Interest (SGI) are services that public authorities of the Member States classify as being of general interest and, therefore, subject to specific public service obligations (PSO). The term covers both economic activities

... and non-economic services. The latter are not subject to specific EU legislation and are not covered by the internal market and competition rules of the Treaty. Some aspects of how these services are organised may be subject to other general Treaty rules, such as the principle of non-discrimination.

(COM (2011) 900 final: 3)

3 This term is used interchangeably to capture the various forms of communications by the European Commission including: opinions, reports, guidelines, working documents, Green Papers and White Papers. It has been observed that for the various forms of documentation – be it, for example, communications, notices or guidelines – the Commission does not necessarily identify with a different type of document but uses them interchangeably (Cosma and Whish 2003).
4 See COM (2000) 580 final; Communication from the Commission, Services of general interest (2001/C 17/04); COM (2001) 598 final; COM (2002) 280 final; COM (2002) 636 final; COM (2003) 270 final; COM (2004) 374 final; COM (2006) 177 final; COM (2007) 725 final; SEC (2008) 2179; SEC (2010) 1284; COM (2011) 146 final; COM (2011) 900 final; Commission Decision of 20 December 2011 on the application of Article 106 (2) of the Treaty of the Functioning of the European Union to State aid in the form of public service compensation granted to certain undertakings entrusted with the operation of services of general economic interest (2012/21/EU).
5 On 1 December 2009 the Court of First Instance was renamed the General Court.
6 Hofman argues that the term 'soft law' is not precise in view of the substantial indirect legal effects of such communications – which the author refers to as administrative guidelines (Hofmann 2006).
7 Hofmann notes that the principle of legal certainty is a more general legal principle cited in cases, and as a fundamental expression of the rule of law it is strongly protected by the ECJ.
8 Following a quantitative analysis of the use of soft law instruments in ECJ and CFI competition case law covering the period 2000–06, it transpired that the European Court was making increased use of such instruments (Ştefan 2008).
9 Article 90 (2) EEC has now become Article 106 (2) TFEU.
10 For an in-depth examination of Article 106 TFEU see, for example, Sauter and Schepel (2009: 142–9), Gareth (2009: 51–67) and Jones and Suffrin (2010: 572–620).
11 To this effect see the discussion in Chapter 4, section 4.5, 'The liberalisation of the network industries as an illustration of the European Union's overriding and unconditional attitude towards the Single Market project'.
12 Articles 2 and 3 EEC were replaced by Articles 2 and 3 EC. Article 2 EC has now been repealed and replaced, in substance, by Article 3 TEU. Article 3 EC para. 1 has now been repealed and replaced, in substance, by Articles 3–6 TFEU.
13 Article 90 (1) EEC has now become Article 106 (1) TFEU.
14 Article 86 EEC has now become Article 102 TFEU.
15 That Member States have not retained complete sovereignty in relation to the creation of legal monopolies was also noted by Edward and Hoskins (1995).
16 Article 14 TFEU headed under Part One – Principles, Title II – Provisions having general application of the Treaty on the Functioning of the European Union, states as follows:

> Without prejudice to Article 4 of the Treaty on European Union or to Articles 93, 106 and 107 of this Treaty, and given the place occupied by services of general economic interest in the shared values of the Union as well as their role in promoting social and territorial cohesion, the Union and the Member States, each within their respective powers and within the scope of application of the Treaties, shall take care that such services operate on the basis of principles and conditions, particularly economic and financial conditions, which enable them to fulfil their

missions. The European Parliament and the Council, acting by means of regulations in accordance with the ordinary legislative procedure, shall establish these principles and set these conditions without prejudice to the competence of Member States, in compliance with the Treaties, to provide, to commission and to fund such services.

17 Article 36 of the Charter of Fundamental Rights of the European Union on 'Access to services of general economic interest' reads as follows: 'The Union recognises and respects access to services of general economic interest as provided for in national laws and practices, in accordance with the Treaties, in order to promote the social and territorial cohesion of the Union.'

18 Article 3 EC para. 1 has now been repealed and replaced, in substance, by Articles 3–6 TFEU.

19 On practical reasonableness refer to the discussion in Chapter 3, more specifically section 5.4.1, 'Morality in natural law theory' and section 5.4.2, 'Practical reasonableness – distinguishing sound from unsound practical thinking'.

20 Refer to endnote 4 above.

21 It is worth acknowledging the fact that the notion of 'public services' in French public law provides a clear distinction between

> public services fulfilling sovereign functions and public services providing public goods or market public services or between constitutional public services and the others.... That notion, following a French tradition that dates back well before the Revolution, although it now operates by different means and in a different context, very definitely helps to reinforce the role and the legitimacy of central authority and the State as compared with those of private initiative and freedom.
>
> (Picard 1998: 92)

22 It is worth noting the similarities of the logic contained in the *restricted exchange* approach and that adopted by the Court in cases involving the financing of services of general economic interest. For example, the notion of maintaining equality was adopted in the *Sociedade Independente de Comunicação SA v. Commission of the European Communities* case (Case T-46/97). In its analysis the Court examined the question of whether a private operator of comparable size to the public body would have carried out the operation in question under the same conditions. The *quid pro quo* logic was adopted by Mr Advocate General Jacobs in *Ministère de l'Économie, des Finances et de l'Industrie v. GEMO SA* (Case C-126/01). The distinction between restricted and generalised exchange was first made by anthropologist Levi-Strauss (1969). An extended critical analysis of restricted and generalised exchange may be found in Ekeh (1974).

23 In effect, public procurement may be considered as another example which serves as the medium in the exchange process.

24 On the notion of social marketing, Bagozzi notes that this does not refer to the mere use or application of marketing techniques or skills. Rather, its meaning is to be found in the unique problems that it confronts – problems which may cut through subject matter or disciplines. In this respect Bagozzi proceeds from the observations made by Popper, a philosopher of science, who noted:

> The belief that there is such a thing as physics, or biology, or archaeology, and that these 'studies' or 'disciplines' are distinguishable by the subject matter which they investigate, appears to me to be a residue from the time when one believed that a theory had to proceed from a definition of its own subject matter. But subject matter, or kinds of things, do not, I hold, constitute a basis for distinguishing disciplines. Disciplines are distinguished partly for historical reasons and reasons of administrative convenience (such as the organisation of teaching and of appointments), and partly because the theories which we construct to solve our

problems have a tendency to grow into unified systems. But all this classification and distinction is a comparatively unimportant and superficial affair. We are not students of some subject matter but students of problems. And problems may cut right across the borders of any subject matter or discipline.

(Popper 1963: 67)

25 Case C-324/07, *Coditel Brabant SA* v. *Commune d'Uccle and Région de Bruxelles-Capitale* para. 28, paraphrasing Case C-458/03, Case C-458/03. *Parking Brixen GmbH* v. *Gemeinde Brixen and Stadtwerke Brixen AG*: para. 36.
26 The Court also made reference to the following case law: Case C-26/03: para. 50, 51).
27 To this effect the following is worth highlighting:

> The General Court in Case T-289/03 at paragraph 178 noted, '... services of general economic interest are distinguished from services in the private interest, even though that interest may be more or less collective or be recognised by the State as legitimate or beneficial ... the general or public interest on which the Member State relies must not be reduced to the need to subject the market concerned to certain rules or the commercial activity of the operators concerned to authorisation by the State.
> (Case T-289/03)

Further, Neergaard (2009) contends that '[t]he element "general" may be considered to indicate the public's interest that the service in question is provided. Page finds that the terms "general interest" and "public interest" are identical' (Page 1982).
28 To this effect see the discussion in Chapter 5, section 5.4.2, 'Practical reasonableness – distinguishing sound from unsound practical thinking'.
29 According to Finnis (2011: 135), what could be said of a *community* could equally be said of *society*.
30 To this effect see the discussion in Chapter 5, section 5.4.3, 'Dignity as the basic moral premise'.
31 The political community refers to the complete community, 'an all-round association in which would be co-ordinated the initiatives and activities of individuals, of families, and of the vast network of intermediate associations' (Finnis 2011: 147). Such a community need not necessarily be confined to the State. According to Finnis (2011: 150), '[t]here is no reason to deny the good of international community in the fourth order'. Integral to personal development is 'both individual self-direction and community with others in family, friendship, work and play' (Finnis 2011: 147).
32 To this effect see the discussion in Chapter 1, section 1.3.1 'Utilitarianism'.
33 In this respect see the discussion in Chapter 4, in particular section 4.3, 'The theory of comparative advantage – a general idea'.
34 Nearly one in seven people in the EU are at risk of poverty. To this effect see the discussion in Chapter 5, in particular section 5.2, 'Poverty across the EU – a snapshot'.
35 See section 6.4.1, 'On economic versus non-economic services – gaining marketing insights on the nature of services'.
36 See (SEC (2007) 1024 final). See also Chapter 4, section 4.5, 'The liberalisation of the network industries as an illustration of the European Union's overriding and unconditional attitude towards the Single Market project'.
37 On the process of exchange see the discussion in section 6.4.1, 'On economic versus non-economic services – gaining marketing insights on the nature of services'.
38 This definition, coined by the author, draws largely from the *marketing* and *public interest* insights discussed in this book.
39 According to Finnis (2011), what could be said of a *community* could equally be said of *society*. The same position is adopted here.
40 In the Cannes European Council of 1995, the Heads of State and Government acknowledged that services of general interest form part of the set of values shared by all countries that help define Europe (Cannes Presidency Conclusions 1995).

41 'Market forces produce a better allocation of resources and greater effectiveness in the supply of services, the principal beneficiary being the consumer, who gets better quality at a lower price. However, these mechanisms sometimes have their limits; as a result the potential benefits might not extend to the entire population and the objective of promoting social and territorial cohesion may not be attained.' (COM (96) 443: 5). 'The market, left to itself, does a good job of supplying many services of general interest for many people. However, sometimes markets fail to deliver socially desirable objectives and, as a result, services are underprovided by the market' (COM (2001) 598 final: 3).

References

Alderson, W., 1957. *Marketing Behaviour and Executive Action*. Homewood, IL: Irwin.

Bagozzi, R.P. 1975, 'Marketing as Exchange' in *The Journal of Marketing*, vol. 39, no. 4, pp. 32–39.

Bateson, J.E.G., 1977. *Do we need service marketing?* Cambridge, MA: Marketing Science Institute.

Beaven, M.H. and Scotti, D.J., 1990. 'Service-oriented thinking and its implications for the marketing mix' in *Journal of Services Marketing*, vol. 4, no. 4, pp. 5–19.

Benn, S. and Peters, R., 1959. *Social Principles and the Democratic State*. London: Allen & Unwin.

Berry, L.L., 1980. 'Service marketing is different' in *Business*, vol. 30, no. 3, p. 25.

Berthon, P., Pitt, L., Katikeas, C.S. and Berthon, J.P., 1999. 'Executive insights: virtual services go international: international service in the marketspace' in *Journal of International Marketing*, vol. 7, no. 3, pp. 84–105.

Booms, B.H. and Bitner, M.J., 1981. 'Marketing Strategies and Organization Structures for Services Firms' in Donnelly, J. and George, W. (eds), *Marketing of Services*. Chicago: American Marketing, pp. 47–51.

Campbell, A.V., 1975. *Moral Dilemmas in Medicine*. Edinburgh: Churchill Livingstone.

Carmen, J.M. and Langeard, E., 1980. 'Growth Strategies of Service Firms' in *Strategic Management Journal*, vol. 1 (January–March), pp. 7–22.

Caruana, A., Ramaseshan, B., Ewing, M.T. and Rouhani, F., 1998. 'Expectations about management consultancy services: testing the assumption of equivalence across Australian and Singaporean firms' in *Journal of Professional Services Marketing*, vol. 18, no. 1, pp. 1–10.

Civitas, E.F., 2007. *The Treaty of Lisbon (2007)*. Available at: www.civitas.org.uk/eufacts/FSTREAT/TR6.htm.

Cleveland, M. and Laroche, M., 2007. 'Acculturation to the global consumer culture: scale development and research paradigm' in *Journal of Business Research*, vol. 60, pp. 249–59.

Cosma, H. and Whish, R., 2003. 'Soft Law in the Field of EU Competition Policy' in *European Business*, vol. 14.

Craig, C.S. and Douglas, S.P., 2006. 'Beyond national culture: implications of cultural dynamics for consumer research' in *International Marketing Review*, vol. 23, no. 3, pp. 322–42.

Dearlove, J. and Saunders, P., 1984. *Introduction to British Politics*. Cambrdige: Polity Press.

Dimock, M.E., 1958. *Philosophy of Administration toward creative* growth. Harper.

Douglas, S.P. and Nijssen, E.J., 2003. 'On the use of borrowed scales in cross-national research: a cautionary note' in *International Marketing Review*, vol. 20, no. 6, pp. 621–42.

Edgett, S. and Parkinson, S., 1993. 'Marketing for Service Industries in *The Services Industries Journal*, vol. 13, no. 3, pp. 19–39.

Edward, D. and Hoskins, S., 1995. 'Art. 90: Deregulation and EC Law. Reflections Arising from the XVI FIDE Conference 1995' in *Common Market Law Review*, vol. 32, p. 157.

Eggert, A. and Ulaga, W., 2002. *Customer perceived value: A substitute for satisfaction in business markets?* United Kingdom, Santa Barbara: Emerald Group Publishing Limited.

Ekeh, P.P., 1974. *Social Exchange Theory: The Two Traditions.* Cambridge, Mass: Harvard University Press.

Enis, B.M., 1974. *Markeing Principles.* Pacific Palisades, California: Good Year Publishing Co.

Feintuck, M., 2004. *'The Public Interest' in Regulation.* Oxford: Oxford University Press.

Finnis, J., 2011. *Natural Law and Natural Rights*, 2nd edition. Oxford: Oxford University Press.

Gabbott, M. and Hogg, G., 1996. 'The glory of stories: using critical incidents to understand service evaluation in the primary healthcare context in *Journal of Marketing Management*, vol. 12, no. 6, pp. 493–503.

Gareth, D., 2009. *What does Article 86 actually do?* Netherlands: TMC Asser Press.

Gronroos, C., 1998. *Marketing services: the case of a missing product.* United Kingdom, Santa Barbara: Emerald Group Publishing Limited.

Gummesson, E., 1987. 'Lip service – a neglected area in service marketing' in *Journal of Services Marketing*, vol. 1, no. 1 (1987), pp. 19–23.

Held, V., 1970. *The Public Interest and Individual Interests.* New York: Basic Books.

Herbig, P. and Genestre, A., 1996. 'An examination of the cross cultural differences in service quality: the example of Mexico and the USA in *Journal of Consumer Marketing*, vol. 13, no. 3, pp. 43–53.

Heywood, A., 2004. *Political Theory, An Introduction*, 3rd edition. New York: Palgrave Macmillan.

Hill, M. and Bramley, G., 1986. *Analysing Social Policy.* Oxford: Basil Blackwell.

Hill, T.P., 1977. 'On goods and services' in *Review of Income and Wealth*, vol. 23, no. 4, p. 315.

Hofmann, H.C.H., 2006. 'Negotiated and Non-Negotiated Administrative Rule-Making: The Example of EC Competition Policy' in *Common Market Law Review*, vol. 43, pp. 153–78.

Houston, F.S., 1987. 'Marketing and Exchange' in *Journal of Marketing*, vol. 51 (October), pp. 3–18.

Information Commissioner's Office, 2009. *Ministerial veto on disclosure of Cabinet minutes concerning military action against Iraq – Information Commissioner's Report to Parliament, 10 June, 2009.* London: The Stationery Office.

Jones, A. and Sufrin, B., 2010. *EU Competition Law: Text, Cases & Materials.* Oxford: Oxford University Press.

Keezer, D.M., 1936. 'Some questions involved in the application of the "Public Interest" Doctrine – Bar Briefs' in *Michigan Law Review*, vol. 12.

Keith, J.E., Lee, D.J. and Lee, R.G., 2004. 'The effect of relational exchange between the service provider and the customer on the customer's perception of value' in *Journal of Relationship Marketing*, vol. 3, no. 1, pp. 3–33.

Kettinger, W.J., Lee, C.C. and Lee, S., 1995. 'Global measures of information service quality: a cross-national study' in *Decision Sciences*, vol. 26, no. 5 (September–October), pp. 569–88.

Kim, Y.H., 2006. 'The Anglo-American Concept of Public Interest and Its Legal Argumentation: Paradigm Shift and Confrontation of Administrative Law' in *Seoul Law Journal*, vol. 55.

Kotler, P., 1972. 'A generic concept of marketing' in *Journal of Marketing*, vol. 36 (April), pp. 46–54.

Kotler, P. and Clarke, R.N., 1987. *Marketing for Health Care Organisations*. Englewood Cliffs, NJ: Prentice-Hall.

Kotler, P. and Levy, S.J., 1969. 'Broadening the Concept of Marketing' in *Journal of Marketing*, vol. 33, no. 1, pp. 10–15.

Lehtinen, U. and Lehtinen, J.R., 1982. *(1982),* 'Service Quality: A Study of Quality Dimensions', unpublished working paper. Helsinki: Service Management Institute, Finland OY.

Leison, B. and Vance, C., 2001. 'Cross-national assessment of service quality in telecommunications' in *Managing Service Quality*, vol. 11, no. 5, pp. 307–17.

Levi-Strauss, C., 1969. *The Elementary Structure of Kinship*. Boston: Beacon Press.

Levitt, T., 1980. 'Marketing success through differentiation of anything', Graduate School of Business Administration, Harvard University, pp. 83–91.

Levy, S.J., 1959. 'Symbols for sale' in *Harvard Business Review*, vol. 37 (July–August), pp. 117–19.

Leys, W.A.R. and Perry, C.M. 1959. *Philosophy and the Public interest*. Chicago: Committee to Advance Original Work in Philosophy.

Lovelock, C. and Gummesson, E., 2004. 'Whither service marketing? In search of a new paradigm and fresh perspective' in *Journal of Service Research*, vol. 7, no. 1, pp. 20–41.

Lovelock, C. and Wright, L., 2001. *Principles of Service Marketing and Management*. Upper Saddle River, NJ: Prentice-Hall.

Mattila, A.S., 1999. 'The role of culture and purchase motivation in service encounter motivations' in *Journal of Services Marketing*, vol. 13, no. 4–5, pp. 376–89.

McCarthy, E.J., 1975. *Basic marketing*. Homewood, IL: Richard D. Irwin.

McCarthy, J.A. and Hattwick, P.M., 1992. 'Cultural value orientations: a comparison of magazine advertisements from the US and Mexico' in *Advances in Consumer Research*, vol. 19, pp. 34–8.

McDougall, G.H.G. and Snetsinger, D.W., 1990. 'The intangibility of services: measurement and competitive perspectives' in *Journal of Services Marketing*, vol. 4, no. 4, pp. 27–40.

Miller, A.S., 1961. 'Fundamental Concepts of Public Law Symposium, No. 1, "Foreword: The Public Interest Undefined"' in *Journal of Public Law*, vol. 10.

Moeller, S., 2010. 'Characteristics of services – a new approach uncovers their value' in *The Journal of Services Marketing*, vol. 24, no. 5, pp. 359–68.

Morales, M. and Ladhari, R., 2010. 'Comparative cross-cultural service quality: an assessment of research methodology' in *Journal of Service Management*, vol. 22, no. 2, pp. 241–65.

Musgrave, R., 1966. 'The public interest: efficiency in the creation and maintenance of material welfare' in C. Friedrich (ed.), *The Formation of Professions*. London: Sage.

Neergaard, U., 2009. 'Services of general economic interest: the nature of the beast' in M. Krajewski, U. Neergaard and J. Van de Gronden (eds), *The Changing Legal Framework for Services of General Interest in Europe*. Netherlands: TMC Asser Press.

Nord, W., 1974. 'Adam Smith and Contemporary Social Exchange Theory in *The American Journal of Economics and Sociology*, vol. 32 (October), pp. 421–36.

Padgett, D. and Allen, D., 1997. 'Communicating experiences: a narrative approach to creating service brand image' in *Journal of Advertising*, vol. 26, no. 4, pp. 49–62.
Page, A.C., 1982. 'Public Undertakings and Article 90' in *European Law Review*, vol. 28.
Palmer, A. and Cole, C., 1995. *Service Marketing: Principles and Practice*. Englewood Cliffs, NJ: Prentice-Hall.
Parasuraman, A., Zeithaml, A. and Berry, L.L., 1985. 'A Conceptual Model of Service Quality and its Implications for Future Research' in *Journal of Marketing*, vol. 49 (Fall), pp. 41–50.
Picard, E., 1998. 'Citizenship, Fundamental Rights, and Public Services' in M. Freedland and S. Sciarra (eds), *Public Services and Citizenship in European Law*. Oxford: Clarendon Press.
Popper, K.R., 1963. *Conjectures and Refutations*. New York: Harper & Row.
Ross, M., 2009. 'A healthy approach to services of general economic interest? The BUPA judgement of the Court of First Instance' in European Law Review, vol. 34, no. 1, pp. 127–40.
Saks, M., 1995. *Professions and the Public Interest – Medical Power, Altruism and Alternative Medicine*. London: Routledge.
Sauter, W., 2008. 'Services of general economic interest and universal service in EU law' in *European Law Review*, vol. 33, no. 2, pp. 167–93.
Sauter, W. and Schepel, S.H., 2009. *State and Market in European Union Law: The Public and Private Spheres of the Internal Market before the EU Courts*. Cambridge: Cambridge University Press.
Schubert, G., 1962. 'Is There a Public Interest Theory?' in C.J. Friedrich (ed.), *Nomos V: The Public Interest*. New York: Atherton Press.
Singh, J., 1995. 'Measurement issues in cross-national research' in *Journal of International Business Studies*, vol. 26, no. 3, pp. 597–619.
Smith, A.M., 2000. 'The impact of scale characteristics on the dimensionality of the service quality construct' in *The Service Industries Journal*, vol. 20, no. 3 (July), pp. 167–90.
Smith, A.M. and Reynolds, N.L., 2001. 'Measuring cross-cultural service quality – a framework for assessment' in *International Marketing Review*, vol. 19, no. 5, pp. 450–81.
Spiegel Online. 'A Less "Anglo-Saxon" EU: Sarkozy Scraps Competition Clause from New Treaty'. Available at: www.spiegel.de/international/europe/0,1518,490136,00.html [accessed 5 April 2015].
Ştefan, O.A., 2008. 'European Competition Soft Law in European Courts: A Matter of Hard Principles' in *European Law Journal*, vol. 14, no. 6, pp. 753–72.
Sugden, R., 1981. *The Political Economy of Public Choice: An Introduction to Welfare Economics*. Oxford: Martin Robertson.
Szyszczak, E., 2007. *The Regulation of the State in Competitive Markets in the EU*. Oxford: Hart Publishing.
Trompenaars, F. and Hampden-Turner, C., 1997. *Riding the Waves of Culture: Understanding Cultural Diversity in Business*. London: Nicholas Brealey Publishing.
Ueltschy, L.C., Laroche, M., Eggert, A. and Bindl, U., 2007. 'Service quality and satisfaction: an international comparison of professional services perceptions' in *Journal of Services Marketing*, vol. 21, no. 6, pp. 410–23.
Ueltschy, L.C., Laroche, M., Tamilia, R.D. and Yannopoulos, P., 2004. 'Cross-cultural invariance of measures of satisfaction and service quality' in *Journal of Business Research*, vol. 57, no. 8, pp. 901–12.

Upah, G.D., 1980. 'Mass Marketing in Service Retailing: A Review and Synthesis of Major Methods' in *Journal of Retailing*, vol. 56 (Fall), pp. 59–76.
Van, D.V. and Leung, K., 1997. *Methods and Data Analysis for Cross-cultural Research.* London: Sage.
Vargo, S. and Lusch, R.F., 2004. 'The four service marketing myths: remnants of a goods-based, manufacturing model' in *Journal of Service Research*, vol. 6 (May), p. 324.
Winsted, K.F., 1997. 'The service experience in two cultures: a behavioural perspective' in *Journal of Retailing*, vol. 73, no. 3, pp. 337–60.
Wong, N., Rindfleisch, A. and Burroughs, J.E., 2003. 'Do reverse-worded items confound measures in cross-cultural consumer research? The case of the material values scale' in *Journal of Consumer Research*, vol. 30, no. 1, pp. 72–91.
Wright, L.K., 1995. Avoiding services marketing myopia. In: Glynn, J.W. and Barnes, J.G., eds, Chicester: Wiley.
Yavas, U., 1998. 'Further evidence on the psychometric properties of SERVQUAL in Turkey: a replication and extension' in *Journal of International Marketing and Marketing Research*, vol. 23, no. 2, pp. 59–70.
Zhang, J., Beatty, S.E. and Walsh, G., 2008. 'Review and future directions of cross-cultural consumer services research' in *Journal of Business Research*, vol. 61, pp. 211–24.

Official documents

Cases before the Court of Justice of the European Union

C-171/00, *P Libéros* v. *Commission [2002]*. ECR I-451.
Case C-179/90, *Merci convenzionali porto di Genova SpA* v. *Siderurgica Gabrielli SpA [1991]*. ECR I-05889.
Case C-107/98, *Teckal Srl* v. *Comune di Viano and Azienda Gas-Acqua Consorziale (AGAC) di Reggio Emilia [1999]*. ECR I-08121.
Case C-18/88, *Régie des télégraphes et des téléphones* v. *GB-Inno-BM SA. [1991]*. ECR I-05941.
Case C-202/88, *French Republic* v. *Commission of the European Communities [1991]*. ECR I-01223.
Case C-260/89, *Elliniki Radiophonia Tiléorassi AE and Panellinia Omospondia Syllogon Prossopikou* v. *Dimotiki Etairia Pliroforissis and Sotirios Kouvelas and Nicolaos Avdellas and others [1991]*. ECR I-02925.
Case C-41/90, *Klaus Höfner and Fritz Elser* v. *Macrotron GmbH [1991]*. ECR I-01979.
Case T-46/97, *SIC – Sociedade Independente de Comunicação SA* v. *Commission of the European Communities [2000]*. ECR II-02125.
Case C-126/01, *Ministère de l'Économie, des Finances et de l'Industrie* v. *GEMO SA [2003]*. ECR I-13769.
Case C-26/03, *Stadt Halle and RPL Recyclingpark Lochau GmbH* v. *Arbeitsgemeinschaft Thermische Restabfall- und Energieverwertungsanlage TREA Leuna [2005]*. ECR I-00001.
Case C-458/03, *Parking Brixen GmbH* v. *Gemeinde Brixen and Stadtwerke Brixen AG [2005]*. ECR I-08585.
Case C-340/04, *Carbotermo SpA and Consorzio Alisei* v. *Comune di Busto Arsizio and AGESP SpA [2006]*. ECR I-04137.

Case C-324/07, *Coditel Brabant SA* v. *Commune d'Uccle and Région de Bruxelles-Capitale [2008]*. ECR I-08457.
Case T-289/03, *British United Provident Association Ltd (BUPA), BUPA Insurance Ltd and BUPA Ireland Ltd* v. *Commission of the European Communities [2008]*. ECR II-00081.
Case C-480/06, *Commission of the European Communities* v. *Federal Republic of Germany [2009]*. ECR I-04747.
Case C-573/07, *Sea Srl* v. *Comune di Ponte Nossa [2009]*. ECR 00000.
Joined Cases C-271/90, C-281/90 AND C C-289/90, *Kingdom of Spain, Kingdom of Belgium and Italian Republic* v. *Commission of the European Communities [1992]*. ECR I-05833.
Joined Cases C-189, 202, 205, 208 AND 213, *Dansk Rørindustri and others* v. *Commission [2005]*. ECR I-05425.

Other case law

94 U.S., 113, 126 (1876).

European Council

SN 211/95. *Cannes European Council, Conclusions of the Presidency*, 26–27 June 1995, Brussels.

European Commission

2001/C 17/04, 'Communication from the Commission, services of general interest in Europe', *Official Journal of the European Union*.
2007/C 161/22, 2007. 'Opinion of the European Economic and Social Committee on the Communication from the Commission Implementing the Community Lisbon programme: Social services of general interest in the European Union, COM (2006) 177 final', *Official Journal of the European Union*.
2012/21/EU, 2012. 'Commission Decision of 20 December 2011 on the application of Article 106 (2) of the Treaty on the Functioning of the European Union to State aid in the form of public service compensation granted to certain undertakings entrusted with the operation of services of general economic interest', *Official Journal of the European Union*.
COM (96) 443 final, 11 September 1996. *Services of General Interest in Europe*. Brussels: European Commission.
COM (1996) 443 final, 11 September 1996. *Communication from the Commission – Services of General Interest in Europe*. Brussels: European Commission.
COM (2000) 580 final, 20 September 2000. *Communication from the Commission – Services of General Interest in Europe*. Brussels: European Commission.
COM (2001) 598 final, 17.10.2001. *Report to the Laeken European Council – Services of General Interest*. Brussels: European Commission.
COM (2002) 280 final, 5.6.2002a. *Report from the Commission on the status of work on the guidelines for state aid and services of general economic interest*. Brussels: European Commission.
COM (2002) 636 final, 27 November 2002b. *Report from the Commission on the state of play in the work on the guidelines for state aid and services of general economic interest (SGEIs)*. Brussels: European Commission.

COM (2003) 270 final, 21 May 2003. *Green Paper on Services of General Interest*. Brussels: European Commission.

COM (2004) 374 final, 12 May 2004. *Communication from the Commission to the European Parliament, the Council, the European Economic and Social Committee and the Committee of Regions – White Paper on Services of General Interest*. Brussels: European Commission.

COM (2006) 177 final, 26 April 2006. *Communication from the Commission – Implementing the Community Lisbon Programme: Social services of general interest in the European Union*. Brussels: European Commission.

COM (2007) 725 final, 20 November 2007. *Communication from the Commission to the European Parliament, the Council, the European Economic and Social Committee and the Committee of the Regions, Accompanying the Communication on 'A single market for 21st century Europe' Services of general interest, including social services of general interest: a new European commitment*. Brussels: European Commission.

COM (2011) 146 final, 23 March 2011a. *Communication from the Commission to the European Parliament, the Council, the European Economic and Social Committee and the Committee of the Regions – Reform of the EU State Aid Rules on Services of General Economic Interest*. Brussels: European Commission.

COM (2011) 900 final, 20 December 2011b. *Communication from the Commission to the European Parliament, the Council, the European Economic and Social Committee and the Committee of the Regions – A Quality Framework for Services of General Interest in Europe*. Brussels: European Commission.

SEC (2007) 1024 final, 12 July 2007. *Commission Staff Working Document – Evaluation of the Performance of Network Industries Providing Services of General Economic Interest 2006 Report*. Brussels: European Commisson.

SEC (2008) 2179, 2 July 2008. *Commission Staff Working Document – Biennial Report on Social Services of General Interest*. Brussels: European Commission.

SEC (2010) 1284, 22 October 2010. *Commission Staff Working Document – Second Biennial Report on Social Services of General Interest*. Brussels: European Commission.

7 Public procurement as the EU's safety valve

7.1 Introduction

Since the end of the Second World War the construction and operation of infrastructure in Europe has been principally achieved by the public sector while the involvement of private investors and operators in this area has been relatively limited. Corporatist regimes have typically promoted large governmental projects. Organised labour movements controlled such public enterprises and eventually turned them into overstaffed and inefficient drains on the public budget (Watkins 2010). However, the situation in the majority of EU Member States – as in a number of other countries around the world – has been one of increasing private participation. The EU region has seen major shifts towards privatisation once public enterprises operating in traditional sectors such as water, transport, energy and telecommunications have been transferred to private ownership.

It is argued that this change in attitude does not only reflect a swing in political trends, nor does it emerge as the only means for increasing extra-budgetary resources for improving investment flows into infrastructure, for increasing public efficiency, or for expanding the private sector. Privatisation emerges as a direct consequence of globalisation (Aman 2003).[1] The global economy that started to take shape in the 1970s obliged States to adapt to the needs of global market forces. Indeed, globalisation as a significant driving force has prompted various changes in society. The relationship between business and society is inherently relational. Businesses cannot exist in isolation from society and society is what it is in relation to its constituting institutions (Buchholz 2004). No absolute line can be drawn between business and society because the origin and foundation of business is social in nature.

As businesses respond to global forces they create new operational modes and a global infrastructure that seeks to maintain cost effectiveness and competitiveness. Likewise, the State is not only faced with domestic pressures – it is also placed under intense pressure to harmonise its regulatory processes so as to better deal with economic and environmental issues that are of global concern. The State is not a passive victim of globalising forces but an active participant in the process (Williams 1996). The end result is an ever-more-blurred divide between the public and private spheres.

It is argued that while globalisation encroaches to a greater or lesser extent upon government's ability to produce independent policies, the situation is further exacerbated within the EU. The notion of 'The EU as a decentred State' (section 7.2) follows on from the discussion in the forthcoming section, in which the ever-increasing subordination of public policies to market forces is put under focus. Within a scenario of ever-changing relationships between the market and the State, the creation of *marchés publiques* as *sui generis* markets is seen to play a highly valid and crucial societal role for the attainment of public interest goals since (it is argued) such goals cannot be left to the whims of market forces. This is the subject matter of section 7.3, '*Marchés publiques* as *sui generis* markets'. Notwithstanding the fact that the regulation of EU public procurement operates within such *sui generis* markets, and that it exposes an economic and legal approach to the integration of public markets, EU public procurement is also used as a policy instrument for adding extra leverage in the drive for achieving other European aims: such as sustainable consumption, production and industry policy; increasing the demand for innovative goods and services; and for the precommercial procurement of innovation. And, adding to the EU's public procurement's task list, it could also be claimed that public procurement serves as the EU's safety valve. Section 7.4 addresses the question: 'To what extent is the EU public procurement regime serving the public interest?', while section 7.5, 'Concluding remarks', presents the case for public procurement's potential within a reordered regime, a regime that operates less rigidly in order to serve as a safety valve for Member States – thus allowing for better harmonisation and synchronisation of socio-economic policies at both EU level and at Member States' level.

7.2 The EU as a decentred State

The process of globalisation encroaches upon governments' domestic power and capacity since it undermines to a greater or lesser extent their ability to implement independent policies. The changing relationships between the market and the State translate into a range of hybrid forms of governance that are characterised by a fusion of public and private values, rhetoric and approaches. Consequently, when it comes to creating public policy, the State becomes 'decentred' and no longer the primary unit of analysis (Aman 2003).

The notion of a 'decentred' state, and the subordination of public policies to market forces, are further accentuated within the EU. Two major conflicting forces in the EU legal order come into play – one at the conceptual level and the other at the operational level.

At the conceptual level, in the EU legal order both the liberal and social democratic theories of the State are considered as fundamentally legitimate. It can be noted that in both liberal and social democratic theory the State is actively involved in dealing with social, political and economic problems. On the one hand, *ordoliberalism*[2] is primarily concerned with the protection of the free market economy – accordingly, the role of law is to deal with the inequities that

Procurement as the EU's safety valve 173

may arise in the distribution of power. On the other hand, *service publique* is concerned with social redistribution and its protection from market pressures through legal means. Both schools of thought construct a clear line of demarcation between the public and private spheres. This is clearly reflected in EU case law. Figure 7.1. attempts to capture in illustrative terms this binary distinction, including the underpinning logic with reference to related caselaw.

Overview to the binary schematic diagram at Figure 7.1

- The first point of departure in conceptualising the forces underlying the EU legal order, and central to the whole schematic of Figure 7.1, features *the State* and the manner in which it is conceptualised at the supranational level. 'The State may act either by exercising public powers or by carrying on economic activities of an industrial or commercial nature by offering goods and services on the market' (Case 118/85: para.7). The distinction herein comprises the fulcrum that eventually determines the specific path to the binary route. At one end, activities that fall under the classification of a non-industrial or non-commercial nature fall within the competence and sovereign powers of Member States. At the other end, activities which are of an industrial or commercial nature fall within the scope of the EU's *shared values*[3] and within the remit of *services of general economic interest*.
- Restrictions on the *fundamental freedoms* enshrined in the treaty may be justified, but 'reasons of a purely economic nature cannot constitute overriding reasons in the public interest justifying a restriction of a fundamental freedom' (Case C-384/08: para. 55). Here, *the underlying rationale behind the nature of the activity in question determines the specific path to be adopted along the binary route, and hence the ultimate destination with its consequent effects.*
- The three conditions defining the nature of a *body governed by public law* are cumulative (Case C-44/96: para. 21). To this effect, the Court draws a distinction between needs in the general interest not having an industrial or commercial character, and needs in the general interest having an industrial or commercial character (Case C-360/96: para. 36). Here, *the underlying rationale behind the nature of the activity in question determines the specific path to be adopted along the binary route, and hence the ultimate destination with its consequent effects.*
- When it comes to defining an *undertaking* 'in the context of competition law, first that concept of an undertaking encompasses every entity engaged in an economic activity, regardless of the legal status of the entity and the way in which it is financed' (Case C-41/90: para. 21). When 'that activity is not an economic activity and, therefore, the organizations to which it is entrusted are not undertakings within the meaning of Article 85 and 96 of the Treaty.' (Joined cases C-159/91 and C-160/91: para. 19). An economic activity refers to 'any activity consisting in offering goods and services on a given market' (Joined cases C-180/98 and C-184/98: para. 75). Here, *the*

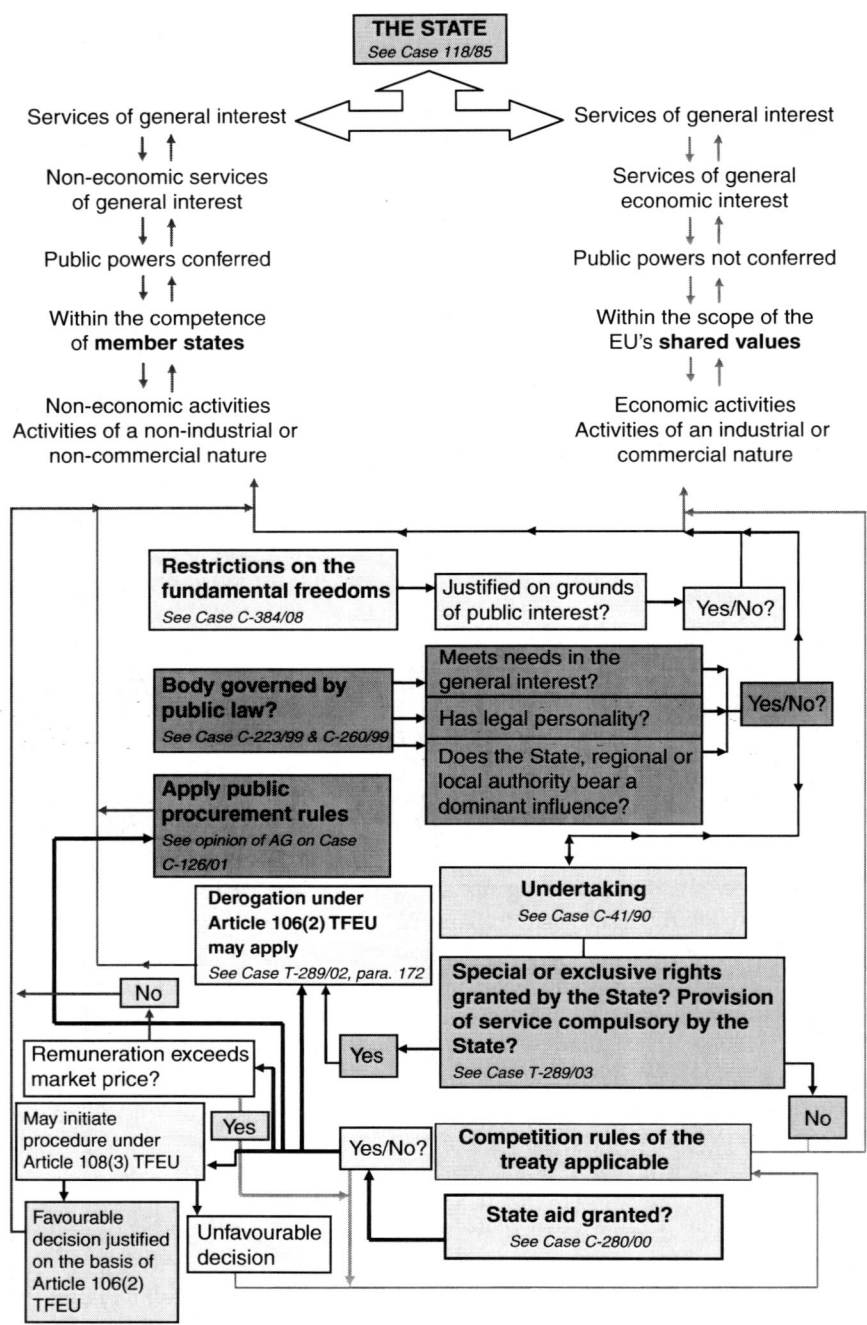

Figure 7.1 Conceptual forces underpinning the EU legal order: a binary distinction on the conduct of the State.

Procurement as the EU's safety valve 175

underlying rationale behind the nature of the activity in question determines the specific path to be adopted along the binary route and hence the ultimate destination with its consequent effects.

- The recognition of activities classified as services of general economic interest do not necessarily presume that *special or exclusive rights* have been granted. 'The grant of a special or exclusive right to an operator is merely the instrument, possibly justified, which allows that operator to perform as SGEI mission' (Case T-289/03: para. 179). On the other hand, the *compulsory* nature of services of general economic interest is recognised as an essential condition for the existence of services of general economic interest within the meaning of Community law (Case T-289/03: para. 188–90). Here, *the underlying rationale behind the nature of the activity in question determines the specific path to be adopted along the binary route and hence the ultimate destination with its consequent effects.*
- On the basis of established case law concerning *Article 106 (2)* TFEU,[4] the Court observed that Member States are to give reasons when a service of general economic interest is identified, and must indicate what makes such a service distinct from other economic activities. Here, *the underlying rationale behind the nature of the activity in question determines the specific path to be adopted along the binary route and hence the ultimate destination with its consequent effects.*
- When it comes to the classification of *State aid*, the Court held in the Altmark Trans case (Case C-280/00: para. 74) that on the basis of established case law all the conditions as set out in Article 107 (1) TFEU need to be fulfilled in order to classify compensation as State aid.[5] Here, *the underlying rationale behind the nature of the activity in question determines the specific path to be adopted along the binary route and hence the ultimate destination with its consequent effects.*
- State aid is not applicable when the financing measures are intended as a *quid pro quo*. In such cases *public procurement procedures* provide the clearest example of a direct and manifest link between State financing and clearly defined obligations.[6]
- State aid may not be applicable when the State aid approach is adopted which necessitates the procedure under *Article 108 (3) TFEU*.[7]
- State aid may not be applicable when the *compensation* viewpoint is adopted. This approach regards State measures as falling within the classification of State aid only to the extent that the *remunerations exceed market price*.[8]

As it transpires, at the *operational level* EU competition rules are steadfastly penetrating the regulatory boundaries that once insulated services of general interest (SGI).[9] Such services now become increasingly exposed to market forces under the pretext of *services of general economic interest* – an illusory concept that could be referred to as a *label*, devoid of true meaning.[10] What was once historically attached by way of definition, organisation and management – and deeply ingrained into the Member States' culture – now becomes commercialised. The commercialisation of the EU citizen's everyday life is made to appear as a natural and inevitable outcome of market forces. Meanwhile, the obligation by the political class to fulfil democratically determined public interest needs that reflect collective values gnaw away as market-driven policies take priority. The making of politics becomes more or less dictated by market forces which seek nothing other than to serve the perceived needs of capital accumulation. The new game that politics has become engaged in requires a highly skilled balancing act. Failure to maintain this balancing act threatens the legitimacy of the government of the day as the gradual destruction of services of general interest – on which social solidarity and active democracy have always depended – are put under pressure.[11] Services of general interest favour and foster the common good. And the sole purpose of the State (and thus that of politics and the law) is the attainment of that common good. But the gradual marginalisation of the common good seriously puts into doubt the authenticity of the political elite.

These two opposing forces – one of which originates at the *conceptual level*, and the other at the *operational level* – conflict. Consequently, the balance at the conceptual and operational level is weakened, thus easing the way to the pressures exerted by the globalising market forces. Such imbalance explains why the notion of a 'decentred' State and the subordination of public policies to market forces become further accentuated within the EU. The demarcation lines between the public and private spheres within the EU become even fuzzier and more confusing as on the one hand, at the conceptual level, a clear-cut line as construed by the EU legal order between the market and the State is drawn up. But on the other, forces at the operational level steadfastly crush down such demarcation lines. This lack of coherence leads to an incompatible state of affairs that goes beyond practical reasonableness. It is unjust. It explains the lack of clarity and the legal uncertainties that have persistently hounded the performance of services of general 'economic' interest. According to Sauter and Schepel, maintaining a clear-cut line of demarcation between the market and the State is where the problem lies (Sauter and Schepel 2009). For Bovis (2005) the roles and the responsibilities of the State are in the process of being redefined.

7.3 *Marchés publiques* as *sui generis* markets

The changing relationship between the market and the State has brought about new forms of governance. Privatisation has been described as a first step away from traditional corporatism. Other forms of governance – namely those falling under the category of 'contracting out' – suggest yet another form of departure from traditional corporatism.[12] Corporatism, it is argued, has emerged as a vital instrument for the State to promote its industrial policy (Bovis 1998). This has led to the creation of *marchés publiques*. *Marchés publiques*, or public markets, are *sui generis* markets for which the attainment of goals in the public interest is the major concern. This concern with the 'public interest' is what distinguishes the public market from the private market. In the case of the latter, the maximisation of profit is the key driver. So, on one hand we have public markets that are driven by actions primarily seeking the fulfilment of *public interest* goals; and on the other we have private markets that are primarily motivated to fulfil *private interest* goals. That the wider needs of society can be met by individuals pursuing their own interests – that is, *private interest* goals in a market-based economy – needs to be understood in the light of what Adam Smith recognised way back in 1776: '[I]t is not from the benevolence of the butcher, the brewer, or the baker, that we expect our dinner, but from the regard to their own interest' (Pike and Neale 1999). So, as long as there is money available to pay for 'desirable' products – irrespective of whether such products are considered socially desirable (for example, drugs) – the market mechanism cannot differentiate between 'right' and 'wrong'. Thus, the attainment of *public interest* goals that operate within *sui generis* markets plays a crucial societal role that cannot be left to the whims of market forces.

Distinctive features distinguishing the public from the private market indicate the boundaries within which the institutionalised nature of public procurement operates. As previously noted, pursuing public interest goals (as opposed to profit) is one of the major thrusts that motivates the public sector. Public markets tend to have monopsony/oligopsony structures in which the State and its organs control a large proportion of the market – few buyers, as represented by government; and many sellers, as represented by economic operators. Competition in private markets can vary from monopoly, to oligopoly, to high levels of competition. Demand in public markets is institutionalised and tends to be cyclical; demand in the private sector tends to be target-oriented and driven by the need to satisfy consumers. Purchasing decisions within public markets are predominantly influenced by policy decisions, and budgetary and bureaucratic constraints. The notion of value for money tends to come into play at a later stage – that is, during the actual procurement process. In private markets purchasing decisions tend to be predominantly influenced (and hence motivated) by price-quality and value-for-money relations. The establishment of prices in public markets is usually determined following calls for tender, or negotiation. 'In consequence, the application of the public procurement regime reinforces the character of services of general interest as non-commercial or industrial and the existence of marchés publics' (Bovis 2009: 166). In such markets, competitive tendering procedures attempt to fulfil public law norms whilst simultaneously mimicking the supply/demand regime that is found in private markets (Bovis 2006: 15). However, the distinctive nature and characteristics of the public procurement market deprive it of the invigorating stimuli that is found in the private market, and instils what Bovis refers to as a static effect to the value-for-money (VFM) process. Although transparency in the public procurement process is used as leverage for VFM – and is claimed to stimulate price competition and all the implied benefits for public authorities to be accrued as a result – when it comes to traditional public procurement it has been argued that the process can, in fact, be counterproductive (Bovis 2006). The actual impact of the public procurement Directives on public procurement *prices* remains inconclusive.[13]

As noted on various occasions, the regulation of EU public procurement exposes an economic and legal approach to the integration of public markets across the EU – with the main objective being to enhance competition and unobstructed market access. In other words, it attempts to promulgate the EU's internal market. EU public procurement is also used as a policy instrument in pursuit of other goals, including: sustainable consumption and production; sustainable industry policy;[14] increasing the demand for innovative goods and services;[15] and for the precommercial procurement of innovation.[16] It could also be claimed that public procurement serves as the EU's safety valve – and in the following section we will look at what is meant by this.

7.4 To what extent is the EU public procurement regime serving the public interest?

As the EU is increasingly shaped in ways that serve the perceived needs of capital accumulation, with the benefit of hindsight and through the understandings deciphered so far it could be argued that the prevailing legal uncertainty in the application of the law on State aid to services of general interest should come as no surprise. As long as the EU's modus operandi remains focused on continuing the juggling act between diametrically opposing forces at the *conceptual* and *operational* levels, the intersection between the public and private sectors is most likely to remain fragile and unstable – unless some sort of equilibrium can be found. Advocate General Jacobs appears to have made an attempt to find such an equilibrium. However, its robustness is seriously questioned – a matter that will be discussed in due course.

In the GEMO case (Case C-126/01) Advocate General Jacobs offered an alternative approach for the applicability of financing of services of general interest – the *quid pro quo* approach. The analysis is based on whether or not there exists a direct and manifest link between State financing and clearly defined public service obligations. The conduct of public procurement procedures are identified as ideal in this respect. It has been argued that the public service obligations imposed by public procurement are so direct and manifest that the financing and the obligation are to be regarded as a single measure. Accordingly, this approach is claimed to bring about a number of advantages. It gives due weight to the importance of services of general interest, strikes a balance between potentially conflicting policies, and is consistent with the general case law on State aid.

In effect, however, it does much more. It is through the *quid pro quo* approach that public procurement serves as a most vital tool for enabling public services to escape the clutches of State aid control. As such, public procurement acts as a modifier because to a certain extent it provides release from the overwhelming pressures that market forces would otherwise exert on the provision of public services. Public procurement, as a stabilising force, helps equalise the balance of competing and opposing forces that are concurrently at work at the conceptual and operational levels. It is in this sense that public procurement can be described as the EU's safety valve.

Nevertheless, the applicability of Community rules to the financing of public services remains the subject of controversy.[17] In particular the counter arguments – as put forth by Advocate General Léger in his opinion on the Altmark case – are noteworthy. Moreover, when his arguments are connected to the understandings as deciphered so far in this book, we come closer to making sense of the situation. In his arguments, Advocate General Léger focuses essentially on four main areas: the criterion of the private investor in a market economy; the concept of 'advantage' in Article 92 (1)[18] of the treaty, the procedural obligations laid down in Article 93 (3)[19] of the treaty; and the *quid pro quo* approach. What follows is a brief exposition of three of his main arguments – namely, the *quid pro quo* approach, the criterion of the private investor in a market economy, and the concept of 'advantage' in Article 92 (1)[20] of the treaty. These three arguments will be put into context in the light of the understandings captured so far.

The quid pro quo approach

Advocate General Léger highlights two difficulties with this approach. The first is in stark contrast to what Advocate General Jacobs claims as the number one advantage – the latter stating that '[T]he proposed distinction has a number of advantages. First it is consistent with general case-law on the interpretation of Article 87 (1)[21] EC' (Opinion of Mr Advocate General Jacobs in C-126/01: para. 121). On the other hand, Advocate General Léger states as follows: '[F]irst, the *quid pro quo* approach appears difficult to reconcile with the Court's case-law on State aid' (Opinion of Mr Advocate General Léger in Case C-280/00: para. 79).

At paragraphs 122 and 123 Advocate General Jacobs opines as follows:

> 122. Under that case-law, bilateral arrangements or more complex transactions involving mutual rights and obligations are to be analysed as a whole. Where for example the State purchases goods or services from an undertaking, there will be aid only if and to the extent that the price paid exceeds the market price.[22] Where the State lends money to an undertaking there will be aid only if and to the extent that it does not ask for an appropriate return as would a private investor.[23] The same global analysis must in my view prevail where the link between State funding and the clearly defined general interest obligations imposed is so direct and manifest that financing and obligation must be regarded as a single measure.

> 123. Under the general case-law on Article 87 (1) EC the causes and aims of a unilateral measure are by contrast not to be taken into account for the classification of the measure as State aid but only for the assessment of its compatibility under Article 87 (2) and (3) EC. Where it is not clear from the outset that State funding is granted as a *quid pro quo* for clearly defined general interest obligations, a State's contention that the funding is in fact intended to offset the additional cost of the general interest tasks assumed

by certain undertakings must be viewed as referring merely to the causes and aims of the measure. Whilst many instances of that second type of funding measure may be justified under Article 86 (2) EC, I consider that they should not fall outside the scope of the State aid rules.

However, Advocate General Léger remains unconvinced and at paragraphs 83 and 84 of his Opinion he argues as follows:

> 83. The first criterion suggested consists in examining whether there is a 'direct and manifest link' between the State funding and the public service obligations. In practice, this amounts to requiring the existence of a public service contract awarded after a public procurement procedure.[24] Similarly, the second criterion suggested consists in examining whether the public service obligations are 'clearly defined'. In practice, this amounts to verifying that there are laws, regulations or contractual provisions which specify the nature and content of the undertaking's obligations.[25]
>
> 84. In those circumstances, the *quid pro quo* approach departs from the Court's case-law on State aid. It amounts to defining aid no longer by reference solely to the effects of the measure, but by reference to criteria of a purely formal or procedural nature. At theoretical level, it means that the same measure may be classified as aid or 'non-aid' depending on whether a contract (of public service) or a legal instrument (defining the public service obligations) exists, although it produces identical effects on competition.

The second difficulty that Advocate General Léger finds in the application of this approach is that, 'the *quid pro quo* approach does not appear to be capable of guaranteeing a sufficient degree of legal certainty' (Opinion of Mr Advocate General Léger in Case C-280/00: para. 85). At paragraphs 86 and 87 of his Opinion he contends as follows:

> 86. The principal criterion underlying this approach is defined in a vague and imprecise fashion. It is clear that this is deliberate and is intended to provide the flexibility needed to comprehend a wide range of situations. Nevertheless, it is extremely difficult to know what is covered by the expression 'direct and manifest link'. Moreover, apart from the case of a public service contract concluded after an award procedure, none of the parties was able to provide a single specific example of this kind of link between State financing and public service obligations.[26]
>
> 87. In those circumstances, the expression 'direct and manifest link' – and hence the very concept of State aid – will be likely to receive widely differing interpretations. These interpretations may also vary according to the cultural (or even personal) attitudes of the various bodies responsible for applying the Treaty rules on State aid.

As observed by Advocate General Léger, the flexibility inherent in the *quid pro quo* approach in essence provides some manoeuvring space – including that for differing cultural interpretations. It is worth noting that culture is not a static phenomenon and European social models are deeply ingrained in their cultures. In effect, this flexibility plays a vital role as it allows for the attainment of equilibrium between the opposing forces that are at work at the *conceptual* and *operational* levels. It helps further explain why this approach allows EU public procurement to serve as a safety valve as it protects to a certain extent the provision of public services – since it enables culture to act as a device protecting Member States from the overwhelming pressures of market forces. And in so doing it reasserts, to a certain extent, their social rights.

Further, we need also to reflect upon Advocate General Léger's difficulty with the term 'direct and manifest link', from which, when connected with the marketing insights relating to the nature of services,[27] we can draw further understandings. As has been revealed through the marketing literature, the *quid pro quo* approach holds that only two parties are involved in the exchange process. In such exchanges, utilitarian or economic meanings are attached – wherein human behaviour is seen to be driven by rational motives in order to achieve maximum satisfaction; and the individuals involved in the exchange process have access to complete information on all the available alternatives and are relatively free from external influences. But as has been argued, in social exchanges – as is the case with public procurement – the exchange involved cannot be reduced to a simple *quid pro quo* notion because complexities are involved which include various tangible and intangible transfers, various media that influence the exchange, and which in the process are separated in part by the passage of time. Nothing is so 'direct and manifest' with public procurement.

The private investor in a market economy

According to EU case law the criterion of the private investor in a market economy is applicable only in cases where the intervention by the State is categorised as an economic one (Opinion of Mr Advocate General Léger in Case C-280/00: para. 21; Case T-46/97). In such cases the Court thus proceeds to examine whether a private operator of comparable size to the public body would have carried out the operation in question under the same conditions. State aid exists only if, and to the extent that, the remuneration paid by the State exceeds the market price. The justification for the use of this criterion is based on the principal of equal treatment between the public and private sectors: the rationale being that the State should not be subject to stricter rules than those applicable to the private sector (Opinion of Mr Advocate General Léger in Case C-280/00: para. 21). On the other hand, in cases where the intervention by the State is categorised as non-economic, the principal of equal treatment between the public and private sectors is not applicable and therefore renders the private operator criterion immaterial (Opinion of Mr Advocate General Léger in Case C-280/00: para. 22, 23, 24).

In his counter arguments Advocate General Léger notes that such rationale is based on erroneous comparisons (para. 27). At paragraphs 25 and 26 of his Opinion he contends as follows:

> 25. It is common ground that the financing of public services is an activity which typically falls within the exercise of public powers. It is for the public authorities to define the services which are to be made available to the collectivity. It is also for them to take the necessary measures to ensure the functioning and financing of those services. It is, moreover, hard to imagine a private operator embarking on his own initiative on such financing activity.
>
> 26. Consequently, I consider that the private operator criterion cannot validly be applied to the financing of public services.

Indeed, Advocate General Léger's counter arguments substantiate further the understandings deciphered so far. First, the strict dividing line that the EU demarcates between the public and private sectors at the *conceptual* level, in reality and for reasons explained above, is very much blurred. This in itself distorts the principle of equality; that is, *if* the application of this principle was to be considered as applicably valid. But, this does not seem to be the case. Second, the application of the principle of equality necessitates that one compares like with like. Given that the public sector operates in a *sui generis* market, this collapses the notion of comparability and therefore invalidates the application of the principal of equality. Third, as noted above by Advocate General Léger at paragraph 24, 'the financing of public services is an activity which typically falls within the exercise of public powers. It is for the public authorities to define the services which are to be made available to the collectivity'. It is worth recalling that public services delivered under the pretext of *services of general economic interest* fall under an illusory concept that is devoid of true meaning.[28]

The concept of 'advantage'

On the concept of 'advantage' in Article 92 (1)[29] of the treaty, Advocate General Léger challenges the argument revolving around the compensation approach. According to this approach it is argued that State measures fall within the classification of State aid only to the extent that the advantage exceeds the additional costs for discharging the imposed public service obligations. As long as State measures are offsetting the costs of the public service obligations this has the effect of bringing the recipient undertaking into a position comparable with that of its competitors. Advocate General Léger refers to the rationale underpinning the compensation approach as based on a 'net' definition of aid, or the 'real' advantage theory wherein the financing and the public service obligations are regarded as a single measure (Opinion of Mr Advocate General Léger in Case

C-280/00: para. 31, 32). However, in his counter arguments at paragraphs 33, 34 and 35 of his Opinion he notes as follows:

> 33. That does not, however, correspond to the approach adopted by the authors of the Treaty in the field of State aid. The relevant provisions of the Treaty are based on a 'gross' theory of aid or the 'apparent' advantage theory.
>
> 34. Using this approach, the advantages given by the public authorities and what the recipient has to contribute in return must be examined separately. The existence of the contribution is of no relevance for determining whether the State measure constitutes aid within the meaning of Article 92 (1). It comes into consideration only at a later stage of the analysis, for assessing whether the aid is compatible with the common market.
>
> 35. The 'gross' theory of aid thus occurs in several provisions of the Treaty, in particular in Article 92 (2) and (3), and in Article 77 of the EC Treaty (now Article 73 EC).[30]

In essence, Advocate General Léger contends that the State aid approach is the appropriate approach for analysing State financing because it ensures coherence with the treaty provisions. On the other hand, he opines that the compensation approach deprives the derogating provisions of the treaty on State aid (namely, Article 93 TFEU, Article 106 (2) TFEU, and Articles 107 (2) and (3) TFEU) from their effect (Opinion of Mr Advocate General Léger in Case C-280/00: para. 46, 52).

The compensation approach is discernible through the application of public procurement procedures (Opinion of Mr Advocate General Jacobs in Case C-126/01: para. 119). The acceptable market/cut-off price becomes established through competitive public tendering. Consequently, EU public procurement serves as a very important gateway that allows the provision of public services to escape from the clutches of State aid control. The notion of the EU public procurement regime acting as the EU's safety valve here again comes into focus.

Advocate General Léger's highly valid and concrete arguments have not in the slightesat deterred the application of the *compensation* approach or the *quid pro quo* approach because they remain applicable when it comes to assessing State aid. Such a response is commensurate with the EU's overriding and unconditional attitude when promulgating the Single Market project. Insofar as EU public procurement is seen to be serving Europe's internal perceived market needs, all else is of secondary importance. The public interest function that the EU actively puts into motion draws heavily on aggregative conceptions of the common good. In this respect, individual freedom, autonomy, rights, and quality of life are only valuable insofar as they increase aggregate utility. The individual is used as the means to increase such aggregate utility. This the author finds problematic because it conflicts with Europe's founding and fundamental value

– the respect for human dignity. The respect for human dignity demands that we treat individuals as an end in themselves and not as a means towards the achievement of other goals. Failure to recognise this dislocates, at the conceptual level, the respect for human dignity.

As Europe becomes highly engrossed in dismantling its non-tariff barriers, social barriers are concurrently erected. Member States' autonomy is severly restricted when it comes to pursuing domestic social policies through public purchasing.[31] Furthermore, and notwithstanding the fact that the benefits deriving from the EU's public procurement regime are highly questionable,[32] Europe's overriding and unconditional attitude prevails in the form of an ever-increasing desire for the capture of even more purchasing power at the supranational level.[33]

These are the tangible ideals that constitute Europe today, the Europe that we experience in our everyday lives once it is shorn of all forms of rhetoric. These are the ideals that are contributing towards Europe's social justice. On the one hand, EU public procurement is serving as a tool that helps dislocate Europe's founding values by way of assigning subordinate status to the goal of respect for the human dignity; on the other hand, EU public procurement is serving as a Community safety valve, modifying (and hence protecting to a certain extent) the provision of public services from the overwhelming effects of market forces. The situation is untenable – the acceptance of Europe's founding values calls for the reordering of economic and social dimensions, but instead we are distancing ourselves from these founding values, and are opting to tread on shaky ground.

But what truly constitutes permissible European ideals? The European Constitution centres on the human person, so does not the respect for human dignity,[34] equality[35] and freedom[36] of participatory action identify with the social conscience of the people of Europe? Do you not agree that these are the values that can help translate into a better European theory of social justice, rather than instead founding our actions upon illusory concepts? For the whole point of this journey, of *verstehen*, is trying to come to grips with our understandings in the hope that eventually we can come up with a better revelation – one that hinges upon practical reasonableness.

7.5 Concluding remarks

The ever-increasing commercialisation of the EU citizen's everyday life – which presses for the subordination of public policies to market forces – poses an obstacle when attempting to further European integration aims. When it comes to EU public procurement, insofar as economic efficiency logic predominates EU public procurement discourse, any other claims purporting to exemplify a European social model (whatever this may mean) will face major constrains. The discussion in this chapter concerning the notion of Europe as a decentred State has revealed that the ever-increasing growth of supranational State intervention encroaches upon Member States' freedom –particularly when it comes to the provision of services of general interest. As a result, public procurement has been identified as a stabilising force that helps equalise the balance of competing and opposing forces concurrently at work at the conceptual and operational levels. It thus helps introduce, to a certain extent, some element of stability. It is in this sense that public procurement is described as the EU's safety valve. However, its compatibility with general treaty provisions has been seriously questioned.

What is now needed is a shift in the emphasis – a reordering of Europe's economic and social dimensions, and a reordering of the State – in line with permissible European moral ideals. For economic activity is all about social activity (Unger 2007: 142). Such logic mandates practical reasonableness. That is, practical thinking that acknowledges the need for Europe's economic logic to dovetail harmoniously with its social logic. In this respect a reordered public procurement regime that serves as the Member States' safety valve (as opposed to the EU's safety valve), presents the case for potentially better harmonisation and synchronisation of Europe's socio-economic policies in conjunction with Member States' socio-economic policies. Through a politics of cooperation and coordination a reordered EU public procurement regime has the potential to realise a social model of integration in the European Union in which the European citizen is the key actor in the integration process.

Notes

1 According to Scholte (2000) globalisation is simultaneously regarded as an effect and a cause.
2 For a discussion on *ordoliberalism* see Chapter 1, section 1.4.1, 'Ordoliberalism'.
3 '... given the place occupied by services of general economic interest in the shared values of the Union', Article 14 TFEU.
4 In its judgement (Case T-289/03: para. 172), the Court referred to the following case law: Case C-179/90, *Merci convenzionali porto di Genova SpA* v. *Siderurgica Gabrielli SpA* [1991] ECR I-05889: para. 27; and C-34/01 to C-38/01, *Enirisorse SpA* v. *Ministero delle Finanze* [2003] ECR I-14243; Joined Cases C-115/97, C-116/97 and C-117/97, *Brentjens' Handelsonderneming BV* v. *Stichting Bedrijfspensioenfonds voor de Handel in Bouwmaterialen* [1999] ECR I-6025: para. 33 and 34.
5 'First, there must be an intervention by the State or through State resources. Second, the intervention must be liable to affect trade between Member States. Third, it must confer an advantage on the recipient. Fourth, it must distort or threaten to distort competition', Case C-280/00: para. 75.
6 See Opinion of Mr Advocate General Jacobs in Case C-126/01, delivered on 30 April 2002 (para. 119).
7 See Case T-46/97.
8 See Case C-53/00.
9 To this effect see the discussion in Chapter 6, 'On the mission of serving the public – services of general interest and Community law'.
10 To this effect see the discussion in Chapter 6.
11 See the discussion in section 1.5, 'Social Europe on the move'. For a more or less similar argument, but one that is based on the effects of the global economy, see also the discussion put forth by Leys (2001).
12 While privatisation denotes a transfer of ownership, contracting out represents a transfer of undertaking only. It is worth noting that in the case of privatisation the control of operations that fall within the public interest domain remain under the control of the State in the form of the regulatory regime. See Bovis (2006).

13 To this effect see the discussion in Chapter 3, and in particular section 3.2, 'EU public procurement and its impact on transparency'.
14 See European Commission, 2008, COM (2008) 400 final.
15 See COM (2011) 572 final; Aho Group (2006).
16 See COM (2007) 799 final.
17 See Opinion of Mr Advocate General Léger in Case C-280/00, delivered on 14 January 2003: para. 4.
18 Article 92 (1) EC has been replaced by Article 107 (1) TFEU.
19 Article 93 (3) EC has been replaced by Article 108 (3) TFEU.
20 Article 92 (1) EC has been replaced by Article 107 (1) TFEU.
21 Article 87 (1) EC has been replaced by Article 107 (1) TFEU.
22 To this effect Advocate General Jacobs cites the following: Opinion of Advocate General Fennelly in Case C-251/97 delivered on 26 November 1998: para. 19, with further references.
23 To this effect Advocate General Jacobs cites the following: Case C-301/87: para. 39–41 of the judgement.
24 To this effect Mr Advocate General Léger refers to the Opinion of Mr Advocate General Jacobs in GEMO: para. 120.
25 To this effect Mr Advocate General Léger refers again to the Opinion of Mr Advocate General Jacobs in GEMO: para. 120.
26 To this effect Mr Advocate General Léger, in footnote 97 of his Opinion, remarks as follows:

> In fact, the sole concrete and 'operational' criterion which can be set in the context of the *quid pro quo* approach is the requirement of a public service contract concluded after an award procedure. The various parties concur, however, in admitting that such a requirement is disproportionate (see also the Opinion of Advocate General Jacobs in *GEMO*, point 129, and the Opinion of Advocate General Stix-Hackl in *Eniresorse* point 157). Furthermore, it must be noted that, in its present state, Council Directive 92/50/EEC of 18 June 1992 relating to the coordination of procedures for the award of public service contracts (OJ 1992 L 209, p. 1) does not apply to public service concessions. It is therefore difficult to lay down such a judge-made requirement in the context of the Treaty provisions concerning State aid.

27 To this effect see the discussion in Chapter 6, in particular section 6.4.1, 'On economic versus non-economic services – gaining marketing insights on the nature of services'.
28 To this effect see also the discussion in section 6.4.1, 'On economic versus non-economic services – gaining marketing insights'.
29 Article 92 (1) EC has been replaced by Article 107 (1) TFEU.
30 Articles 92 (2), 92 (3) and 77 of the EC Treaty have now been replaced by Articles 107 (2), 107 (3) and 93 TFEU.
31 To this effect see the discussion in Chapter 5, in particular section 5.6, 'The quest for poverty reduction – putting EU public procurement into perspective'.
32 To this effect see the discussion in Chapter 3.
33 GPP is now seen as an integral part of the New Action Plan on Sustainable Consumption and Production and Sustainable Industry Policy (See European Commission, Communication to the European Council and the European Parliament, the European Economic and Social Committee and the Committee of Regions on Sustainable Consumption and Production and Sustainable Industry Policy Action Plan, 397/3 (2008). Indeed, one of the greatest challenges facing the EU today is the integration of environmental sustainability and economic growth and welfare. With a view to moving towards an energy- and resource-efficient economy, the EU has put forth a range of legislation to foster resource-efficient and

eco-friendly products, and to raise consumer awareness. However, it is argued that the introduction of such mandatory obligations on Member States may have an impact on public procurement markets by way of restricting considerably the public procurers' choice and competiton in procurement markets whilst simultaneously limiting the effect of other potential considerations in the award decison. Although the public procurement Directives provide a common framework for public purchasers on procedural rules on how to buy, the following legislation mandates the public procurer on what to buy:

> Energy End Use Efficiency and End Services – Directive 2006/32/EC;
> EU Regulation 106/2008, Community energy efficiency labelling programme for office equipment so called (Energy Star);
> Directive 2009/33/EC on promotion of clean and energy-efficient vehicles;
> Energy Labelling Directive – Directive 92/75/EEC;
> Energy Performance of Buildings – Directive 2002/91/EC.

In the proposal for a Directive of the European Parliament and of the Council on public procurement,

> [t]he traditional distinction between so-called prioritary and non-prioritary services ('A' and 'B' services) will be abolished. The results of the evaluation have shown that is no longer justified to restrict the full application of procurement law to a limited group of services. However, it became also clear that the regular procurement regime is not adapted to social services which need a specific set of rules.

See COM (2011) 896 final, p. 8. Refer also to the discussions in Chapter 3, section 3.3, 'EU public procurement and its impact on cross-border procurement'.
34 On the value of respect for human dignity – each and every person as a rational human being, has a dignity. Human dignity is inviolable. It is 'superior to human rights and fundamental freedoms who owe their origin and existence to the dignity of the human person' (Aquilina 2010). See also the discussion in Chapter 5, in particular section 5.4.3, 'Dignity as the basic moral premise'; and section 5.5, 'Respect for human dignity – a legally enforceable fundamental right'.
35 On the value of equality – what we are concerned with here is equality vis-à-vis the person in their totality, i.e. a totality that recognises the individual not just as a physical being but also as a social being, at the very core of which lies their human dignity. It calls for the recognition of the human being as an end in itself and not as a means to an end. More specifically, we need to refer to an equality that takes into account the *capability to function*. Capabilities to function assert freedom. The notion of capability to function refers to that conceived by Professor Amartya Sen as discussed in Chapter 5, section 5.3, 'The nature of Poverty – definitions abound'.
36 On the value of freedom of participatory action – what we are concerned with here is a freedom that enables the full participation of the individual in society, a freedom that defines and serves the ends of its citizens, liberates the individual, and provides space for initiative and action. Such space for initiative and action unleashes the individual's capability to function – which in itself asserts freedom. This is the freedom that finds its epitome when expressed through the flourishing of the individual.

References

AHO Group, 2006. *Creating an innovative Europe: Report of the independent expert group on R&D and innovation appointed following the Hampton Court Summit*, January.

Aman, A.C.J., 'Globalization, Democracy, and the Need for a New Administrative Law in *Indiana Journal of Global Legal Studies*, vol. 10, no. 1 (Winter 2003), pp. 125–56.

Aquilina, K., 2010. *Respect for Human Dignity and the Law.* State Care. [Homepage of State Care], Available at: www.statecareandmore.eu/index.php/blogs/respect-for-human-dignity-and-the-law-by-prof-kevin-aquilina-.html23 [accessed November 2010].

Bovis, C., 1998. 'The Regulation of Public Procurement as a Key Element of European Economic Law' in *European Law Journal*, vol. 4, no. 2, pp. 220–42.

Bovis, C. 2005, 'Financing services of general interest, public procurement and state aids: The delineation between market forces and protection' in *European Law Journal*, vol. 11, no. 1, pp. 79–109.

Bovis, C., 2006. *EC Public Procurement Case Law and Regulation.* Oxford: Oxford University Press.

Bovis, C.H., 2009. 'State Aid and Public Procurement in the Financing of Services of General Economic Interest' in Krajewski, M., Neergaard, U. and Van de Gronden, J. (eds), *The Changing Legal Framework for Services of General Interest in Europe.* The Hague: TMC-Asser Press.

Buchholz, A.R., 2004. *Stakeholder Theory and Public Policy: How Governments Matter.* Netherlands: Kluwer Academic Publishers.

Leys, C., 2001. *Market-Driven Politics: Neoliberal Democracy and the Public Interest.* UK: Verso.

Pike, R. and Neale, B., 1999. *Corporate Finance and Investment – Decisions and Strategies.* Great Britain: Prentice Hall.

Sauter, W. and Schepel, S.H., 2009. *State and Market in European Union Law: The Public and Private Spheres of the Internal Market before the EU courts.* Cambridge: Cambridge University Press.

Scholte, J.A., 2000. *Globalisation: a critical introduction.* London: Macmillan Press Ltd.

Unger, M.R., 2007. *Free trade reimagined: the world division of labor and the method of economics.* Princeton, NJ: Princeton University Press.

Watkins, T., 'The economic system of Corporatism'. Available at: www.sjsu.edu/faculty/watkins/corporatism.htm [accessed 25 March 2010].

Williams, M., 1996. 'Rethinking Sovereignty' in Kofman, G. (ed.), *Globalisation: Theory and Practice.* London: Continuum International Publishing Group, pp. 109–20.

Official documents

Cases before the Court of Justice of the European Union

Case 118/85, *Commission of the European Communities v. Italian Republic [1987].* ECR 02599.

Case C-179/90, *Merci convenzionali porto di Genova SpA v. Siderurgica Gabrielli SpA [1991].* ECR I-05889.

Case C-126/01, *Ministère de l'Économie, des Finances et de l'Industrie v. GEMO SA [2003].* ECR I-13769.

Case C-251/97, *French Republic v. Commission of the European Communities [1999].* ECR I-06639.

Case C-280/00, *Altmark Trans GmbH and Regierungspräsidium Magdeburg v. Nahverkehrsgesellschaft Altmark GmbH, and Oberbundesanwalt beim Bundesverwaltungsgericht [2003].* ECR 07747.

Case C-301/87, *French Republic* v. *Commission of the European Communities [1990]*. ECR I-00307.
Case C-360/96, *Gemeente Arnhem and Gemeente Rheden* v. *BFI Holding BV [1998]*. ECR I-06821.
Case C-384/08, *Attanasio Group Srl* v. *Comune di Carbognano*. ECR 00000.
Case C-41/90, *Klaus Höfner and Fritz Elser* v. *Macrotron GmbH [1991]*. ECR I-01979.
Case C-44/96, *Mannesmann Anlagenbau Austria AG and Others* v. *Strohal Rotationsdruck GesmbH [1998]*. ECR I-00073.
Case C-53/00, *Ferring SA* v. *Agence centrale des organismes de sécurité sociale (ACOSS) [2001]*. ECR I-09067.
Case T-289/03, *British United Provident Association Ltd (BUPA), BUPA Insurance Ltd and BUPA Ireland Ltd* v. *Commission of the European Communities [2008]*. ECR II-00081.
Case T-46/97, *SIC – Sociedade Independente de Comunicação SA* v. *Commission of the European Communities [2000]*. ECR II-02125.
Joined Cases C-115/97, C-116/97, and C-117/97 *Brentjens' Handelsonderneming BV* v. *Stichting Bedrijfspensioenfonds voor de Handel in Bouwmaterialen [1999]*. ECR I-6025.
Joined Cases C-159/91 and C-160/91 *Christian Poucet* v. *Assurances Générales de France and Caisse Mutuelle Régionale du Languedoc-Roussillon [1993]*. ECR I-00637.
Joined Cases C-180/98 to C-184/98 *Pavel Pavlov and Others* v. *Stichting Pensioenfonds Medische Specialisten [2000]*. ECR I-06451.
Joined Cases C-34/01 to C-38/01 *Enirisorse SpA* v. *Ministero delle Finanze [2003]*. ECR I-14243.

European Commission

COM (2007), 799 final, *Communication to the European Council and the European Parliament, the European and Economic and Social Committee and the Committee of Regions – Pre-commercial procurement: Driving innovation to ensure sustainable high quality public services in Europe*. Brussels: European Commission.
COM (2008), 400 final, 16 July 2008. *Communication to the European Council and the European Parliament, the European and Economic and Social Committee and the Committee of Regions of 16 July 2008, Public Procurement for a Better Environment*. Brussels: European Commission.
COM (2011), 572 final, *Communication to the European Council and the European Parliament, the European and Economic and Social Committee and the Committee of Regions – Partnering in Research and Innovation*. Brussels: European Commission.
COM (2011), 896 final, 20 December 2011. *Proposal for a Directive of the European Parliament and of the Council on public procurement*. Brussels: European Commission.
European Commission, *Communication to the European Council and the European Parliament, the European and Economic and Social Committee and the Committee of Regions on Sustainable Consumption and Production and Sustainable Industry Policy Action Plan* (2008), 397/3. Brussels.

Part III
The solution

8 On public-private partnerships
A European theory of a socially just alternative

8.1 Introduction

It is hoped that during this journey of *verstehen* we have, to a greater or lesser degree, been enlightened and in the process configured our beliefs – beliefs that confer justifications which now make it possible to proceed a step further in attempting to move towards a theory that is based upon practical reasonableness. For it is on the basis of practical reasonableness that we can work our way towards a theory of justice – more specifically, we aim towards a European theory of social justice. By such a theory it is meant that due account is given to various specific features that the European Union ought to be highly concerned with when regulating or promoting a European agenda and which henceforth manifests in some way or other, directly or indirectly, in Europe's theory of social justice.

Our concern here is with a theory that seeks to define and meet the ends of its citizens, that capitalises on Member States' diversity, and operates on the basis of principles and conditions that enable the flourishing of its citizens by incorporating key values as discussed and understood in this book; that is, the respect for human dignity,[1] equality[2] and freedom[3] of participatory action. These three values are tightly enmeshed and cannot be disentangled. Any attempt to treat them separately is to deprive the very essence of their integrity. A European theory of social justice can be realised through various institutional formats: and public-private partnerships (hereafter referred to as PPPs) present this opportunity. Indeed, PPPs provide the framework of argument that can give way to this European theory of social justice.

The discussion in the forthcoming section – section 8.2, 'On Public-Private Partnerships', attempts to put into perspective the ever-increasing trend towards PPPs across the globe – not least across Europe. Section 8.3, 'UK, London: Thameslink rolling stock procurement programme – the case in a nutshell', narrows the discussion by focussing on a particular UK PPP project that managed to generate controversy and debate. The UK case brings to the fore two central issues which are discussed in section 8.3.2, 'Best value for money – long-term best value?', and section 8.3.3, 'On the meaning and content of the fundamental right to equality'. Section 8.4 then proceeds to

'Arguing for a European theory of social justice', while section 8.4.1 is about 'Advancing a European theory of a socially just alternative'. Section 8.5 sets out our 'Concluding remarks'.

8.2 On public-private partnerships

The subject of PPPs has generated debate and controversy from various quarters, as well as attracting media attention. For some, it is thought of as a procurement approach that disguises private financing while making use of creative accounting in order to cover up government budget deficits. For others, it is regarded as an important tool for improving economic competitiveness, increasing efficiencies, expanding innovation opportunities, mitigating risk, and delivering value for money.

PPPs are fast becoming a global phenomenon. They refer to a wide variety of contractual formats that involve complex legal and financial arrangements between public authorities and private sector undertakings. In essence, such contractual relations translate into a method for the acquisition of public services wherein undertakings are engaged to take the risks they are best equipped to manage – relative to investment and operations. Concurrently, the public sector relinquishes its former role of service provider to concentrate on determining levels of public services and to ensure their timely delivery under contractual conditions that generate efficiency gains.

At Community level the term 'Public-Private Partnership' is not defined. It remains an evolving concept, but in general terms it is referred to as 'forms of cooperation between the public authorities and the world of business which aim to ensure the funding, construction, renovation, management or maintenance of an infrastructure or the provision of a service' (COM (2004) 327 final: 3). The Green Paper 'Community Law on Public-Private Partnerships and Community Law on Public Contracts and Concessions' (COM (2004) 327 final) classifies the set-ups that are generally known as PPPs under two major models. One model refers to PPPs by way of their purely contractual nature wherein the partnership between the public and private sector is based solely on contractual links. This includes contractual relationships classified as 'concessions'; and those that are commonly referred to as private finance initiative (PFI) projects. The other model refers to PPPs by way of their institutional nature and involves cooperation between the public and the private sector within a distinct entity.

PPPs have been widely developed in the UK. Its programme began in earnest in the early 1990s with a politically led initiative aiming to attract private sector finance and management skills for the delivery of public services and infrastructure. Up to the end of 2008, 935 PFI and PPP projects in the UK had been signed off, with a capital value of £66 billion (McKenzie 2009). Since 1996, 10–15 per cent of public sector capital investment has been attributable to PFI/PPPs (McKenzie 2009). Over the period 1987–2008 the major sectors engaging in PFI/PPP procurement have been transport (25.2 per cent), health (21.9 per cent), education (17.2 per cent) and defence (14.1 per cent) (McKenzie 2009). Ongoing reviews of the European PPP market show that the UK was the most active market in terms of both the number of projects, and their value, for the years 2012–14 (European PPP Expertise Centre 2013, 2014, 2015). Some 24 transactions were closed in 2014 (compared to 31 in 2013) – to an estimated value of €6.6 billion in 2014 (€6 billion in 2013) (European Expertise Centre 2014).

The PPP market in Europe has also been growing steadily. Between 2001–08, the number of deals signed across Europe (excluding the U.K) totalled 215 – to a cumulative value of €37 billion (McKenzie 2009). This represents less than two-thirds of the €61 billion in the UK over the same time period. Spain and France are reported to have had the greatest cumulative value of PPP deals signed by end of 2008, each at €4.1 billion, with Italy at €3.6 billion, and Ireland at €3.3 billion. The largest PPP contracts are found in transport infrastructure. By the beginning of 2007 approximately €68 billion worth of PPP projects were being procured in Europe (excluding the UK) (McKenzie 2009).

In 2014 the aggregate value of PPP transactions that reached financial close across the EU28, the countries of the Western Balkans, and Turkey, amounted to €18.7 billion. This represents an increase of 15 per cent over 2013 (European Expertise Centre 2014). As noted above, while the UK captured the largest PPP market in Europe both in terms of value and number of projects, Turkey represented the second largest PPP market in terms of value (€3.5 billion) with Germany taking third place (€1.5 billion). In terms of the number of projects in 2014 (following the UK – total number 24), France recorded ten deals, Germany and Greece seven deals apiece, and Denmark six deals (European Expertise Centre 2014). The transport sector is the most active in terms of value, and represented €11.8 billion worth of transactions in 2014 (European Expertise Centre 2014). An upward trend both in the number of projects and their value can be noted in the healthcare sector – a totasl of 15 projects in this sector, with an aggregate value of €2.2 billion, were reached in 2014 (European Expertise Centre 2014).

The following discussion will narrow the focus on a particularly high-profile UK PPP project that managed to spark debate and controversy across the UK. By putting into context real-life experiences alongside the understandings deciphered in this book it is hoped that we will be able to reflect and put into better perspective our programmed ways of reasoning, principles and patterns, in order to enlighten further our understandings and progress towards a potentially better European theory of social justice.

8.3 UK, London: Thameslink rolling stock procurement programme – the case in a nutshell

On 9 April 2008 the Department for Transport (DfT) displayed a Contract Notice (reference, 2008/S 71–096012) in the *Official Journal of the European Union* for and on behalf of the train operating company operating the Thameslink/GN franchise. Interested parties were invited to submit expressions of interest for the supply and maintenance of between 900 and 1,300 new vehicles for an estimated period of seven to ten years – together with the arrangement of the necessary finance. However, in the matter of financing, the DfT noted that it reserved the right to decide whether or not the selected bidder would be required to arrange finance, 'in which case the ITT may require bids for supplying and maintaining the new rolling stock without the need to arrange finance' (Contract Notice, reference 2008/S 71–096012).[4] In addition, the Contract Notice specified that the procurement might also include the development of one or more train depots. The 'negotiated procedure' was to be adopted as the procurement method, and the best offer was to be chosen on the basis of the most economically advantageous tender – in terms of the criteria stated in the specifications or in the invitation to tender or to negotiate. According to the Contract Notice, the tender was divided into lots and tenders were to be submitted for all lots. Variants were also accepted. The trains, and associated services, were expected to be in service by December 2015 – and the contract was envisaged for award by mid-2009.

The £6 billion Thameslink programme, originally known as Thameslink 2000, is a major expansion programme which comprises major infrastructure improvements including the rebuilding of London Bridge Station. The initiative also seeks to provide additional capacity for passengers on the Thameslink route running north–south through London, by providing for longer (up to 243 m) and more frequent (up to 24 trains per hour) trains (Department for Transport 2011). The Thameslink fleet is also expected to release carriages to other parts of the network, including the north-west of England and the Thames Valley routes (The Rt. Hon. Theresa Villiers 2011).

In November 2008 the Invitation to Tender was released and three bids were submitted (Department for Transport 2011). In October 2009 two bidders were shortlisted – two consortia: one led by Siemens plc (hereafter referred to as Siemens), and the other by Bombardier Transportation UK Ltd. (hereafter referred to as Bombardier). On 16 June 2011, the Minister of State for Transport announced Siemens plc with Cross London Trains (XLT) – a special purpose company comprising of Siemens Project Ventures GmbH, Innisfree Ltd and 3i Infrastructure plc – as preferred bidder for the supply of the new Thameslink trains (The Rt. Hon. Theresa Villiers 2011). It was stated that '[t]he choice of Siemens Plc with Cross London Trains (XLT) as preferred bidder represents the *best value for money* for taxpayers' (The Rt. Hon. Theresa Villiers 2011, emphasis added). As a direct result of this announcement, Siemens declared that it envisaged the creation of up to 2,000 new jobs in their UK operations and across the UK supply chain, in particular in the north-east of England (The Rt. Hon. Theresa Villiers, 2011).

In the meantime Siemens' announcement as preferred bidder spelled disaster for the workforce at the Bombardier plant at Derby, and for its various suppliers scattered throughout the country. Shortly after the announcement, in July, Bombardier announced 1,400 redundancies (Transport Committee 2011). According to Derbyshire County Council, 13,500 supply chain jobs were at risk (Transport Committee 2011). In view of the fact that the Bombardier plant in Derby was the UK's last remaining train manufacturing facility, the consequent job and skill losses threatened the whole future of train manufacturing in the UK: 'The Government is concerned that the loss of a UK train design facility is likely to have long term adverse implications for the cost of the railway, because of the specific design requirements of British trains' (Transport Committee 2011). According to the Transport Committee, when bundling train manufacture and financing in a single procurement package the market will most likely be skewed in favour of larger multinational firms at the expense of 'excellence' in train design and domestic manufacturing.[5] The committee thus recommended 'that the Government work with the railway industry to establish how train manufacturers can create finance partnerships which offer good value to the taxpayer whilst promoting *long-term best value* (Transport Committee 2011, emphasis added).

8.3.2 Best value for money – long-term best value?

Value-for-money objectives sit at the very heart of PPP contracting. According to HM Treasury (2006) this is defined as 'the optimum combination of whole-of-life costs and quality (or fitness for purpose) of the good or service to meet the user's requirement'. In essence, value-for-money (VFM) is not about choosing the lowest priced bid – it is concerned with the trade-off between initial cost, future repair and maintenance costs, and overall reliability and flexibility.

However, it is worth noting that unlike the private market, the distinctive parameters within which the public procurement market operates deprive it of the invigorating stimuli present in the private market. Consequently, we get what Bovis refers to as a static effect to the VFM process. Although openness in public procurement through the principle of transparency is used as leverage for VFM, and is claimed to stimulate price competition – with the consequent benefits being enjoyed by public authorities – when it comes to public procurement it has been argued that this process can be counterproductive. Within the context of the public procurement rules, transparency in conjunction with the notion of predictability, combined with stability of public demand, in effect creates an environment that facilitates collusion and other anti-competitive behaviour by bidders (Albano *et al.* 2006).

It thus becomes increasingly clear that much more needs to be achieved from the value-for-money objectives through PPPs in order to increase social, environmental and economic development. Broader objectives that go beyond the whole-of-life costs and quality of the good or service being purchased need to be met. Given that the main characteristic of PPP contractual arrangements is that they bundle investment expenditure with life-cycle operational costs, the grounds for its justification is only evident when the most efficient mix of costs leads to cost-cutting with simultaneous increases in social welfare gains.[6]

PPPs are not the panacea for all our problems. On the other hand, we should not lose sight of the fact that PPPs can be made to work for society at large. For instance, they have been instrumental in poverty reduction – there are ample examples to prove this point. It is all a matter of getting the right PPP framework, one that is conducive to fundamental values that do not render the individual as the means for elevating free trade as an end in itself. For what society is founded upon is the common good, which is essential for human flourishing. This is the driving force that motivates each and every individual to reach their internal satisfaction. This satisfaction needs to be distinguished from the utilitarian type of satisfaction that aims for the greatest happiness of the greatest number.

In an attempt to drive this point forward, the following discusses two successful pro-poor PPP initiatives that provide food for thought.

Bompart *et al.* describe a successful needs-driven innovation for patients in resource-poor settings through a PPP which was instrumental in developing a new anti-malarial combination within the shortest possible time frame. The PPP that was set up made it possible to bring together different strengths and make the most out of skills and resources in order to meet new global health challenges for poverty-related diseases. From the outset, when the PPP was formed, two bold commitments were made. First, the product was not to receive patent protection. This eventually turned out to be one of the key factors behind its success. Second, the partners set a target price of US$1 for an adult treatment and less than 50 cents for children. The roles and responsibilities of each partner and the rules for decision-making were clearly laid out early on. This proved very useful since differences in opinion about how to reach common goals led to debates and delays in decision-making on more than one occasion. However, the partners also learned how to collaborate. This turned out to be another crucial factor behind their success, since progress seemed to be made when there was dialogue and when the partners worked together rather than in isolation. As a result of the partnership, as of late 2010 the new anti-malarial combination (ASAW Winthrop) had been registered in 30 sub-Saharan African countries and in India, with over 80 million treatments distributed across 21 countries. The challenges brought by the introduction of the new drug meant that the PPP continued to evolve by adding new partners (Bompart *et al.* 2011).

In Durban, the second most populous city in South Africa, PPPs are used as one of the mechanisms to achieve urban development (Houghton 2011). Durban faces major socio-economic challenges including poverty, very high HIV/AIDS infection rates, unemployment, severe housing shortages and crime. These challenges strongly influence Durban's urban development imperatives – imperatives that seek to be socially oriented and particularly focused on uplifting the lives of the poorest urban citizens. In 1999, the private sector in Durban formulated a 'Business Vision' for the city and presented this to local and provincial government. As a result, a strategic partnership between business and government was formalised as the Durban Growth Coalition – which went on to address successfully the planning and implementation of various flagship developments within the city. The Durban Growth Coalition has continued to evolve to include local and provincial government representatives, medium-sized businesses, and internationally and locally renowned business partners such as Mondi Paper and Tongaat Hulett Property Developments. Overall, the Coalition's vision is to unblock development in Durban, encourage economic growth, and 'realise the city's potential as a world class port and leisure centre.' (Houghton 2011: 81).

The above examples illustrate how PPPs can be utilised as effective mechanisms capable of uplifting the lives of the poor and addressing social inequalities, and hence act as an effective means for moving towards social justice. Social considerations have been weaved into their PPP programme from the very outset, and were key to their success. Such success also translated into economic benefits. In order for PPPs to work one requires an enabling environment in which 'community is not founded upon law; rather, law is founded upon community' (McCabe 2009: 6). And what community is founded upon is the common good as constitutive of human flourishing.

Therefore, when it comes to the notion of a public procurement regime driving Europe's internal market agenda, let us not delude ourselves to the point of obsession. Our walk and our talk need to be in line with Europe's founding values. It is all about human living. It is now high time to reorder Europe's economic and social dimensions. This essentially boils down to politics.

8.3.3 On the meaning and content of the fundamental right to equality

The Thameslink rolling stock procurement case clearly demonstrates the major impact public procurement bears on a country's industrial policy. Public procurement decisions are capable of being realised in different directions, and have different consequences for social life, and the distribution of wealth and power – at times leading to dramatic consequences. That public procurement exchanges go far beyond the simple *quid pro quo* notion found in the restricted exchange paradigm – which involves a reciprocal economic exchange between two parties – is clearly evidenced by this case.[7]

> Public procurement contracts are a special category of contracts wherein one of the parties represents the public interest and is manifest through complex exchanges that occur in social relationships and which in the process are separated in part by the passage of time.

Failure to recognise this fundamental issue in the theories that we construct to solve our problems is to suppress society's building capacity. How can we, 'justify the choice of one route over another by claiming that it is the market route. There are too many market routes' (Unger 2007: 94).

But, as the argument goes,

> [T]he competition to supply trains and maintenance services for the Thameslink programme was designed and launched ... in accordance with EU procurement procedures.
> (The Rt. Hon. Theresa Villiers 2011)

> The impact of the award of a contract on employment or unemployment necessarily cannot be taken into account as a relevant consideration.
> (Jonathan Faull, Director General, European Commission in Transport Committee 2011)

The solution

> A tender can be crafted to encourage participation of small and medium sized companies, subcontracting arrangements, but anything which indirectly requires location or origin in a particular country is obviously discriminatory.
>
> (Jonathan Faull, Director General, European Commission in Transport Committee 2011)

Discrimination appears to be the key word.

At para. 16 of a judgement of the European Court of Justice, the following was held:

> 16. According to the established case-law of the court the general principle of equality, of which the prohibition on discrimination on grounds of nationality is merely a specific enunciation, is one of the fundamental principles of community law. This principle requires that *similar situations* shall not be treated differently unless differentiation is objectively justified.
>
> (Case 810/79, emphasis added)

Further, in Case 330/91 at para. 14, the Court stated:

> 14. Moreover, it follows from the Court's judgment in Case 152/73 *Sotgiu v. Deutsche Bundespost* [1974] ECR 153 (at paragraph 11) that the rules regarding equality of treatment forbid not only overt discrimination by reason of nationality or, in the case of a company, its seat, but all covert forms of discrimination which, by the application of other criteria of differentiation, lead in fact to the same result.
>
> (Case C-330/91)

Herein follows the pertinent question – how can we be so sure that it is *discrimination* that actually confronts us? The main test to the discrimination argument revolves around its definition. In its investigations into the Thameslink rolling stock procurement case the Transport Committee noted the following: '[I]t is hard to escape the conclusion that Siemens' A+ credit rating made a significant contribution to its success in winning the Thameslink procurement' (Transport Committee 2011). Could it be argued that the A+ credit rating led to the creation of a discriminatory situation? Because according to EU public procurement standards the procurement process should, on the contrary, guarantee a 'level playing field'. (Directorate-General for Employment, Social Affairs and Equal Opportunities, Directorate-General for the Internal Market and Services 2010: 25).

Here is where we need a thorough rethink of current EU doctrine. It goes against Community public procurement policy, and the Treaty itself (notably Article 34 TFEU and Article 56 TFEU), to incorporate preference schemes in order to ameliorate the situation of SMEs, for example. This situation contrasts sharply with that of the US federal public procurement system. In the US,

A socially just alternative 201

socio-economic policy – which includes specific programmes of positive action in favour of various 'disadvantaged' businesses – is an ongoing manifestation in federal procurement. The main provisions in support of small businesses in the US are set out in the Small Business Act, which asserts as the declared policy of Congress that the government should aid,

> counsel, assist, and protect, insofar as is possible, the interests of small business concerns in order: to preserve free competitive enterprise; and, to ensure that a *fair proportion* of the total purchases and contracts or subcontracts for property and services for the Government ... be placed with small business enterprises.
>
> (The Small Business Act of 1953 in GHK and Technopolis 2007: 102, emphasis added)

Public procurement rules in Europe are concerned with providing equal access to opportunities. While EU law permits positive action by purchasers it does not allow for positive discrimination. The rationale behind such logic is 'to guarantee a level playing field, so that purchasers offer under-represented businesses the same opportunities to compete for public contracts as other qualified suppliers. In this way, competition can be encouraged, drawing more companies into the tendering process' (Directorate-General for Employment, Social Affairs and Equal Opportunities, Directorate-General for the Internal Market and Services 2010: 25). It therefore transpires that the 'guarantee' of a level playing field – by way of offering the same opportunities to compete for public contracts – confines the notion of equality only with respect to *access* to participation in public procurement contracts. However, in order to realistically guarantee a level playing field, various inclusion criteria other than the accessibility criterion for participation in public procurement contracts merit consideration. The point of entry – that is, the opportunity to compete in a fair manner – is heavily dependent upon, and hence determined by, other factors.

> equality is no longer merely an equality of rights, a purely legal notion of formal equality in the definition and application of legal rules – a form of equality which is in any case now much discredited, not because it no longer has any value ... but because it has proved inadequate to ensure what is now perceived as social harmony, namely no longer solely the absence of injustices suffered by the most disadvantaged to the benefit of the most advantaged, but a degree of integration of every individual into the collectivity that will achieve the overall satisfaction of all its members.
>
> (Picard 1998)

For it is equality vis-à-vis the person in their *totality* that we are concerned with – a totality that recognises the individual not just as a physical being but also as a social being at whose very core lies their human dignity. It calls for the recognition of the human being as an end in itself and not as a means to an end. The latter appears to be the case when the notion of equality is allowed to rest solely upon the merits of the accessibility criterion for participation in public procurement contracts in order to serve the free trade dogma. More specifically, we need to refer to an equality that takes into account the *capability to function*.[8] Capabilities to function assert freedom, a freedom that liberates the individual and provides space for initiative and action. Hence, 'the principle of equality thus changes from a ban on discriminatory forms of treatment that create inequalities to an obligation to impose discriminatory forms of treatment that have an equalising effect, i.e. compensatory or positive discrimination' (Picard 1998: 93). It calls for profound changes in economic and social structures, not least an indefinite expansion of the public sphere (Picard 1998). This is how society can decide to expand upon individual freedoms, and how society will in return benefit.

When it comes to conceptualising the notion of equality it is only natural that such a conception embraces a broad equation. In this respect we may refer to J. Stacey Adams' equity theory, through which much of the thinking on equity and fairness has been developed (Griffin 1993). According to this theory, in order to seek social equity in terms of rewards received for performance, people view their outcomes and inputs as a ratio and then compare their own ratio to someone else's. Therefore, we end up with a comparison that undergoes the following process:

$$\frac{\text{Outcomes (self)}}{\text{Inputs (self)}} \stackrel{?}{=} \frac{\text{Outcomes (other)}}{\text{Inputs (other)}}$$

This formulation is subjective and based on individual perceptions. Outcomes represent what the individual receives from the exchange, while inputs represent what the individual contributes to the exchange. According to this theory individuals assign weights to various outcomes and inputs. This ratio is then compared with the perceived ratios of outcomes and inputs of others who are in the same or similar situation in order to determine whether they have been equitably treated. When the two ratios are perceived as equal there is equity. When this is not the case the individual concerned may feel under-rewarded or over-rewarded, and as a result becomes motivated to alter the equation – for example by distorting the original ratios by rationalising, trying to get the other person to change his or her outcomes or inputs, leaving the situation, or changing the object of comparison. It is worth noting that the notion of equity and fairness does not simply revolve around a single variable, such as that of ensuring equal access to participation in public procurement contracts. The formulation is much more complex, and individuals, by their nature, incorporate a much broader spectrum in order to balance out what they perceive as fair.

This naturally ingrained methodology of arriving at an internalised sense of fairness/equality should direct and guide our thinking when it comes to promulgating public policies. Broadening the notion of equality – rather than confining it to a single criterion – appears to present a more just approach that is in sync with our social nature. It therefore transpires that when it comes to public procurement contracts the notion of equality needs to be seen through a much broader lens. In this respect the lens of *capabilities* – or *capabilities to function* – is much more fitting. Because capabilities to function assert freedom – a freedom that can make human flourishing possible. This notion of equality recognises the individual not just as a physical being but also as a social one, at whose very core lies human dignity. It also calls for the recognition of the human being as an end in itself and not as a means to an end. Free trade will flourish when deep-seated commitments underlie public policy that is guided by a vision of human flourishing.

8.4 Arguing for a European theory of social justice

A European theory of social justice can be realised through various institutional formats. PPPs are one of the formats that can exemplify such. Our concern here is engaging in a social justice model that seeks to define and meet the ends of its citizens, that capitalises on Member States' diversity, and that operates on the basis of principles and conditions that enable the flourishing of its citizens through the incorporation of key values as discussed and understood in this book; that is, the respect for human dignity, equality and freedom of participatory action. These are the values that conceptualise the key umbrella concept that infuses the notion of the public interest. This socially just model finds philosophical underpinnings grounded in natural law theory. It is worth noting that the PPPs conceptualised within this framework mark a fundamental departure from the way in which they are currently institutionalised. The public procurement framework that is presented here takes into consideration the distributive objectives of societal welfare as an *ex ante* mechanism. This is not the case with the ongoing EU public procurement regime.

The EU public procurement regime, as currently conceived, essentially embraces a neoliberalism that rests on utilitarian logic. Neoliberalism is primarily concerned with the protection of the free market economy, and the role of law is to maintain a healthy level of competition. But the free market economy, which is based on the theory of comparative advantage, is confronted with controversies that cannot be left ignored.[9] In addition, and as mentioned before, its justifications are grounded on the utilitarian view of social justice. In essence this holds that in order to obtain the social good, social institutions are to be arranged in such a way as to maximise the *greatest happiness*. Its focus is with the derivation of the maximum distribution of wealth, and in the process the individual is recognised as a means towards this end. According to utilitarianism, values such as individual freedom, autonomy, rights, and quality of life, are only valuable insofar as they increase aggregate utility – and therefore acquire a subordinate status in relation to the maximisation of aggregate utility.[10]

The alternative that is being argued for here is based on a socially just model in which the principles find philosophical underpinnings grounded in natural law theory. On the basis of the understandings deciphered through this journey of *verstehen*, it has been revealed that the EU public procurement regime turns the hallowed principles of Europe's social market model on their head – it superimposes potential socially dynamic welfare effects whilst dislocating fundamental European values.[11] This has led to the creation of a vacuum that encroaches upon the attainment of treaty principles and fundamental human rights. Evidently, the need to place 'Europeans at the heart of the market once again' (Monti 2010: 3) has featured as an important factor in the relaunching of Europe's Single Market, for which Professor Mario Monti (2010), in his report to President Barroso, advocates 'a social market economy approach' in pursuit of the newly proposed strategy.[12] However, it is argued that if one is guided solely by philosophical underpinnings that essentially hold on to the maximisation of the *greatest happiness*, respect for human dignity acquires secondary status at the conceptual level. Such an approach helps to maintain the status quo, as clearly evidenced by a glance at the poverty data.[13] For poverty is fundamentally linked with the question of how society distributes and redistributes its resources and opportunities; and its continued existence therefore exposes the inadequacy of our current systems. The full realisation of one's humanity, wherein the dignity of the human person is accorded full respect, turns out to be the common denominator that plays a pivotal role – intricately linking policy actions with the question of poverty.

Thus, the notion of PPPs as advanced and discussed hereunder, seeks to make up for the social justice fissures that neoliberalism fails to fulfil. In doing so it provides a naturally evolving conceptual order to the economic integration of the EU. For economic integration essentially refers to economic life within the existing Nation States[14]. How this economic life is achieved is not confined to one market route: there are many.[15] The market route identified here is grounded on a socially just model that finds philosophical underpinnings grounded in natural law theory, and is one that reaffirms 'economic activity is social activity' (Unger 2007: 142).

If we were to ask the informed and fair-minded observer about the market route that EU citizens should opt for, would their choice be based on utilitarian logic (one that utilises the individual as the means for deriving aggregate utility) or would it be the one *that exploits the potential and provides the greatest opportunities for all those wanting to engage in it in a sustained manner*[16] (in other words, a market route that seeks to achieve the flourishing of each and every individual as conceived by natural law theory)? It is presumed that the answer would point in the direction of the latter, for who would not want to be given a genuine chance in life, irrespective of social class or origin? This is the socially just model that departs conceptually from utilitarian interpretations of social justice. This departure is fundamentally justified because it sits at the very heart of Europe's founding values:

> The Union is founded on the values of respect for human dignity, freedom, democracy, equality, the rule of law and respect for human rights, including the rights of persons belonging to minorities. These values are common to the Member States in a society in which pluralism, non-discrimination, tolerance, justice, solidarity and equality between women and men prevail.
> (Article 2 TEU)

Only when an acceptable level of European social justice is achieved through the unconstrained recognition of social rights can Europe progress any further. Thus, the reordering of Europe's economic and social dimensions, that this book calls for, essentially endorses a socially just model that seeks to achieve the flourishing of each and every individual who is willing to engage in it. It is a socially just model that recognises the human being as an end in itself, and at the core of which lies human dignity: 'All human beings are born free and equal in dignity and rights. They are endowed with reason and conscience and should act towards one another in a spirit of brotherhood' (United Nations, Universal Declaration of Human Rights, Article 1).

Conceived through such a framework, a socially just model of public procurement has the potential to translate into a European theory of social justice that is capable of tilting the balance towards a more just equilibrium in the EU legal, social and economic order. Such a model seeks to achieve a positive impact on societal welfare, one that is in harmony and capitalises upon the diverse cultures of European Member States. Therefore, when Professor Mario Monti highlights that the 'success of the European model depends on its ability to combine economic performance with social justice and to involve economic operators and the social partners in achieving this goal' (Monti 2010: 4), the way of achieving such a goal necessitates that we tackle the issue at grass roots level. That is to say, by engaging Europe in a social justice model whose principles find their philosophical underpinnings justified on grounds that were established and enshrined in Europe's founding values.

8.4.1 Advancing a European theory of a socially just alternative

In advancing a European theory that is based on a socially just model that has philosophical underpinnings grounded in natural law theory and institutionalised through PPPs, the principles that the theory will engage in are those derived and put forth by John Rawls. Rawls' argument for 'justice as fairness' holds that the just arrangements of major social institutions in a liberal society form the basic structure of society within which justice is located.[17] Rawls' conception of society draws on social institutions which he maintains need to be fair for all cooperating members of society irrespective of their race, gender, religion, class of origin, and so on. Social institutions need to stand up to public scrutiny.

In order to derive principles of justice based on the notion of fairness, Rawls presents two principles. Absolute or *lexical priority* is assigned to the first principle: the *liberty principle*. The second principle, the *equality principle*, focuses on two particular aspects of justice; the first part relates to the *principal of fair equality of opportunity*, while the second – also referred to as the *difference principle* – advances that social and economic inequalities between citizens are to be limited as long as they favour the least well-off members of society. In cases of conflict the *principal of fair equality of opportunity* takes priority over the *difference principle*. For Rawls a property-owning democracy is necessary in order to realise the principles of justice as fairness. This he distinguishes from welfare state capitalism. It is argued that whilst welfare state capitalism secures a social baseline through *ex post* redistributive taxation, a property-owning democracy sets limits to the accumulation of wealth across a concentrated narrow band of citizens by dispersing capital holdings across the population and therefore making use of *ex ante* redistribution of capital. 'The intent is not simply to assist those who lose out through accident or misfortune (although that must be done), but rather to put all citizens in a position to manage their own affairs *on a footing of a suitable degree* of social and economic equality' (Rawls 2001: 138).

Whereas Rawls grounds his arguments in favour of a property-owning democracy regime over that of welfare state capitalism, there have been others who believe that both regimes can complement each other and that property-owning democracies should be regarded as 'useful extensions of, rather than replacements for, the welfare state' (O'Neill 2009: 390).[18] This view is congruent with that adopted in this book, which also aims to demonstrate how Rawls' principles of justice as fairness through the regime of a property-owning democracy can be institutionalised through public procurement and more specifically through the PPP regime. The following thus attempts to set out how public procurement, manifested through the PPP regime as an *ex ante* mechanism, can be made more socially just by linking the discussion to Rawls' elaborations in support of a property-owning democracy.

In advancing the notion of a property-owning democracy, Rawls, in *Justice as Fairness* (2001: 149–150), presented a socio-economic system which requires (at least) the following three institutional or policy-based features:

1. Wide dispersal of capital: The *sine qua non* of a POD is that it would entail the wide dispersal of the ownership of the means of production, with individual citizens controlling substantial (and broadly equal) amounts of productive capital (and perhaps with an opportunity to control their own working conditions).
2. Blocking the intergenerational transmission of advantage: A POD would also involve the enactment of significant estate, inheritance, and gift taxes, to limit the largest inequalities of wealth – especially from one generation to the next.
3. Safeguards against the corruption of politics: A POD would seek to limit the effects of private and corporate wealth on politics, through campaign finance reform, public funding of political parties, public provision of forums for political debate, and other measures to block the influence of wealth on politics (perhaps including publicly funded elections).

Policies of type (3) are consistent with Rawls' first principle of justice and therefore aim to protect the fair value of political liberties. Policies of type (1) and (2) aim to put into operation the second principle of justice: the equality principle. In setting out the linkages with the PPP regime we will start by focusing on public procurement policies that have the potential to realise Rawls' second principle of justice: that is, type (1) and type (2) policies. Discussion of potential public procurement policies that realise type (3) policies, will follow.

PPPs as the means for satisfying type (1) policies

As mentioned earlier, policies in this respect need to satisfy the equality principle, which in effect focuses on two particular aspects of justice – the principle of fair equality of opportunity and the difference principle. The former takes precedence in cases of conflict.

One of the major concerns that the notion of equality brings to mind in the context of the EU public procurement regime is the under-representation of SMEs participating in above-EU threshold public procurement – a fact long acknowledged by the Commission.[19] This clearly indicates that a narrow band of European citizens are enjoying the fruits of productive resources. Such dominance comes in breach of Rawls' difference principle which postulates that social and economic inequalities between citizens are to be limited as long as they favour the least well-off members of society. Therefore, policies aiming to satisfy the difference principle necessitate a move towards the greater dispersal of control over productive resources. Such a move directs our attention to policies that are aimed at realising Rawls' principle of fair equality of opportunity.

What is actually meant by the term 'fair equality of opportunity'? In Rawls' view, membership of any particular socio-economic group should be based on one's own abilities and efforts, irrespective of social class or origin. Accordingly he notes: '[S]upposing there is a distribution of native endowments, those who have the same level of talent and ability and the same willingness to use these gifts should have the same prospects of success regardless of their social class of origin' (Rawls 2001: 114–15). Therefore, a PPP regime that aims to preserve *the fair equality of opportunity* over time needs to have a 'keen concern for limiting the influence of social background on individual life chances' (O'Neill 2009: 385). In effect, it could be argued that the *fair equality of opportunity* principle essentially comprises two fundamental concepts: *equality* and *fair opportunity*. One can only claim that he or she has been accorded *fair opportunity* if the safeguards to the notion of *equality* have been secured. In the case of the latter, according to European Court of Justice case law, 'this principle requires that *similar situations* shall not be treated differently unless differentiation is objectively justified' (COM (2011) 896 final: para. 16). It is at this point that we now come full circle to our previous arguments on the matter.[20] This argumentation gives further credence to our previous claims, in that one cannot adopt a contracted view – i.e. one that confines the notion of equality solely on the basis of ensuring *equal access to opportunities* as interpreted by the Commission. It is too simplistic an interpretation.

For it is an equality vis-à-vis the person in their totality that should concern us. This totality recognises the individual not just as a physical being, but also as a social being at whose very core lies human dignity. It calls for recognition of the human being as an end in itself, and not as a means to an end. More specifically, we need to refer to an equality that takes into account the *capability to function*. Capabilities to function assert freedom, a freedom that liberates the individual and which therefore provides space for initiative and action.

This conception is also consistent with Rawls' assertion that citizens situated in this way will 'have a lively sense of their worth as persons and ... be able to advance *their ends* with self confidence' (Rawls 2001: 59).

Therefore, within the context of a PPP regime, on the basis of the above arguments the realisation of type (1) policies justifies the adoption of so-called *preferential schemes* in order to ensure the wide dispersal of capital. Such preferential schemes can include set-asides; that is, 'when a percentage of the overall procurement budget or a percentage of a single contract value is reserved to targeted group(s) (SME, domestic, women owned, etc.' (Fana and Piga 2012: 22). It may also refer to bid preferences/subsidies; that is, 'when targeted firms get a percentage discount on their bid' (Fana and Piga 2012: 22). It is worth noting, however, that generally speaking the usage of the term 'preference schemes' – and other similar terms – are a misnomer because of the negative connotations and consequent misleading effect. In contrast it appears more fitting to use such terms as 'appropriation schemes', 'anti-discriminatory', and affirmative action'. Such terms have a better potential to communicate the right signals – signals that, generally speaking, reflect institutional measures undertaken for the sake of preserving the *equality principal*.

PPPs as the means for satisfying type (2) policies

Policies falling within this category also aim to satisfy the equality principle, in this case by *blocking the intergenerational transmission of advantage*. To this effect Rawls advocated various forms of inheritance and gift taxes. It is not within the scope of this book to argue in favour or against such policies. However, we will argue about policies that have the potential to bear the same effect; that is, to *block the intergenerational transmission of advantage* via *ex ante* mechanisms made possible through the PPP regime.

Indeed, the arguments set out above in satisfying type (1) policies can very well have the effect of satisfying type (2) policies. Nevertheless, we can take this a step further by asking a simple question – what is the nature of the *intergenerational transmission of advantage* that PPPs might bring about, and, having established this, what policies can be implemented that are capable of negating this? The answer becomes clear as soon as we acknowledge the fact that public procurement – and especially PPPs – are essentially concerned with complex exchanges that occur in social relationships, and which in the process are separated in part by the passage of time. The *intergenerational transmission of advantage* can comprise any measure that blocks the *complex exchanges that occur in social relationships*. Let us for a very brief moment revert to the Thameslink rolling stock procurement case. The following transcripts make the point:

> *Professor Williams.* All I have is an envelope and that tells me that Bombardier has a B++ credit rating and Siemens an A+ credit rating. You can then play around with rates of interest and various other things, and on the back of my envelope it looks like it could be anything like £500 million ... the

fundamental mistake of issuing a bundled contract where you have multiple policy objectives, where you want low cost finance and you want the trains built appropriately, and you bundle it all together in one contract with one number at the end as the decision principle. Of course, you lose sight of a fair number of your objectives.

(Transport Committee 2011)[21]

Professor Williams The bundling introduced a bias in favour of Siemens because they had the superior credit rating and that gave them an advantage of maybe several hundred million pounds on the deal. Apart from that, the other issue which all your witnesses are emphasising, is that value for money was defined very narrowly as price for quality, as though it were you or I choosing a toaster at John Lewis or my central administrator choosing stationery supplies. That calculus is entirely appropriate for a small-scale decision by you or me at John Lewis. It is not appropriate for a £1.5 billion contract which is relevant to the future of train building in the UK.

... the scale makes this a kind of procurement industrial policy ... these considerations have some considerable weight. Each Bombardier worker pays £17k of taxes a year and makes £10k a year of tax contributions. Average pay in the rail supply industry is £44k total compensation. These are material considerations, material sums, which should have been taken into account.

(Transport Committee 2011)[22]

It is at this point that we now come full circle to our previous arguments relating to the notion of *value for money*.[23] Within the context of a PPP regime, the realisation of type (2) policies needs to take account of the *value-for-money principle* – a principle that incorporates broad objectives that go beyond the whole-of-life costs and the quality of the good or service being purchased. Hence, justification on the basis of the value-for-money principle is only acceptable when the most efficient mix of costs leads to cost-cutting with simultaneous increases in social welfare gains.

Furthermore, in addition to the above-mentioned policy and on the basis of the arguments put forth, policies that seek to *block the intergenerational transmission of advantage* need also to *mandate* that major contracts be divided into lots.

PPPs as the means for satisfying type (3) policies

As previously noted, policies of type (3) are consistent with Rawls' first principle of justice and therefore aim to protect the fair value of political liberties. Policies falling under this category attempt to safeguard against the corruption of politics. In this respect Rawls advocated policies that seek 'campaign finance reform, public funding of political parties, public provision of forums for political debate, and other measures to block the influence of wealth on politics (perhaps including publicly funded elections)' (Rawls 2001: 149–50). When it comes to public procurement and PPPs it is a known fact that 'the financial risks at stake and the close interaction between the public and the private sectors make public procurement a risk area for unsound business practices, such as conflict of interest, favouritism and corruption' (COM (2011) 15 final: 48). Thus, all type (3) policies as advocated by Rawls are applicable within the context of promulugating social justice policies in PPPs. Indeed, one may consider various alternative devices which are consistent with realising Rawls' first principle of justice. In this respect Roberto Mangabeira Unger (1987) advanced a three-tiered economic order. The first tier would consist of a social investment fund controlled democratically by elected executive and representative bodies responsible for fixing the institutional and economic framework within which the rest of the system operates, and that lends capital to funds at the second tier. The second tier in turn comprises a system of subordinate investment funds controlled by semi-independent bodies that borrow from the central fund and that lend to enterprises within the limits set by the central fund. The third tier is composed of firms that borrow capital from the subordinate investment funds and that transact with one another within the rules fixed by the funds. The system aims at achieving a wide dispersion of power, while seeking to avoid direct links between the central fund and firms themselves.

Policies that seek only to address social justice issues through the enactment of type (1) and type (2) policies cannot deliver social justice because the absence of type (3) policies will deprive them of all force. Indeed, the PPP regime clearly illustrates the case that type (1), (2) and (3) policies are so closely intertwined that only through a combination of all three, as discussed, is there the capacity to deliver more just socio-economic arrangements.

8.5 Concluding remarks

Having embarked on a journey of *verstehen* this book culminates by advancing a European theory of a socially just alternative. Such theory finds philosophical underpinnings grounded in natural law theory, and is institutionalised through the PPP regime which puts into operation principles derived by John Rawls in *Justice as Fairness*.

It is now possible to move a step further and conceptualise PPPs by way of presenting a definition that reflects the underpinning philosophical rationale that drives its *public interest* function when put into operation – a rationale that is grounded in natural law theory. This definition (see below) builds and refines further the definition that was put forth by the European Commission in its Green Paper (COM (2004) 327 final) on PPPs:

> Public–Private Partnerships are forms of cooperation between the public authorities and the world of business which aim to best meet clearly defined public interest needs through:
>
> (1) the optimum allocation of resources, risk and rewards by way of funding, construction, renovation, management or maintenance of infrastructure or the provision of a service and;
> (2) the simultaneous increases in social welfare gains.

A socially just alternative 211

The PPP regime has made it possible to clearly explicate how a socially just model can be institutionalised through the infusion of a *public interest function* that incorporates the key umbrella concept as brought to the fore and discussed in this book; namely, one that incorporates the values of respect for human dignity, equality, and freedom of participatory action. Indeed, the naturally occurring question as to whether such logic could extend to other public interest functions – for instance to public procurement in general – may arise. This all boils down to how we are to interpret the public interest function.[24] For as the discussion on public interest has revealed, the concept is very vague, and overly used and abused. Unless we can supply meaningful content from which to derive workable meanings, the notion will remain that way.

It therefore follows that if the public interest function in the EU public procurement regime were to be guided by philosophical underpinnings conceived in natural law theory – in which the individual is seen as an end in itself – a total rethink on how the EU public procurement regime is conceived and put into operation would become necessary. However, the EU public procurement regime, as currently construed, essentially embraces neoliberal principles that are grounded in utilitarian logic wherein the individual is used as a means to promulgate the European Single Market.

Thus, when it comes to deciding upon which philosophical argument should underpin and henceforth guide public interest functions, such decisions need to be based upon sound practical thinking. This book advocates a *public interest* function that takes into account social concerns explicated through a *common good* that fulfils, first and foremost, the values of human dignity, equality and participatory action and that capitalises on making the best possible use of public procurement as a dynamic and powerful policy instrument. In doing so it reaches out towards the achievement of a socially just model of European integration, one that occurs within the pan European social space and which intensifies the role of the citizen both in their capacity as a national citizen and as a European citizen. However, for this to occur it is necessary for there to be a fundamental departure in the way that the current EU public procurement regime is conceived. This requires a change in attitude that moves away from an overriding and unconditional approach revolving around a European economic efficiency logic, and towards a socially just alternative that calls for a reordering of its economic and social dimensions.

Notes

1 On the value of respect for human dignity – each and every person as a rational human being has dignity. Human dignity is inviolable. It is 'superior to human rights and fundamental freedoms who owe their origin and existence to the dignity of the human person' (Aquilina 2010). See also the discussion in Chapter 5, in particular section 5.4.3, 'Dignity as the basic moral premise'; and section 5.5, 'Respect for human dignity – a legally enforceable fundamental right'.
2 On the value of equality – what we are hereconcerned with here is an equality vis-à-vis the person in their totality, a totality that recognises the individual not just as a physical being but also as a social being at whose very core lies human dignity. It calls for the recognition of the human being as an end in itself and not as a means to

an end. More specifically, we need to refer to an equality that takes into account the *capability to function*. Capabilities to function assert freedom. The notion of capability to function refers to ideas conceived by Professor Amartya Sen, as discussed in Chapter 5, section 5.3, 'The nature of poverty – definitions abound'.
3. On the value of freedom of participatory action – what we are concerned with here is a freedom that enables the full participation of the individual in society, a freedom that defines and serves the ends of its citizens, liberates the individual and provides space for initiative and action. Such space for initiative and action unleashes the individual's capability to function, which in itself asserts freedom. This is the freedom that finds its epitome when expressed through the flourishing of the individual.
4. ITT stands for Invitation to Tender.
5. The Transport Committee is appointed by the House of Commons to examine the expenditure, administration, and policy of the Department for Transport and its associated public bodies.
6. In this respect see also Hart (2003).
7. On the notion of 'exchange' see the discussion in Chapter 6.
8. The notion of *capability to function* refers to that conceived by Professor Amartya Sen, as discussed in Chapter 5, section 5.3, 'The Nature of poverty – definitions abound'.
9. See discussion in Chapter 4, in particular section 4.3, 'The theory of comparative advantage – a general idea'.
10. To this effect see Chapter 1, section 1.3.1, 'Utilitarianism'.
11. See the discussion in chapter 5, in particular section 5.6, 'The quest for poverty reduction – putting EU public procurement into perspective'.
12. In this respect see COM (2010) 608 final. See also the discussion in Chapter 1, section 1.4, 'On Europe's social model'.
13. Poverty in the EU features as a real problem. Nearly one in seven people in the EU are at risk of poverty. For a discussion of this see Chapter 5, in particular section 5.2, 'Poverty across the EU – a snapshot'.
14. For Myrdal, economic integration refers to economic life within the existing Nation States (Myrdal 1956: 94).
15. According to Unger Mangabeira (2007: 94), 'There are too many market routes'.
16. Paraphrasing previous arguments as discussed in Chapter 4.
17. For egalitarian liberal perspectives on social justice see the discussion in Chapter 1, section 1.3.2, 'Egalitarian liberal perspectives'.
18. The author also notes that this is very much in line with James Meade's opinion about policies concerning a property-owning democracy, and quotes his view in this respect: 'These measures are needed, for the most part, to supplement rather than to replace the existing Welfare-State policies' (Meade 1964: 75).
19. To this effect see the discussions in Chapter 3, in particular section 3.4, 'EU public procurement and its impact on small- and medium-sized enterprises', and Chapter 5, in particular section 5.6, 'The quest for poverty reduction – putting EU public procurement into perspective'.
20. To this effect see in particular the discussion in section 8.3.2, 'Best value for money – long term best value?'
21. See Professor Karel Williams, Director, ESCR Centre for Research on Socio-Cultural Change, University of Manchester, as witness in response to question 11, minutes taken on the 7 September 2011. Transport Committee minutes of evidence – HC1453. Available at: www.publications.parliament.uk/pa/cm201012/cmselect/cmtran/1453/11090701.htm [accessed 8 March, 2012]. Parliamentary information licensed under the Open Parliament Licence v3.0.
22. Ibid. in response to question 17. Parliamentary information licensed under the Open Parliament Licence v3.0.

23 To this effect see in particular the discussion on the matter in section 8.3.2, 'Best value for money – long term best value?'
24 To this effect see the discussion in Chapter 6, section 6.4.2, 'The public interest – fiction or fact?'

References

Albano, G.L., Buccirossi, P., Spagnolo, G. and Zanza, M., 2006. 'Preventing Collusion in Procurement' in: Dimitri, N., Piga, G. and Spagnolo, G. (eds), *Handbook of Procurement*. Cambridge: Cambridge University Press.

Aquilina, K., 2010. 'Respect for Human Dignity and the Law' [Homepage of State Care]. Available at: www.statecareandmore.eu/index.php/blogs/respect-for-human-dignity-and-the-law-by-prof-kevin-aquilina-.html23 [accessed November 2010].

Bompart, F., Kiechel, J.R., Sebbag, R. and Pecoul, B., 2011. 'Innovative public-private partnerships to maximise the delivery of anti-malarial medicines: lessons learned from the ASAQ Winthrop experience' in *Malaria Journal*, vol. 10, no. 143, pp. 1–9.

Department for Transport, 2011. 'Thameslink Rolling Stock Project'. Available at: www.dft.gov.uk/publications/thameslink [accessed 8 March 2012].

European PPP Expertise Centre, 2013. *Market Update – Review of the European PPP Market in 2012*. Luxembourg: EPEC.

European PPP Expertise Centre, 2014. *Market Update – Review of the European PPP Market in 2013*. Luxembourg: EPEC.

European PPP Expertise Centre, 2015. *Market Update – Review of the European PPP Market in 2014*. Luxembourg: EPEC.

Fana, M. and Piga, G., 2012. *How could simplification of the rules increase SME's possibilities of and interest in participating in competition for public contracts?* Copenhagen: Copenhagen Business School.

GHK, A.T., 2007. *Evaluation of SME Access to Public Procurment Markets in the EU, Final Report*. Brussels: European Commission.

Griffin, R.W., 1993. *Part V, The Leading Process*. Boston, London: Houghton Mifflin Company.

Hart, O., 2003. 'Incomplete Contracts and Public Ownership: Remarks and an Application to Public-Private Partnerships' in *Economic Journal*, vol. 113, pp. 69–76.

Houghton, J., 2011. 'Negotiating the Global and the Local: Evaluating Development Through Public-Private Partnerships in Durban, South Africa' in *Urban Forum*, vol. 22, pp. 75–93.

McCabe, H., 2009. *The Good Life*. London: Continuum.

McKenzie, D., *PFI in the UK & PPP in Europe 2009*. International Financial Services London.

Meade, J., 1964. *Efficiency, Equality and the Ownership of Property*. London: George Allen and Unwin.

Monti, M., 2010. *A new strategy for the single market: At the service of Europe's economy and society – Report to the President of the European Commission*. Brussels.

Myrdal, G., 1956. *An International Economy: Problems and Prospects*. London: Routledge & Kegan Paul.

O'Neill, M., 2009. *Liberty, Equality and Property-Owning Democracy*. London: Blackwell Publishing Inc.

Picard, E., 1998. 'Citizenship, Fundamental Rights, and Public Services' in Freedland, M. and Sciarra, S. (eds), *Services and Citizenship in European Law*. Oxford: Clarendon Press.

Rawls, J., 2001. *Justice as Fairness: A Restatement.* Cambridge, MA: Harvard University Press.
Rt. Hon. Theresa Villiers, 2011. *Thameslink rolling stock.* UK: Department for Transport.
Transport Committee. 2011. 'Eleventh Report, Thameslink rolling stock procurement and the proceedings of the Committee ordered by the House of Commons, printed 6 December 2011'. Available at: www.publications.parliament.uk/pa/cm201012/cmselect/cmtran/1453/145302.htm [accessed 8 March, 2012]. Parliamentary information licensed under the Open Parliament Licence v3.0.
Treasury, H.M, 2006. *Value for Money Assessment Guidance.* Norwich: Controller of Her Majesty's Stationery Office.
Unger, M.R., 1987. *Fake Necessity.* Cambridge: Cambridge University Press.
Unger, M.R., 2007. *Free trade reimagined: the world division of labor and the method of economics.* Princeton, NJ: Princeton University Press.
United Nations., *Universal Declaration of Human Righs, Article 1.*

Official documents

Cases before the Court of Justice of the European Union

Case 810/79. *Peter Überschär v. Bundesversicherungsanstalt für Angestellte [1980].* ECR 02747.
CASE C-330/91. *The Queen v. Inland Revenue Commissioners, ex parte Commerzbank AG [1993].* ECR I-04017.

European Commission

COM (2004) 327 final, 30 April 2004. *Green Paper on Public-Private Partnerships and Community Law on Public Contracts and Concessions.*
COM (2010) 608 final, 27 October 2010. *Towards a Single Market Act for a highly competitive social market economy.* Brussels: European Commission.
COM (2011a) 15 final, 27 January 2011. *Green Paper on the modernisation of EU public procurement policy. Towards a more efficient European Procurement Market.* Brussels: European Commission.
COM (2011b), 896 final, 20 December 2011. *Proposal for a Directive of the European Parliament and of the Council on public procurement.* Brussels: European Commission.
Directorate-General for Employment, Social Affairs and Equal Opportunities and Directorate-General for the Internal Market and Services, 2010. *Buying Social – A Guide to Taking Account of Social Considerations in Public Procurement, European Commission.* Brussels: European Commission.
European Commission, TED – Tenders Electronic Daily. *Official Journal of the European Union.*

9 Conclusions

The importance of having a clear political philosophy underpinning political action in order to address fundamental questions regarding the *public interest* comes out clearly from this book. Ultimately, whatever philosophy the policy-makers and legislators choose to embrace – or fail to embrace – will have an inescapable impact on the individual in relation to the society they live in. The discussion in the last chapter culminated in the production of a European theory of social justice that is in alignment with the European Union's founding values. The theory has clear philosophical underpinnings that draw on natural law theory. It operates on the basis of principles and conditions that enable the flourishing of EU citizens by incorporating key values that are mutually reinforcing and cannot be disentangled – these values being respect for human dignity, equality, and freedom of participatory action. Evidently, such values have come into play only as a result of their impact upon the direct and indirect experiences that the European citizen is forced to endure vis-à-vis Europe's public procurement regime.

When it comes to understanding the extent to which the public procurement regime is serving the *public interest*, practical reasonableness leads us in a direction that suggests the human person is not just a mere subject, not just a means for balancing the equation of supply and demand. The human person entails respect for their dignity and for their human rights. It is in the very nature of human beings to build relationships and to interact with the community. And it is within this communion that the human person can aspire to the highest levels of accomplishment and flourishing.

Public procurement contracts represent a special category – more specifically, they represent complex exchanges that occur in social relationships and which in the process are separated in part by the passage of time, wherein one of the parties represents the public interest. On the basis of the understandings deciphered by this book, it was noted that EU public procurement as a vital tool for promulgating the internal market comes at the expense of the public interest, insofar as the public interest function in question is one that seeks to achieve a common good in which the individual is seen as an end in itself and not as a means to an end – as is the case when Single Market integration aims appear as the ultimate objective. The author finds the latter position problematic since it conflicts with European founding values wherein respect for human dignity necessitates that individuals be treated as an end in themselves and not as a means for achieving ulterior goals. On the one hand, EU public procurement is seen as serving as a tool that helps dislocate Europe's founding values; while on the other hand it serves as the EU's safety valve, modifying (and hence protecting, to a certain extent) the provision of public services from overwhelming market forces. The situation is untenable as long as it distances itself from permissible European ideals as contained within the Constitution. Respect for human dignity, equality, and freedom for participatory action all identify with the social conscience of the people of Europe.

9.1 The validity of our actions needs to be limited by time and concrete results

The adoption in 1971 of Directive 71/305/EEC on the coordination of procedures for the award of public works contracts marked the beginning of an evolution in EU public procurement regulation. The argument used at the time was that by guaranteeing transparent and non-discriminatory procedures economic operators across the Single Market would fully benefit from basic freedoms in competing for public contracts. During the first half of the 1980s the role of public procurement in the completion of the Single Market was further accentuated. Its regulation played a crucial part in exposing an economic and legal approach to the integration of public markets with the main object being to enhance competition and unobstructed market access. The Single Market Act of 2011 identified 12 levers for boosting European growth and confidence levels. Public procurement stood out as one of the 12 levers – and as one of the market-based instruments seeking to play a key role in the Europe 2020 strategy for smart, sustainable and inclusive growth. A proposal for a revised and modernised public procurement legislative framework – one that would incorporate greater simplicity and flexibility – was put forth by the Commission in December 2011. The proposal was to replace existing EU public procurement rules, and included for the first time proposals for legislation on concession contracts. The new public procurement legislative framework was agreed by the Council in 2012 and approved by the European Parliament in January 2014. The new legislation seeks to increase the efficiency of public spending, to deliver the best possible value for money, to facilitate the participation of SMEs and cross border procurement, and to make better use of common societal goals such as the protection of the environment, higher resource and energy efficiency, combating climate change, promoting innovation, employment and social inclusion, and ensuring the best possible conditions for the provision of high quality social services.

The proposal for a revised and modernised public procurement legislative framework is claimed to comply with the proportionality principle.

> [T]he proposal complies with the proportionality principle since it *does not go beyond what is necessary* in order to achieve the objective of ensuring

the proper functioning of the Internal Market through a set of European-wide coordinated procurement procedures.

(COM (2011) 896 final: 6, emphasis added)

However, it is worth noting that efforts to utilise Europe-wide coordinated procurement procedures – aimed at ensuring the proper functioning of the internal market – have now been in effect for 40 years. Notwithstanding this, three key problems were identified (SEC (2011) 1586 final: 3). These are as follows:

1   Insufficient cost-efficiency – current EU rules generate estimated savings of approximately €20 billion on a spend of €420 billion p.a., but procedures may be unduly burdensome as the associated cost is around €5.6 billion.[1]
2   Missed opportunities for society – current rules may not always allow stakeholders to optimise the use of their resources and/or make the best purchasing choices.[2]
3   National rather than EU PP market – more than 98 per cent of contracts awarded according to EU rules are won by national bidders (approximately 96 per cent of total value).[3]

In addition to the above it is worth recalling the fact that when it comes to small- and medium-sized enterprises these remain under-represented in above-EU threshold public procurement,[4] a matter that has long been acknowledged.[5] Furthermore, it has been claimed that a new Directive on concessions is appropriate because for the first time there are a comprehensive, clear and unambiguous set of provisions in an area which has so far been characterised by the sort of continuous uncertainty and erroneous interpretation that has often left room for unlawful practices (SEC (2011) 1588 final: 4).

Such 'problems' have long been in existence: they are chronic and structural in nature. It is hence argued that, given the nature of such problems, the claim that EU actions go no further than what is strictly necessary is difficult to uphold. Remedial treatment through the internal market route alone cannot fix the 'problems' since they go beyond proportionality. Any meaningful claims to the Single Market project mandate accountability that factors in clear timelines and concrete results.

Furthermore, in its proposal for a revised and modernised public procurement legislative framework it is claimed that the proposal complies with the subsidiarity principle. Accordingly, EU public procurement procedures above certain thresholds are said to provide European-wide transparency and objectivity, considerable savings, improved outcomes, and will serve as an important tool for the achievement of the internal market. Once again, such claims are seriously questioned and they have been the subject of scrutiny in this book. Furthermore, when one delves into the notion of the internal market – at the heart of which sits the theory of comparative advantage – there appear to be conflicting claims.[6]

218 *The solution*

How can actions that yield an overriding and unconditional attitude at the supranational level – by way of integrating public procurement markets – be legitimated? This is where rationality loses out to irrationality. We become lost in a high level of operational ambiguity and thrive on broad discretionary powers that make it possible to offer explanations for any conclusion we choose to reach.

9.2 On a plane of practical reasonableness

This book attempts to prove how a reordering of the European Union's economic and social dimensions within the sphere of the EU public procurement regime has the potential to realise a socially just model of integration in the European Union in which the European citizen is the key actor in that process. The reordering of Europe's economic and social dimensions – which this book calls for – essentially endorses a socially just model that seeks to put into motion a public interest function that recognises the human being as an end in itself. This stands in stark contrast to the public interest function that the EU public procurement regime actively puts into motion since it draws heavily on aggregative conceptions of the common good. Counter arguments to this book's stance in favour of capturing the EU public procurement regulatory framework within a social model may arise largely from three different positions:

1 The inherent flexibility of the EU acquis in relation to procurement – which has been in existence since the inception of the public procurement regulatory framework – may be argued to be already balanced inasmuch as it allows domestic policies to be taken into account in public contract awards. Social service contracts which are listed in Annex IIB of Directive 2004/18/EC are not subject to all the detailed rules of the Directive. Only certain specific rules of the Directive are applicable to such services; namely, compliance with technical specifications and publication of the Contract Award Notice. Furthermore, when it comes to the award of contracts for social services with cross border interest there remains much room for manoeuvre for contracting authorities when compared to other sectors. In such cases compliance with the full set of provisions as laid out in Directive 2004/18/EC is not required, other than the requirements as mentioned above and respecting basic principles of Community law; namely, the principle of transparency, equal treatment and non-discrimination.

In the case of contracts which include mixed services – that is, a social service component and other services that are fully covered by the procurement Directives – the Directive will only apply to a limited extent (as noted above) if the value of the social service component is greater than the value of the other service.

Furthermore, EU public procurement legislation allows Member States to reserve contracts to sheltered workshops where most of the employees concerned are disabled (such workshops seek to contribute efficiently towards the integration or reintegration of people with disabilities in the labour market). Contracting authorities are also allowed to lay down special conditions relating to the performance of a contract – provided that these are compatible with Community law and are indicated in the contract notice or in the specifications. The conditions governing the performance of a contract may, in particular, concern social and environmental considerations.

In addition, contracting authorities can legally award their contracts in accordance with the most economically advantageous offer they receive, not solely by virtue of the lowest offer. Contracting authorities can afford themselves in-house arrangements to deliver public services as well as public-public co-operation. EU law also allows public undertakings to organise and deliver services as they see fit (Article 106 (2) TFEU). Sectoral regulation covering transport allows the notion of the internal operator delivering transport services.

Following such line of advance it may be argued that given the already-ingrained levels of flexibility in EU public procurement legislation, any reported failures of its effectiveness and social applications may be attributed to ineffective application on the part of either the Member States, the EU institutions, or both.

2 Notwithstanding the overarching aims of the EU's public procurement strategy – which are driven to promulgate the Single Market – the new rules on public procurement and concession contracts, approved by the European Parliament on 15 January 2014, seek to incorporate greater simplification and flexibility whilst increasing efficiency of public spending, delivering best possible value for money, facilitating participation of SMEs and cross border procurement, and making better use of common societal goals such as the protection of the environment, higher resource and energy efficiency, combating climate change, promoting innovation, employment and social inclusion, and ensuring the best possible conditions for the provision of high quality social services. This adds further impetus to the social application of the EU public procurement regime.

3 If one takes (for instance) expenditure values for 2010, EU public procurement expenditure was reported to be in the region of 19 per cent of EU GDP. However, only 3.7 per cent of this can be attributed to expenditure that is directly related to EU public procurement regulation. This reflects that a significant amount of public procurement remains below the EU applicable public procurement thresholds, thus there remains ample flexibility at EU Member States' disposal. In the case of contracts whose value falls below the applicable thresholds of the public procurement Directives, public authorities need only comply with the basic rules and principles of Community law; that is, the principles of equal treatment, non-discrimination and transparency.

Following the above lines of argument, and given the significant amount of flexibility already enjoyed by EU Member States, any claims that a reordered public procurement regime that takes into account social concerns could reverse – or at least retard – the levels of social decline and poverty, are superfluous. Moreover, social policies rest with Member States' sovereignty and are immune from supranational intervention.

The above counter arguments obscure the real weaknesses inherent in EU public procurement regulation. The discussion that follows attempts to address this.

As a follower of political fashion, public procurement policy has over the years been used as a vital instrument to secure national economic and social welfare policies. It has a long history of being used to drive forward social justice goals. Notwithstanding this, the use of public procurement policy to serve competition and market access goals, on the one hand, and its use to serve as a socio-economic lever for domestic policy on the other, has very often been the subject of friction at both international and EU level.

EU public procurement, estimated at 19 per cent of EU GDP, has the potential for significant strategic investments both in the economic and social policy dimensions – particularly when one bears in mind the highly dynamic and multi-faceted uses of public procurement as a policy tool. Against such a scenario this book puts into context the question of poverty. Poverty features as a real problem across the EU. One in seven people across the EU are at risk of poverty. The persistent levels of poverty across the EU – which have maintained their momentum for well over the past decade – raise fundamental political questions. The recent wave of social injustices that have come about as a result of the current economic crisis is another case in point, and one that cannot be left ignored.

Poverty reflects the inadequacy of our systems, which, in the author's view, is indicative of the system failures of market regulation that are too heavily based on neoliberal economics. The discussion below elaborates further on this issue, and attempts to explain why the author holds such a position by presenting two major supporting arguments.

1. In the so called '*fight*' against poverty and social exclusion, the EU treads very cautiously and recognises the legitimate freedom of Member States in pursuing their own social policy goals. And yet, in the same breath, Member States are constrained when it comes to the use of vital policy tools, such as public procurement, that have the power to steer a State's social policy agenda. Public procurement has the potential to serve the aims and objectives stipulated in the European treaties – such as social cohesion, combating long-term unemployment and achievement of acceptable standards of living. But because public procurement can also serve Europe's internal market aims the latter takes precedence. It is argued that when the EU limits the use of public procurement as a policy tool at Member States' disposal, such restrictions represent a straightforward socio-economic burden on Member States. For at the same time as dismantling the so-called *non-tariff trade barriers*, the EU concurrently erects social barriers by restricting Member States' public purchasing autonomy in the pursuit of their own national social policies.

Public procurement as a vital policy tool which is indissolubly linked to national policies, and in particular social policies, can assist towards poverty reduction. This is the basis of this book's logic and justifications for regulating EU public procurement. It is not a matter of social versus economic uses of public procurement, or about favouring 'protectionism' *per se*, but rather about making optimal use of public procurement as a policy instrument which is supported by EU regulation that benefits the EU citizen. The *European citizen* is the fulcrum that stands at the heart of attempts to meet European integration aims. The Single Market route is *not* the only market route that is capable of leading Europe towards political and social integration. There are various market routes available, and all are there for the taking. Such routes need not necessarily be bound by economic liberal theories that essentially underpin the Single Market rationale, for what in effect is economic integration about? It is about economic life within the existing Nation States. This is not to be interpreted as a call for nationalism but simply that European citizens are the fundamental basis for how life is lived and thus the social dimension cannot be neglected. Enabling European citizens to attain reasonable objectives for themselves constitutes the common good. And the conditions that need to be obtained if each citizen is to attain his or her objectives relate to the common good of the political community – a matter that needs to be addressed at both EU level and by Member States.

Poverty across Europe features as a major obstacle to social cohesion, harmonious development, the attainment of acceptable standards of living, and, not in the least, EU integration objectives. As argued above, the persistent levels of poverty across the EU, and current social injustices, are indicative of system failures relating to market regulation – which is too heavily based on neoliberal economics. What follows below elaborates on this issue by presenting the second supporting argument.

2 Despite the fact that there appears to be general agreement that the provision of public services exert a highly valid and crucial societal role that cannot be left solely to the whims of market forces, a growing proportion of public authority tasks – including social services, by way of services of general economic interest – now fall under Community rules on competition and the internal market. In this respect such tasks become subjected to market imperatives. The notion of a 'decentred' State and the subordination of public policies to market forces become further accentuated within the EU – economic efficiency logic dominates. On the other hand, public procurement as a vital public policy tool concerned with the delivery of public services is being utilised to promote Single Market objectives. Here again economic efficiency logic dominates.[7] This draws on utilitarianism and is concerned with the achievement of aggregate utility.[8] Therefore, the public interest function that the EU actively puts into motion draws heavily on aggregative conceptions of the common good. In this respect individual freedom, autonomy, rights, and quality of life are only valuable insofar as they increase

aggregate utility. Because to derive aggregate utility the individual is used as the means. This the author finds problematic since it conflicts with European founding values wherein the respect for human dignity necessitates that we treat individuals as an end in themselves and as a means towards the achievement of ulterior goals. The discussion on poverty[9] has revealed it to be more than a state of hunger or nakedness that relies for its resolution on whatever remnants are thrown out by the wealthy. Respect for human dignity is as important as the satisfaction of hunger. The full realisation of one's humanity, wherein the dignity of the human person is accorded full respect, is the common denominator that plays a pivotal role in intricately linking policy actions with the question of poverty. It is therefore on the basis of the logic supporting this second argument, that the author further contends that the persistent levels of poverty across the EU, and current social injustices, are indicative system failures of a market regulation that is too heavily based on neoliberal economics.

The public interest function that this book endorses, and sets out, is one that seeks to achieve a common good in which the interdependent and harmonious flourishing or fulfilment of each individual can only be made possible through community cooperation and coordination. It calls for the incorporation of the key umbrella concept – namely, the respect for human dignity, equality and freedom of participatory action – to underpin and thus guide such public interest functions. The key umbrella concept corresponds to embracing the fight against poverty and social exclusion, whilst enabling the participatory engagement of citizens.

Hence, a social model of integration in the European Union achieved through a reordering of the economic and social dimensions of the public procurement regime makes it possible to capture a common good – one that generates ripple effects that extend into a deepening of European integration. This social model embraces a public interest function that fulfils first and foremost the values of human dignity, equality and freedom of participatory action. Furthermore, as a highly dynamic and powerful policy tool it ensures best use of public procurement. Indeed, the dynamic nature of public procurement as a policy tool facilitates the possibility to reinforce Member States' diversity. Diversity is one of Europe's distinctive features. In challenging times, diversity makes it possible to put into motion our tailor made coping mechanisms. It enables a number of ways in which to organise work, and combine ideas and machines, to shape how we want our economies to function. Therefore, EU public procurement regulation should seek to reinforce the highly dynamic nature and adaptive features of this highly powerful tool. In doing so it will reinforce the very diverse nature and the socio-economic needs of EU Member States. The overarching goal of the EU public procurement regime should be to facilitate optimal use of the powerful and dynamic tool that is public procurement – and in a way that serves better as a safety valve for Member States rather than the EU as a whole.[10] It is through the common good of the political community, both at the EU level and at

Member State level, that the interdependent and harmonious flourishing of all individuals across the EU can be better enhanced.

The intellectual rationale underpinning European integration theories, and their consequent impact in guiding European policies, has reflected a shift in its *raison d'être* over the years. Neofunctionalist arguments supposed the supranational state as the main actor in the integration process. Such arguments were eventually challenged, most prominently by liberal intergovernmental theory – which posited that constituent States were the main actors in the integration process. However a social model of integration, as discussed in this book, places the European *citizen* as the main actor in the integration process. The ability for individual citizens to flourish is seen as a cornerstone for European growth.

This European theory of social justice manifests itself as a social model of European integration since it institutionalises Rawls' principles of 'justice as fairness' through the regime of a property-owning democracy, and, more specifically, through the PPP regime. The intellectual rationale underpinning the logic of public procurement contracts therefore takes into consideration the distributive objectives of societal welfare – albeit in a limited manner as far as public procurement is concerned. But the adoption of a public procurement regime through a PPP system that takes into account social concerns can only be seen as one example of the multitude of social and economic uses of public procurement. Using public procurement as a tool for addressing these social concerns should not come at the expense of limiting its several other uses, because to do so would limit its dynamic nature as a policy instrument.

In advancing a socially just model of EU integration, PPPs provided the framework of argument. Notwithstanding this, there is no reason why the same underpinning logic for advancing a socially just model of EU integration cannot be extended to public procurement in general. The most essential element is that we remain guided throughout by a public interest function that embraces the key umbrella concept; namely, the respect for the human dignity, equality and freedom of participatory action. Therefore, in shaping a public procurement regime that extends to a socially just model of EU integration – and, more specifically, one that acts as an *ex ante* mechanism that takes into consideration the distributive objectives of societal welfare – such a regime needs to be based on the notion of a property-owning democracy, as advanced by Rawls in his book *Justice as Fairness*. This regime incorporates a socio-economic system that requires at least the following three institutional or policy-based features:

Type (1) policy-based features seek the wide dispersal of capital. Policies in this respect are consistent with Rawls' equality principle as outlined in *Justice as Fairness* and which in effect focus on two particular aspects of justice: the principle of fair equality of opportunity, and the difference principle. The former takes precedence in cases of conflict. On the basis of the discussion put forth in this book the realisation of type (1) policies justifies the adoption of so-called *preferential schemes* in order to ensure the wide dispersal of capital.[11]

Type (2) policy-based features seek to block the intergenerational transmission of advantage. Policies in this respect also seek to satisfy the equality principle. On the basis of the discussion put forth in this book the realisation of type (2) policies need to take into account the value-for-money principle that incorporates broad objectives that go beyond the whole-of-life costs and the quality of the good or service being purchased. Hence, justifications on the basis of the value-for-money principle are only acceptable when the most efficient mix of costs leads to cost-cutting with simultaneous increases in social welfare gains. In addition to the above, and on the basis of the arguments put forth in this book, policies that seek to block the intergenerational transmission of advantage need also *mandate* that major public contracts be divided into lots.

Type (3) policy-based features seek to impose safeguards against the corruption of politics. Policies in this respect are consistent with Rawls' first principle of justice – which aims to protect the fair value of political liberties and to safeguard against the corruption of politics. Policies that seek only to address social justice issues through the enactment of type (1) and (2) policies cannot deliver social justice because the absence of type (3) policies will deprive them of all force.

As argued, there are various market routes available and all are for the taking. Such routes need not necessarily be bound by economic liberal theories that essentially underpin the Single Market rationale. Hence, there is no reason why the EU and Member States should limit themselves when it comes to the use of such a powerful and dynamic instrument as public procurement – as long as they are guided by a clearly defined public interest function.

Domestic public procurement regulation has been highly influenced by EU public procurement regulation. EU public procurement should further pursue its objective of increasing open market access opportunities by reinforcing transparency, objectivity and non-discrimination between competing participants in tenders, increasing efficiency in public procurement, and supporting common goals such as the protection of the environment, the generation of higher resource and energy efficiencies, combating climate change, and promoting innovation. But it should not limit or suppress Member States from making additional socio-economic uses of public procurement as a mechanism for promoting domestic public interest needs. In this respect Member States should lay down the scope and extent of such additional alternative uses. Public procurement for social reasons falls under the sovereign competence of Member States. The overarching balance between utilisation of public procurement as a policy tool at EU level in support of common EU goals, and its use in support of Member States' domestic goals, needs to be guided by a public interest function that recognises the full dignity of the human person as an end in itself.

Deriving a balance between the social and economic uses of public procurement at EU level, and at Member State level, is possible through a politics of cooperation and coordination. Claims that such a scenario attempts to serve 'two masters' – and is therefore contradictory in nature – collapses in view of the fact that it is the EU citizen who features as the key actor in this balancing act. For this is all about policy-making that is guided by a public interest function that seeks to achieve one common good – the EU's common good.

Such a balancing act appears to be well incorporated and workable in international procurement regulations occurring mainly through bilateral trade negotiations. The approach adopted during such negotiations is to maintain the basic model as contained in the Government Procurement Agreement (GPA), thus securing the procurement aspect of the bilateral agreement. However, when it comes to the actual market access objectives of procurement, these are contained in the annexes. In such agreements, the US specifies almost exactly the same exclusions from coverage – notably that such agreements do not apply to set-asides on behalf of small- or minority-owned businesses. Indeed, the GPA has never detained the adoption of socio-economic procurement preferences by those willing to do so, whilst making it possible to further regional, international and bilateral procurement regulation. A case in point is the procurement chapter of the North American Free Trade Agreement (NAFTA) agreed in October 1992 – which includes Mexico, Canada and the US into a single free trade area. The main text of the procurement chapter follows closely the text of the 1979 GPA model – with the main difference being in the market access provisions. NAFTA makes use of a negative listing method by way of listing in the annex all that is excluded by the agreement. Provisions made by the US exclude set asides on behalf of small and minority businesses. In the case of Canada the agreement is not applicable to any measures adopted or maintained with respect to Aboriginal peoples.

It is noteworthy how the GPA model itself evolved over the years.[12] It is very apparent that the need to create a balance between market access aims, on the one hand, and the fulfilment of socio-economic domestic policy aims on the other, featured as the main bone of contention during a 24-year time period between the beginnings of the GPA in 1955 and the 1979 Tokyo Round Negotiations when the text of the final draft was adopted.

Several countries sought exemptions in the 1979 GPA. The United States and Canada included set-asides as exceptions in their annexes to the Agreement, but the European Community did not seek to include similar exceptions for small business or minority set-aside programmes.

The 1994 GPA adopted largely the same approach in that several countries sought exemptions from coverage for particular public procurement preferences, notwithstanding the fact that it now covers previously excluded areas – namely construction works and services, procurement by states (in federally organised countries) and local administration. To date the GPA is the only binding plurilateral agreement concerning public procurement that includes WTO members who are parties to the Agreement.

Hence, when one considers that the major EU argument for eliminating 'protectionist' public procurement behaviour was because it undermined transparency and fairness – and thus impacted negatively on the creation of the Single Market and, most importantly, Europe's vision of political and economic integration – such argumentation needs to be considered in the light of where Europe stands today relative to what others are successfully achieving insofar as public procurement is concerned. The major question we need ask ourselves is whether or not the underlying rationale and present justifications for regulating EU public procurement are realistic and capable of meeting proclaimed expectations. It is hoped that this book has assisted in putting into perspective a more balanced and realistic view that essentially needs to be factored in when distinguishing sound from unsound practical thinking; that is, between acts that are reasonable, all things considered, and acts that are unreasonable, all things considered. The various potential uses of public procurement as a vital policy instrument – and in particular its social use – should not be regarded as a barrier to EU economic growth but rather as a crucial safety valve at the disposal of Member States for the benefit of both EU citizens and as a method for pursuing EU integration aims.

Notes

1 The reliability of such estimates is seriously questioned. Reliance on the actual initial price paid is insufficient. What counts is the final price that the public purchaser actually pays. There can be major discrepancies between the initial award price and the actual final price – especially for works and service contracts where cost overruns can flow during the contractual period. The Directives are silent when it comes to the post-contractual phase. Measuring such variations would be a mammoth task. To this effect see the discussion in Chapter 3, section 3.2, 'EU public procurement and its impact on transparency'.
2 That the EU public procurement regime creates missed opportunities for society is further reiterated by this book. However the proposals, as set out herein, are on a totally different wavelength from those being proposed by the Commission. To this effect see the discussion in Chapter 8, 'On public-private partnerships: for a European theory of a socially just alternative', and the discussion in this chapter, section 9.2, 'On a plane of practical reasonableness'.
3 From the understandings deciphered by this book it was revealed that deeply ingrained cultural preferences feature as one of the main trade barriers. To this effect see the discussion in Chapter 4, 'Free trade: what about it – myths or realities?'
4 To this effect see the discussion in Chapter 3, section 3.4, 'EU public procurement and its impact on small- and medium-sized enterprises'.
5 To this effect see for instance COM (1989) 400 final: para. 41, Directorate-General for Employment, Social Affairs and Equal Opportunities, Directorate-General for the Internal Market and Services 2010: 25.
6 See Chapter 4 and in particular section 4.3, 'The theory of comparative advantage – a general idea'.
7 To this effect see the discussions in Chapter 6, 'On the mission of serving the public – services of general interest and community law', and Chapter 7, 'Public procurement as the EU's safety valve'.
8 To this effect see the discussion in Chapter 1, in particular section 1.3.1, 'Utilitarianism'.
9 See the discussion in Chapter 5, and in particular section 5.2, 'Poverty across the EU – a snapshot', and section 5.3, 'The nature of poverty: definitions abound'.
10 To this effect see the discussion in Chapter 7, 'Public procurement as the EU's safety valve'.

11 To this effect see the discussion in Chapter 8, in particular section 8.4.1, 'Advancing a European theory of a socially just alternative'.
12 To this effect see the discussion in McCrudden (2007): 183–230 (Chapter 8, 'Evolution of the Government Procurement Agreement Model and Procurement Linkages').

Reference

McCrudden, C., 2007. *Buying social justice: Equality, government procurement, & legal change*. New York: Oxford University Press.

Official documents

European Commission

COM (1989) 400 final, 24 July 1989. *Public Procurement Regional and Social Aspects (Communication from the Commission)*. Brussels: European Commission.

COM (2011) 896 final, 20 December 2011. *Proposal for a Directive of the European Parliament and of the Council on Public Procurement*. Brussels: European Commission.

Directorate-General for Employment, Social Affairs and Equal Opportunities, and Directorate-General for the Internal Market and Services, 2010. *Buying Social – A Guide to Taking Account of Social Considerations in Public Procurement, European Commission*. Brussels: European Commission.

SEC (2011a) 1586 final, 20 December 2011. *Commission staff working paper executive summary of the impact assessment accompanying the document Proposal for a Directive of the European Parliament and of the Council on Public Procurement and the Proposal for a Directive of the European Parliament and of the Council on procurement by entities operating in the water, energy, transport and postal sectors*. Brussels: European Commission.

SEC (2011b) 1588 final, 20 December 2011. *Commission staff working document impact assessment of an initiative on concessions accompanying the document proposal for a Directive of the European Parliament and of the Council on the award of concession contracts*. Brussels: European Commission.

Index

Page numbers in *italics* denote tables, those in **bold** denote figures.

absolute advantage 86–7
absolute poverty 111–12, 113–14
access to jobs, lack of 29; *see also* households with very low work intensity measure
Adams, J. Stacey 202
additional works, direct awards of 71
advantage: absolute 86–7; comparative advantage theory 84, 86–90; concept of 182–3
aggregation 68, 69
air transport reforms 93, 95–6
Almunia, Joaquín 105
Althusser, Louis 12–13
anti-malarial drugs 198
Aquinas, Thomas 117–19, 123, 143, 155
Aristotle 116, 117–19, 143, 155
Atkins Report (1988) 4–5, 51, 53
Augustine 155
austerity measures 24–5, 27–8
Austria: poverty *109*, *110*; unemployment 25, *26*
award criteria 66

Bagozzi, R.P. 144–6, 159, 162n24
Barnier, Michael 76
Barroso, José Manuel 91
basic goods 119, *120*, 157
Belgium: competition rules 139; poverty *108*, *110*, 111; social protection expenditure 27; unemployment *26*
Benn, S. 155
Bentham, Jeremy 15, 154
Bernhofen, D.M. 88
bid preferences 208
Bombardier Transportation UK Ltd. 196
Bompart, F. 198

border effects 83–4
Bovis, Christopher 176, 177, 197
Brown, J.C. 88
Bulgaria: poverty 107, *108*, *110*, 111; social protection expenditure 27; unemployment *26*
Burtt, E.J.J. 85–6

Cairnes, John E. 86
CAN *see* Contract Award Notices (CAN)
Canada 225
capabilities to function 114, 115, 124, 125, 126n10, 202–3, 207
capital, redistribution of 10, 20, 206, 207–8
case law: Category 'B' services 75; concept of advantage 182–3; fair equality of opportunity principle 207; in-house doctrine 150–2; private investor in market economy criterion 181–2; *quid pro quo* approach 178, 179–81, 186n26; services of general interest 5–6, 138–40, 173–5, **174**; soft law 136–7
Category 'A' services 73–4, 79n13
Category 'B' services 73–5, 79n13
Cecchini Report (1988) 4–5, 52, 69, 83
Chadwick, Edwin 17
Charter of Fundamental Rights 31, 48, 120–1, 126n1, 141
Churchill, Winston 41–2
CN *see* Contract Notices (CN)
Cockfield, Lord 5, 52
cohesion 58–9, *58*
Cohesion Fund 7, 70
cohesion policy 56–7, 70
collectivism 12

Index 229

commercialisation 176
common action, unity of 157
common good 11, 123, 157, 176, 211
common interest model of public interest 154–5, 156
community 156–7
Community Charter of the Fundamental Social Rights of Workers 46
comparative advantage theory 84, 86–90
compensation approach 175, 182–3
competition effect 82–3
competition rules 137–40, **174**, 175; *see also* special and exclusive rights
competitive tendering procedures 177
competitiveness ranking 27
'Completing the Internal Market' White Paper (1985) 51–2, 92
complex exchange 144
concessions 194
consequentialism 16, 17
consumer bias, as trade barrier 74, 83, 84, 98, 125
Contract Award Notices (CAN) 65, 66, 71
Contract Notices (CN) 66, 67
contracted works, significant changes in 71
contracting out 176
corporatism 176
corruption in politics, safeguards against 206, 209–10
cost-benefit analysis 154
cost-effectiveness analysis 154
Council of Europe 42
Court of Auditors of the European Union 7, 70–1
Cox, A. 50, 82
Croatia: poverty *108*, *110*, 111; unemployment 25, *26*
cross border public procurement 7, 29, 51, 72–5
Cross London Trains (XLT) 196
cultural preferences, as trade barrier 72, 98
culture 125; and service quality 148–50; unity of 156
Cyprus: poverty *108*, *110*, 111; unemployment *26*
Czech Republic: poverty 107, *108*, *110*, 111; unemployment *26*

de Gaulle, Charles 44
Deardorff, A.V. 88–9
decentred state concept 172–6, **174**
Delhey, J. 13–14, 58–9, *58*
Denmark: national debt 24; poverty *108*, *110*, 111; Public-Private Partnerships 195; public procurement and social policy 122; social protection expenditure 27; unemployment *26*; welfare reform measures 24
Department for Transport (DfT), UK 195–7
dialectic materialism 12
difference principle 19, 124, 205, 207
dignity *see* human dignity
Dimock, M.E. 153
direct awards 70–1
direct effect doctrine 14
Directives on public procurement 50–1, 52–3, 61n27, 79n13, 216
Director General for Regional Policy 29, 70
distributive justice 15, 20, 21
Durban, South Africa 198
Dworkin, Ronald 21

economic liberal theories 17
economic theories: difficulties with 85–6; neoliberal 5, 6, 11, 51, 54, 83, 84, 203–4; theory of comparative advantage 84, 86–90
education *see* services of general interest
effective demand theory 86
efficiency gains 82–3
Eisenhower, Dwight D. 152
elections, European Parliament 25
electricity market liberalisation 97
employment: health and social services sector 27; regional disparities 29; unemployment 25, *26*, 29; *see also* households with very low work intensity measure
'Empty Chair Crisis' 44
EMU *see* European Monetary Union (EMU)
environmental sustainability 186n33
equality 10, 11, 117, 187n35, 199–203
equality principle 19, 205, 207–8; *see also* fair equality of opportunity principle
equity theory 202
ERDF *see* European Regional Development Fund (ERDF)
established procurement procedures 67
Estonia: poverty *108*, *110*; social protection expenditure 27; unemployment *26*
Europe 2020 strategy 64, 91–3, 106–7, 121
Europe Economics 68, 69, 71
European Agriculture Guidance and Guarantee Fund 57

230 *Index*

European Atomic Energy Community (EURATOM) 42
European citizen, as key actor 9, 14, 221
European Coal and Steel Community (ECSC) 42
European Court of Human Rights 48
European Court of Justice 14, 44, 48; Category 'B' services 75; concept of advantage 182–3; fair equality of opportunity principle 207; in-house doctrine 150–2; private investor in market economy criterion 181–2; *quid pro quo* approach 178, 179–81, 186n26; services of general interest 5–6, 138–40, 173–5, **174**; soft law 136–7
European Defence Community (EDC) 42
European Economic Area (EEA) countries 76
European Economic Community (EEC) 42
European Federalist Movement 41
European Monetary Union (EMU) 44–5
European Parliament elections 25
European Political Cooperation (EPC) treaty 42
European Regional Development Fund (ERDF) 7, 57, 70–1
European Social Fund 44, 57
exchange paradigm 144–6, 159
expenditure: public procurement 64–5, 67; social protection 25–8; *see also* welfare reform measures

fair equality of opportunity principle 19, 205, 207–8
false necessity 13
Feintuck, M. 156
financial crisis 23–5, 29
Finland: poverty 107, *109*, *110*, 111; unemployment *26*
Finnis, John 9, 116, 117, *118*, 119, *120*, 156–7, 158
fiscal trade barriers 52
Fisher, G.M. 112
flourishing, human 10–11, 30, 115–19
formal equality 117
France: national debt 24; poverty *108*, *110*; Public-Private Partnerships 195; public services 140–1, 162n21; small- and medium-sized enterprises (SMEs) 75; social protection expenditure 27; unemployment *26*; welfare reform measures 24
free trade 30, 82–98; and Europe 2020 strategy 91–3; liberalisation of network industries 93–8, 138–40; theory of comparative advantage 84, 86–90
free trade agreements 51, 76, 225
freedom of participatory action 11, 187n36
functionings 114, 126n10; *see also* capabilities to function
fundamental freedoms, restrictions on 173, **174**
fundamental right to equality 199–203

General Agreement on Tariffs and Trade rules (GATT) 51
general will 155
generalized exchange 144
Germany: electricity market liberalisation 97; national debt 24; postal sector reforms 95; poverty *108*, *110*; preference schemes 6; Public-Private Partnerships 195; public procurement and social policy 122; service quality 149–50; social market economy 22–3; unemployment 25, *26*; welfare reform measures 24
Geroski, P. 74, 83, 98, 125
Geyer, R. 45, 49
gift taxes 206, 208
Gillingham, J. 45
globalisation 171–2
golden rule of Jesus of Nazareth 16
governance 176
Government Procurement Agreement (GPA) 76, 225
Grech, Louis 91
Greece: competition rules 139–40; national debt 24; poverty 107, *108*, *110*, 111; Public-Private Partnerships 195; social protection expenditure 27; unemployment 25, *26*; welfare reform measures 24

Häberle, Peter 125
Hague Congress (1948) 42
Hague Summit (1969) 44
Hayek, Friedrich 15, 33n22
Head, K. 74, 83–4, 98, 125
health services: employment 27; *see also* services of general interest
Heckscher–Ohlin model 88
Hegel, G.W.F. 155
Held, V. 154, 155
heterogeneity of services 146, 147
high speed rail networks 96–7
Hill, T.P. 147, 158
historical materialism 12

Houghton, J. 198
households with very low work intensity measure 107, *108–9*, 111, 126n5
HPI *see* Human Poverty Index (HPI)
Human Development Reports 114
human dignity 11, 30, 31, 125, 184, 187n34, 205; as basic moral premise 117–19; as legally enforceable fundamental right 120–1; and public procurement 121–4
human flourishing 10–11, 30, 115–19
Human Poverty Index (HPI) 114
Hungary: poverty *108*, *110*, 111; unemployment *26*

Iceland 76, *109*
ideal markets 92–3
ideal theory 18, 33n28
ideal type concept 116
Ilzkovitz, F. 84
impartiality of interest 16, 33n24
in-house doctrine 150–2, 158
individualistic conceptions of society 11–12
Information Commissioner, UK 152–3
inheritance taxes 206, 208
inseparability of services 146–7
intangibility of services 146, 147
intelligence, unity of 156
intergenerational transmission of advantage, blocking 206, 208–9
International Air Transport Association (IATA) 95–6
international public procurement 7, 76–7, 225
'invisible hand' 144
Ireland: national debt 24; poverty *108*, *110*; unemployment *26*; welfare reform measures 24
Italy: competition rules 139; national debt 24; poverty *108*, *110*, 111; public procurement and social policy 122; unemployment *26*; welfare reform measures 24

Jacobs, Sir Francis 178, 179
Japan 51, 76
jobs, lack of access to 29; *see also* households with very low work intensity measure
Joerges, C. 22–3
justice as fairness theory 18–21, 205–10

Kant, Immanuel 117

Keezer, D.M. 152
Kelly, G.A. 116
Keynes, John Maynard 86
Kiyota, K. 88
Kotler, P. 143–4

language recognition 125
Latvia: poverty 107, *108*, *110*, 111; social protection expenditure 27; unemployment *26*
law and morality 123, 127n15
Léger, Philippe 179–83, 186n26
legitimate authority 123
Levi-Strauss, C. 144
Levitt, T. 147–8
Levy, S.J. 143–4
Leys, W.A.R. 152
liberal intergovernmental theory 3, 52
liberalisation of network industries 93–8, 138–40
liberty principle 19, 20, 205, 209–10
Liechtenstein 76
light regime 79n13
Lisbon Treaty 22, 31, 47, 105, 120–1, 141
Lithuania: poverty *108*, *110*; social protection expenditure 27; unemployment *26*
low-cost airlines 96
low-cost business strategies 95
Luxembourg: poverty 107, *108*, *110*, 111; unemployment 25, *26*
Luxembourg Compromise 44

Maastricht Treaty *see* Treaty of the European Union (TEU)
McCabe, H. 199
Malta: poverty *108*, *110*; social protection expenditure 27; unemployment 25, *26*
Malthus, Thomas 86
MAPPS database 68
marchés publiques 176–8
market-based approach to public services 141, 172–6, **174**
market fragmentation, causes 83–4, 98, 125
marketing 143–50
marriage 115
Marx, Karl 86, 155–6
Marxian economics 12
Marxism 12
Mayer, T. 74, 83–4, 98, 125
Meade, James 20
media of exchange 144, 146, 159
Mexico 225

Mill, John Stuart 15, 16, 86
Millennium Declaration, UN 112
Miller, A.S. 153
mixed meaning of exchange 145
mobile phones 93
mobility of labour, restrictions on 90
Moeller, S. 147
monetary poverty 29
Monnet, Jean 42
monopoly rights *see* special and exclusive rights
Monti, Mario 21, 91, 204
morality: dignity as basic moral premise 117–19; and law 123, 127n15; in natural law theory 115–16; unitary model of public interest 155
Moravcsik, Andrew 46
Morin, Edgar 125
Müller-Armack, A. 22
Myrdal, G. 9, 86

NAFTA *see* North American Free Trade Agreement (NAFTA)
national debt levels 24–5
natural law theory 115–19, *118*, *120*, 125, 156–7, 203–4
necessaries 113–14
Neergaard, U. 142
negotiated procedure procurement method 196
neofunctionalist theory 42, 46
neoliberal economic theories 5, 6, 11, 51, 54, 83, 84, 203–4
Netherlands: postal sector reforms 95; poverty 107, *109*, *110*, 111; public procurement and social policy 122; unemployment 25, *26*
network industries: liberalisation of 93–8, 138–40; *see also* services of general interest
New Poor Law (1934), UK 17
non-tariff barriers 50, 51, 52, 74, 83–4
North American Free Trade Agreement (NAFTA) 225
Norway 76, *109*
number of bidders model 68
Nussbaum, Martha 126n10

Official Journal of the European Union (OJEU) 8, 65, 66, 67, 121, 195
Open Method of Coordination (OMC) 49
openness 68, 69
opportunity costs 87, 99n6
order, unity of 156

ordoliberalism 22–3, 172–3
outcome model 68
overdetermination 12–13

Pareto criterion of optimality 17, 97, 155
participatory action, freedom of 11, 187n36
people at risk of poverty measure 8–9, 32n12, 107–11, *108–9*, *110*, 126n3
perishability of services 147
Perry, C.M. 152
personal construct theory 116
Peters, R. 155
Peterson, J. 13
physical trade barriers 52
Picard, E. 160, 162n21, 201, 202
PIN *see* Prior Information Notices (PIN)
Plato 143, 155
Poland: poverty *109*, *110*; social protection expenditure 27; unemployment 26
political integration, defined 13
'polluter pays' principle 97
Popper, Karl 162n24
Portugal: national debt 24–5; poverty *109*, *110*, 111; unemployment 25, *26*; welfare reform measures 24–5
positive discrimination 200–2; *see also* special and exclusive rights
postal sector reforms 95
poverty 8–9, 29, 105, 204, 220–1; conceptualising 111–14; households with very low work intensity measure 107, *108–9*, 111, 126n5; levels across EU 106–11, *108–9*, *110*; people at risk of poverty measure 8–9, 32n12, 107–11, *108–9*, *110*, 126n3; and public procurement 121–4; severe material deprivation measure 29, 107, *108–9*, 111, 126n4
poverty gap *110*, 111, 126n6
PPPs *see* Public-Private Partnerships (PPPs)
practical reasonableness 115, 116–17, *118*, *120*, 185, 193
preference schemes 5–6, 9, 200–2, 208; *see also* special and exclusive rights
preponderance model of public interest 154, 156
primary goods 20, 34n29
principle of fair equality of opportunity 19, 205, 207–8
principle of proportionality 123, 216–17
principle of subsidiarity 123
Prior Information Notices (PIN) 66

private finance initiative (PFI) projects 194
private investor in market economy criterion 181–2
privatisation 171, 176
progressive taxation 20
property-owning democracy 10, 20, 56, 205–6
proportionality principle 123, 216–17
protectionist behaviour 6, 51, 52
public interest 9, 11, 30, 55, 150–8, 176, 178–84, 210–11
public markets 176–8
Public-Private Partnerships (PPPs) 193–211; blocking intergenerational transmission of advantage 208–9; fundamental right to equality 199–203; redistribution of capital 207–8; safeguards against corruption in politics 209–10; and social justice model 203–10; Thameslink rolling stock procurement, UK 195–7, 199–200, 208–9; value-for-money principle 197–9, 209
public procurement expenditure 64–5, 67
public procurement regulation development 50–3
public services *see* services of general interest
publication of notices 66

qualified majority voting 47
quality improvements 8
Quesnay, François 86
quid pro quo approach 178, 179–81, 186n26

railway transport reforms 96–7
Ramboll Report (2011) 72–4, 75
Rawls, John 10, 18–21, 33n26, 34n29, 56, 114, 124, 205–10
Raz, Joseph 123, 127n15
Reagan, Ronald 51
redistribution of capital 10, 20, 206, 207–8
redistributive taxation 10, 20
regional policy 56–7
relative poverty 111, 112–13
relevance of the needed job condition 123
religion and morality 115–16
reordered public procurement regime 28–30, 54–6, 185, 218–26
Resnick, S.A. 13
responsibility 21
restricted exchange 144
restructuring effect 83

Ricardian model 87–8
Ricardo, David 86, 87–8
right to freedom 160
right to local self-government 150–2
Rödl, F. 22–3
Romania: poverty 107, *109*, *110*, 111; unemployment *26*
Rossi, Ernesto 41
Rousseau, Jean-Jacques 155

Saks, M. 155–6
Sauter, W. 138, 176
savings 8, 68–9
Scharpf, F.W. 46–7, 49, 56
Schepel, S.H. 176
Schubert, G. 153
Schuman, Robert 30–1, 42
SEA *see* Single European Act (SEA)
second best theory 97, 100n18
Second World War 41
selection criteria 66
self-government, right to local 150–2
Sen, Amartya 16, 17, 20, 33n28, 113–14, 115, 124, 125
service publique 140–1, 160, 173
service quality 148–50
services of general interest 135–60; economic versus non-economic services 142–50, 173–5, **174**; internal market tensions 140–1; public interest 150–8; special and exclusive rights 5–6, 50, 137–40, **174**, 175
set asides 76, 208, 225
severe material deprivation measure 29, 107, *108–9*, 111, 126n4
sheltered workshops 218–19
Siemens plc 196, 200
Single European Act (SEA) 3, 45–6, 52, 57
Single Market Act 85, 91, 216
Single Market strategy 4, 9, 82–4; relaunch of 21, 22, 91–3
Sismondi, Jean Charles Léonard de 86
Slovakia: poverty *109*, *110*, 111; small- and medium-sized enterprises (SMEs) 75; unemployment *26*
Slovenia: poverty *109*, *110*; small- and medium-sized enterprises (SMEs) 75; unemployment *26*
small- and medium-sized enterprises (SMEs) 7, 75–6, 79n14, 124, 200–2, 207
Small Business Act, US 201
Smith, Adam 86–7, 113–14, 144, 177

234 *Index*

Social Action Programme 44–5, 46
Social Chapter 47
social contract 18
social exclusion 29, 107
social formation theories 11–14
social inclusion targets 105, 106–7
social integration 58–9, *58*
social investment fund 210
social justice model 10–11, 54–6, 203–10
social justice theories 14–15; egalitarian liberal perspectives 18–21; utilitarianism 15–17
social market economy 21–3, 204
social marketing 145, 162n24
social minimum policy regime 17
social model, Europe's 21–3, 124, 125
social policies 23–5, 43–9; and public procurement 121–4
Social Protection Committee 49
social protection expenditure 25–8; *see also* welfare reform measures
social relationships, exchanges in 145, 159
social services: employment 27; *see also* services of general interest
social spaces 13–14, 58
soft law 136–7
solidarity-based approach to public services 140–1
soul 119
South Africa 198
South Korea 76
Spain: competition rules 139; national debt 25; poverty 107, *108*, *110*, 111; Public-Private Partnerships 195; social protection expenditure 27; unemployment 25, *26*; welfare reform measures 25
special and exclusive rights 5–6, 50, 137–40, **174**, 175
Spinelli, Altiero 41
State aid 138, **174**, 175, 178, 179–80, 181, 182–3
static efficiency 89, 90
static trade effect 82
statistical public procurement reports 7, 29, 78n2
subsidiarity principle 123
subsidies 208
substantive equality 117
success condition 123
sum-ranking 16, 17
supremacy doctrine 14
Supreme Court, US 152
sustainability 186n33

Sweden: postal sector reforms 95; poverty 107, *109*, *110*, 111; social protection expenditure 27; unemployment *26*
Switzerland *109*
symbolic meaning of exchange 145
Szyszczak, E. 140

tastes, national and regional, as trade barrier 74, 83, 84, 98, 125
technical specifications 66–7
technical trade barriers 52
TED *see* Tenders Electronic Daily database (TED)
telecommunications sector: and competition rules 138–9; liberalisation of 93, 94–5; service quality 149–50
Tenders Electronic Daily database (TED) 8, 65, 66, 68
TEU *see* Treaty of the European Union (TEU)
TFEU *see* Treaty on the Functioning of the European Union (TFEU)
Thameslink rolling stock procurement, UK 195–7, 199–200, 208–9
Thatcher, Margaret 51
theory of comparative advantage 84, 86–90
theory of effective demand 86
theory of second best 97, 100n18
tied amity *58*, 59
tied hostility *58*, 59
total public expenditure on works, goods and services 64–5, 67
Townsend, P. 112–13
trade agreements 51, 76, 225
trade barriers 52, 83–4; cultural preferences as 72, 98; national and regional tastes as 74, 83, 84, 98, 125
transparency 7–8, 29, 66–71, 177
transport system reforms 96–7; *see also* air transport reforms
Treaty Establishing the European Community (TEC) *see* Treaty of Rome
Treaty of Amsterdam 47, 141
Treaty of Lisbon 22, 31, 47, 105, 120–1, 141
Treaty of Nice 47
Treaty of Rome 3, 42, 43–4, 50, 123, 137–8
Treaty of the European Union (TEU) 31, 31n1, 47, 48, 204
Treaty on the Functioning of the European Union (TFEU) 47, 48–9, 50, 136, 137–8, 141

Tripartite Social Summits 48
Turkey 195

unemployment 25, *26*, 29
Unger, Roberto Mangabeira 13, 30, 89–90, 199, 204, 210
unitary model of public interest 155–7
United Kingdom: electricity market liberalisation 97; national debt 25; poverty *109*, *110*; preference schemes 6; public interest cases 152–3; Public-Private Partnerships 194–7, 199–200, 208–9; public services 141; small- and medium-sized enterprises (SMEs) 75; Social Chapter 47; unemployment *26*; welfare reform measures 25
United Nations Development Programme 114
United Nations Millennium Declaration 112
United States: competition from 51; North American Free Trade Agreement 225; preference schemes 200–1; public interest cases 152; service quality 149–50; set asides 76, 225
Universal Declaration of Human Rights 121, 205

'user pays' principle 97
utilitarian meaning of exchange 145
utilitarianism 15–17, 19, 117, 123, 154, 157, 203–4

value-for-money principle 10, 55, 177, 197–9, 209
veil of ignorance 18
Ventotene Manifesto 41
veto power of Member States 44, 45
VFM *see* value-for-money principle

Weber, Max 116
welfare reform measures 24–5, 27–8
welfare state capitalism 10, 20, 205–6
welfarism 16, 17
wished-for markets 92–3
Wishlade, F.G. 57
Wolff, R.D. 13
Wood, Alan 72
Wood Report (2004) 72, 98, 125
World Summit for Social Development (1995) 112
World Trade Organisation (WTO) 76, 225

youth unemployment 25, *26*

eBooks
from Taylor & Francis
Helping you to choose the right eBooks for your Library

Add to your library's digital collection today with Taylor & Francis eBooks. We have over 50,000 eBooks in the Humanities, Social Sciences, Behavioural Sciences, Built Environment and Law, from leading imprints, including Routledge, Focal Press and Psychology Press.

Choose from a range of subject packages or create your own!

Benefits for you
- Free MARC records
- COUNTER-compliant usage statistics
- Flexible purchase and pricing options
- All titles DRM-free.

Benefits for your user
- Off-site, anytime access via Athens or referring URL
- Print or copy pages or chapters
- Full content search
- Bookmark, highlight and annotate text
- Access to thousands of pages of quality research at the click of a button.

Free Trials Available
We offer free trials to qualifying academic, corporate and government customers.

eCollections
Choose from over 30 subject eCollections, including:

Archaeology	Language Learning
Architecture	Law
Asian Studies	Literature
Business & Management	Media & Communication
Classical Studies	Middle East Studies
Construction	Music
Creative & Media Arts	Philosophy
Criminology & Criminal Justice	Planning
Economics	Politics
Education	Psychology & Mental Health
Energy	Religion
Engineering	Security
English Language & Linguistics	Social Work
Environment & Sustainability	Sociology
Geography	Sport
Health Studies	Theatre & Performance
History	Tourism, Hospitality & Events

For more information, pricing enquiries or to order a free trial, please contact your local sales team:
www.tandfebooks.com/page/sales

www.tandfebooks.com